S0-BCK-569

CLASSIC SPEECHES

CLASSIC SPEECHES

22 Selections from
Brigham Young University
Devotional and Fireside Speeches

Volume One

Order from
Publications & Graphics
218 UPB
Brigham Young University
Provo, UT 84602–1919

ISBN 0–8425–2323–5

Brigham Young University Publications & Graphics, Provo, Utah 84602–1919
11–94 15M 94–806

PRINTED IN THE UNITED STATES OF AMERICA

CONTENTS

FREQUENTLY USED ABBREVIATIONS

CR—*Conference Reports of The Church of Jesus Christ of Latter-day Saints.*

DBY—Young, Brigham. *Discourses of Brigham Young.* Selected by John A. Widtsoe. Salt Lake City: Deseret Book Company, 1941.

GD—Smith, Joseph F. *Gospel Doctrine.* 5th ed. Salt Lake City: Deseret Book Company, 1939.

GI—McKay, David O. *Gospel Ideals.* 2nd printing. Salt Lake City: Improvement Era, 1954.

GS—Grant, Heber J. *Gospel Standards.* Compiled by G. Homer Durham. Salt Lake City: Improvement Era, 1941.

HC—Smith, Joseph. *History of The Church of Jesus Christ of Latter-day Saints.* 7 vols. 2nd ed. revised. Edited by B. H. Roberts. Salt Lake City: The Church of Jesus Christ of Latter-day Saints, 1932–51.

Hymns—*Hymns.* Revised and enlarged. Salt Lake City: The Church of Jesus Christ of Latter-day Saints, 1948 and 1985.

JD—*Journal of Discourses.* 26 vols. London: Latter-day Saints' Book Depot, 1854–86.

MD—McConkie, Bruce R. *Mormon Doctrine.* 2nd ed. Salt Lake City: Bookcraft, 1966.

PPP—Pratt, Parley P. *Autobiography of Parley P. Pratt.* Edited by his son Parley P. Pratt. Salt Lake City: Deseret Book Company, 1973.

Sing—*Sing with Me: Songs for Children.* Salt Lake City: The Church of Jesus Christ of Latter-day Saints, 1970.

Teachings—Smith, Joseph. *Teachings of the Prophet Joseph Smith.* Selected by Joseph Fielding Smith. Salt Lake City: Deseret Book Company, 1938.

TETB—Benson, Ezra T. *The Teachings of Ezra Taft Benson.* Salt Lake City: Bookcraft, 1988.

TSWK—Kimball, Spencer W. *The Teachings of Spencer W. Kimball.* Edited by Edward L. Kimball. Salt Lake City: Bookcraft, 1982.

Introduction

The bells on the Carillon Tower ring out every Tuesday at 11 A.M. as thousands of students, faculty, and staff walk together to devotionals and forums at Brigham Young University's Marriott Center. There, they celebrate, in Professor Richard Cracroft's words, "the reality of the often ignored and too little heralded but very real outpouring of the Spirit of God upon the believing inhabitants of the earth." They "leave the meeting with [their] eternal perspective refurbished and revitalized."

A beautiful library of wisdom and knowledge has resulted from these assemblies. We've selected twenty-two of them, taken generally from the 1970s and early 1980s. Our rationale for selection in this first volume has been imperfect—some are frequently requested for reprint, and we are aware of how some have affected individuals in a profound way. For example, President Gordon B. Hinckley's "The Widow's Mite" encouraged one person to leave the university until he could live the standards. Elder Jeffrey R. Holland's "For Times of Trouble" gave hope to another who was struggling with extraordinary difficulties.

Other addresses have prompted wonderful discussion and provided needed course correction, such as President Boyd K. Packer's talk "The

Arts and the Spirit of the Lord." Of course, Volume 1 would be incomplete without the vision of "The Second Century of Brigham Young University" by President Spencer W. Kimball or a talk by the heroic missionary/apostle Elder LeGrand Richards.

The most recent address in this volume is by President Howard W. Hunter. Though given in 1993, this talk became an instant classic and, we think you'll agree, belongs with this collection. On February 7, 1993, students gathered to listen to President Hunter. Elder James E. Faust later said,

> *When President Hunter was at the pulpit, an intruder carrying a briefcase in one hand and something black in the other stepped on the stand and shouted, "Stop right there." He then ordered everybody to leave the stand but President Hunter,* [who] *stayed quietly and resolutely at the pulpit. The assailant demanded that President Hunter read aloud a prepared statement,* [which he] *firmly declined to do. The assailant picked the wrong man. I know of no man in this world that is more resolute, unflappable, and courageous than President Hunter.*
>
> *You will recall that when the assailant was momentarily distracted,* [President Hunter] *was pushed from the stand* [and] *lowered by the security guards and others to the floor for safety. After the incident, I am told that President Hunter's pulse was seventy beats per minute! . . .*
>
> *President Hunter collected himself and then began his prepared message saying: "Life has a fair number of challenges in it." And then his irrepressible sense of humor surfaced and he added, "As demonstrated." . . . He went on with his message as though nothing had happened.*

Although not all our firesides and devotionals have had such an exciting beginning, the real thrill has been to learn from prophets, apostles, presidents, and colleagues as they speak about the gospel of Jesus Christ to a vast audience of believers. Good reading.

—REX E. LEE
President, Brigham Young University

CLASSIC SPEECHES

Flaxen Threads

CARLOS E. ASAY

I THANK President Condie for that very generous introduction. It was so flattering that it reminds me of an experience I had recently with President Marion G. Romney. I walked into the Church Office Building, stepped on the elevator, and he was there. He looked a little bit weary, so I thought I would cheer him up. I asked him how he was.

He said, "Oh, about average."

I said, "Well, President, average for you is superior for most of us."

He smiled, looked at me, and said, "Boy, you are very kind, but you are not the least bit honest."

President Condie mentioned that I am somewhat at ease on a basketball court, or at least I used to be. When I left the University of Utah years ago, I tried very hard to stay in shape. I continued to play basketball in an effort to retain my skills. But I sustained an injury and was forced to undergo a back operation. The operation was torture and the long period of convalescence much the same. Finally, when the doctor was ready to give me release, I asked him if I could play basketball again. He looked at me, smiled a little bit, and said, "Carlos, you go home, and you read 1 Corinthians 13:11."

I returned home, opened my Bible, and read:

> When I was a child, I spake as a child, I understood as a child, I thought as a child: but when I became a man, I put away childish things.

That was enough to retire me.

It is a pleasure and a distinct honor, my brothers and sisters, to be in your presence this evening; and I hope and pray that the Spirit of the Lord will help me deliver the message I have in mind.

I have invited two young men, Elder Brockman and Elder Robey, to help me introduce my subject. Will you two please step forward? You will note that both have their wrists bound together. Though you may not be able to see the material that I have used in binding my friends, it is the same for each—flaxen thread.

Elder Robey's wrists are tied with only one strand of the flaxen material. I will now invite him to muster all his strength and courage and break free. *[Pause]* Did you notice how easy and effortless that was?

Elder Brockman's wrists are tied with twenty strands of the flaxen thread. I now ask him to do what Elder Robey did. *[Pause]* If you were closer to the pulpit, you would see that my captive is really trying to break his cords. You would also observe that, as he strains to break the thread, it is beginning to make indentations in his wrists, and, if he were to continue much further, I think it would cut and draw blood. Thank you very much.

I have engaged you in this simple demonstration to make a point. Suppose each strand of thread used in binding these young men represented one bad habit. From the demonstration, we might conclude that a single bad habit has limited restricting power. A number of bad habits, however, has great power—almost limitless power.

"The chains of habit," said one man, "are seldom heavy enough to be felt until they are too strong to be broken" (Samuel Johnson).

Plato, it is said, once rebuked a person for engaging in a gambling game. When the person protested that he had only played for a trifle, Plato replied, "The habit is not a trifle" (*Home Book of Quotations,* Burton Stevenson (ed.) [New York: Dodd, Mead, 1956], p. 845).

When I taught at this institution, I worked with students who *fitted, floated,* or *failed.* Those who fitted came with purpose, high resolve, and good work habits. Those who floated appeared on the scene for a semester or two and faded away to something less challenging when their grades finally caught up with them. Those who failed lacked the commitment and discipline required of a person in an institution of higher learning.

It seemed to me that most of the failures were shackled by poor habits. Some were not in the habit of attending class regularly; some were not in the habit of reading required texts; some were habitually late in submitting assignments; some were not in the habit of budgeting time and energies; and some were not even conditioned to work. In all too many cases, so it seemed to me, one weakness seemed to breed upon another, and what appeared at first to be a flaxen habit proved to be a strong inhibiting cord.

A Spanish proverb reads: "Habits are at first cobwebs, then cables." I suspect that most students come here with pure intent. They register, select their courses of study, and attend their classes with high hopes of attaining declared goals. But, when one becomes careless, when one permits resolve to sag, slouchy habits appear, and academic anemia sets in. This malady comes web by web until learning and growing are choked off by the cables of intellectual inactivity.

More than a decade ago, a young man wrote President Ernest L. Wilkinson of this institution and asked what he should do to become a successful leader. President Wilkinson responded with some wise counsel. He included in his counsel this quote from the philosopher and psychologist William James:

> The hell to be endured hereafter, of which theology tells, is no worse than the hell we make for ourselves in this world by habitually fashioning our characters in the wrong way. Could the young but realize how soon they will become mere walking bundles of habits, they would give more heed to their conduct while in the plastic state. We are spinning our own fates, good or evil,

> and never to be undone. Every smallest stroke of virtue or of vice leaves its never so little scar. The drunken Rip Van Winkle, in Jefferson's play, excuses himself for every fresh dereliction by saying, "I won't count this time!" Well! he may not count it, and a kind Heaven may not count it; but it is being counted none the less. Down among his nerve-cells and fibres the molecules are counting it, registering and storing it up to be used against him when the next temptation comes. Nothing we ever do is, in strict scientific literalness, wiped out. Of course, this has its good side as well as its bad one. As we become permanent drunkards by so many separate drinks, so we become saints in the moral, and authorities and experts in the practical and scientific spheres, by so many separate acts and hours of work. Let no youth have any anxiety about the upshot of his education, whatever the line of it may be. If he keep faithfully busy each hour of the working-day, he may safely leave the final result to itself. He can with perfect certainty count on waking up some fine morning, to find himself one of the competent ones of his generation, in whatever pursuit he may have singled out. [Letter from Ernest L. Wilkinson to Bryce V. Redd, 2 March 1971, pp. 2–3. Quoted from William James, *The Principles of Psychology,* Great Books of the Western World, vol. 53 (Chicago: Encyclopaedia Britannica, 1952), p. 83]

I would remind you "walking bundles of habits" that there is a relationship between thoughts, actions, habits, and characters. After the language of the Bible we might well say: "Thought begat Action; and Action took unto himself Habit; and Character was born of Habit; and Character was expressed through Personality. And, Character and Personality lived after the manner of their parents."

A more conventional way of linking the above concepts is found in the words of C. A. Hill: "We sow our thoughts, and we reap our actions; we sow our actions, and we reap our habits; we sow our habits, and we reap our characters; we sow our characters, and we reap our destiny" (*Home Book of Quotations,* p. 845).

I have often referred to and preached of a "missionary character"—one of the most desired characters of all, in my opinion. This character, I feel, is the sum of all the good habits acquired through selfless day-by-day service and obedient living. It is molded slowly, as the ambassador of righteousness shares the gospel of Jesus Christ and seeks to save souls.

As missionaries completed their work in the Texas North Mission, where I served, I would invite them to sit down, to reflect, and to list all of the habits that they felt they had acquired during their terms of service. Most lists would include phrases like this:

The habit of rising and retiring early.

The habit of praying frequently.

The habit of studying the scriptures regularly.

The habit of exercising daily.

The habit of working hard, consistently—and on and on it would go.

When the list was complete, I would ask the missionary to identify those habits that he felt he should break and discard upon his return home and his subsequent release. Nearly every missionary would eye his list carefully and respond something like this: "President, I can see only one habit that I can afford to place aside."

"What is that?" I would ask.

Invariably the missionary would conclude, "I can drop my daily tracting."

If character is truly born of habit—and it is—it is vital that all of us understand the process of habit formation. Not only will this process, if applied, enable us to refine character, but it will also assure us success in our missions in the mission field, at home, at school, or wherever.

Now, I am no expert on the subject of habit. Nevertheless, I would like to share with you some steps that I feel are involved in the cultivation of a desirable habit.

First, you must *define the desired habit.* You must identify it, verbalize it, and write it down. You should be as specific as possible. For example, you might write: "I shall attend all of my classes this semester and arrive on time." Or, "I shall attend Church worship services every Sunday without fail this year." Chances of successfully acquiring the new habit depend much upon how clearly you plant it in your mind and in your heart. Fuzzy or vague resolves are usually short-lived. You know that as well as I. A firm and definite declaration of intent has staying power. Joshua did not say to the children of Israel: "Choose, if you like, within the next month or so, whom ye will serve. But as for me and my house, we may, if all goes well, serve the Lord." With firm resolve and clarity of purpose he declared:

> Choose you this day whom ye will serve . . . : but as for me and my house, we will serve the Lord. [Joshua 24:15]

Second, you must *bind yourself to act* and to honor your declared resolve. Through the Prophet Joseph Smith the Lord taught the Saints how to benefit from meetings and conferences. He instructed that the Saints meet together and instruct and edify one another; and, so that the instruction would not be spent and lost, he asked that we bind ourselves to act. The Lord's words are: "And ye shall bind yourselves to act in all holiness before me" (D&C 43:9). I feel that one binds himself best to a desired action by sharing his resolve with a friend, with a wife, with a husband, with a bishop, or with someone else who can monitor his progress. I also feel that one finds strength as he shares his desires with God and begs for divine assistance.

Third, you must *put the new mode of conduct into operation.* Just thinking about church or class attendance is not sufficient. Thoughts must be supported by action. The old adage "Practice makes perfect" certainly applies in this case. And with each planned and proper action, one repetition after another, comes added strength. President Heber J. Grant often quoted this statement from Emerson:

> That which we persist in doing becomes easier for us to do; not that the nature of the thing itself is changed, but that our power to do is increased. [*GS,* p. 355]

President Grant practiced what he preached. He tells this story of how he attempted to polish some singing skills:

> Upon my recent trip to Arizona, I asked Elders Rudger Clawson and J. Golden Kimball if they had any objections to my singing one hundred hymns that day. They took it as a joke and assured me that they would be delighted. We were on the way from Holbrook to St. Johns, a distance of about sixty miles. After I had sung about forty tunes, they assured me that if I sang the remaining sixty they would be sure to have nervous prostration. I paid no attention whatever to their appeal, but held them to their bargain and sang the full one hundred. One hundred and fifteen songs in one day, and four hundred in four days, is the largest amount of practicing I ever did.
>
> Today [1900] my musical deafness is disappearing, and by sitting down to a piano and playing the lead notes, I can learn a song in less than one-tenth the time required when I first commenced to practice. [*GS,* p. 354]

Fourth, you must *bolster your will or desire* by riveting your mind upon the virtues of the desired habit. A man does not lick the smoking habit by relishing the pleasure of a cigarette. But rather, he gains resolve by thinking about the added health and vitality and money savings that he will realize when free of the habit. Motivation to lose weight comes by anticipating the increased good looks and vitality, not by savoring caloric foods and exotic dishes.

In the scriptures, we read of good desires and wills. Alma taught:

> I know that he [God] granteth unto men according to their desire, . . . yea, I know that he allotteth unto men . . . according to their wills. [Alma 29:4]

So, when you have made your resolve, build your case, and build your will. Gather data, identify reasons, and do whatever you can to justify your struggle in acquiring the new habit.

Fifth, you must *not look back or permit exceptions to occur* once you have embarked upon your new course of action. No exceptions! Famous last words for the alcoholic are: "Just one more sip. I'll drink only this one, and then it's back on the wagon." Can't you just hear Lot's wife saying, as they raced away from Sodom, "Hold up for a minute; let me take one more look at the city." That was a fatal and very salty mistake (see Genesis 19:15–26).

Once we have determined the new habit or the improved pattern of living, we must guard against any inclination to deviate. No exceptions must be tolerated and no excuses invented. For every breach of our new resolution returns us to point zero, or below, and adds strength to the behavior we are trying to conquer.

"Look not behind thee" (Genesis 19:17) were the Lord's words to Lot and his company, and those words apply to you and to me as we seek to improve our lot.

Sixth, you must *plunge wholeheartedly into the new program of conduct.* Wholeheartedly: You do not let go of old habits gradually and move into new ones slowly. You do not taper off from the old, because that only prolongs the struggle. It also provides opportunities for the old habit to increase its hold. The new habit, if it is to survive, must be favored in every possible way and repeated in its complete form as often as possible.

I have suggested to you six steps that may assist you in cultivating new habits. Let me review the process quickly: (1) *Define* the desired habit, (2) *bind* yourself to act, (3) *put* the new conduct into operation, (4) *bolster* your will or desire, (5) *do not look back,* and (6) *plunge* wholeheartedly into the new conduct.

As you follow these steps, please bear in mind the need to take one resolve at a time. The big problem with most of our New Year's resolutions is that the list is generally too long and too ambitious. It seems that our tendency to forsake resolves increases as the list grows. I believe that one resolve made and kept is better than a dozen made and abandoned. Therefore, move forward in your progress one step, one habit at a time.

I find wisdom and inspiration in the lyrics of a song written in honor of some United States astronauts. You may recognize these words:

> One small step for man,
> One giant leap for mankind.
> There isn't a thing that man cannot do,
> If he takes one small step at a time.

[R. Harris, "One Small Step," sung by Mormon Tabernacle Choir, Columbia MS 7399]

You should also bear in mind the need to take advantage of your rather "plastic" state. Please understand that everyone becomes more and more fixed in his habits as he becomes older. While you are younger and relatively malleable, form habits that will work to your advantage rather than habits that will enslave. Make every effort to maintain the tendency to grow and to improve.

I like the words of Hubbard:

> It may not be out of place to say that every man (and [every] woman) is controlled by Habit. When Habits are young they are like lion cubs, easily managed, but later there comes a time when they manage you. Bad Habits may put you on the Avernus Jerkwater, No. 23, with a ticket one way to Nowhere.
>
> Good Habits are mentors, guardian angels, and servants that regulate your sleep, your work, your thought. [*Selected Writings of Elbert Hubbard,* vol. 2 (New York: William H. Wise, 1922), p. 195]

At the beginning of this presentation, I conducted a simple demonstration. I used a flaxen thread in handcuffing two young men. The thread was used to illustrate the binding power of bad habits. Permit me now to turn your minds to sin, the older and the uglier brother of bad habits.

Sin, much like habit, can enter one's life in a seemingly innocuous way. It can begin small and occupy only a corner of our lives. Yet, if left unattended, countenanced, and allowed to flourish, it can consume one's soul.

An ancient American prophet understood perfectly well this concept of which I speak. He referred to the devil as the founder of sin and works of darkness and warned: "He [the devil] leadeth them by the neck with a flaxen cord, until he bindeth them with his strong cords forever" (2 Nephi 26:22).

Those who become followers of the evil one do not generally reach their captive state with one misdeed. They lose their freedom one sin at a time—one error after another—until almost all is lost. Flaxen cords are transformed into awful chains of steel as one allows oneself to follow the downward course. Each easy step away from the line of goodness and truth makes it more and more difficult to recover.

More than 2500 years ago, the prophet Nephi predicted the conditions of our day. Among other things he said,

> There shall be many which shall say: Eat, drink, and be merry, for tomorrow we die; and it shall be well with us.
>
> And there shall also be many which shall say: Eat, drink, and be merry; nevertheless, fear God—he will justify in committing a little sin; yea, lie a little, take the advantage of one because of his words, dig a pit for thy neighbor; there is no harm in this; and do all these things, for tomorrow we die; and if it so be that we are guilty, God will beat us with a few stripes, and at last we shall be saved in the kingdom of God. [2 Nephi 28:7–8]

Nephi labeled such teachings as "false and vain and foolish doctrines" (2 Nephi 28:9) and stated further:

> The devil will grasp them with his everlasting chains. . . .
>
> And others will he pacify, and lull them away into carnal security, that they will say: All is well in Zion; yea, Zion prospereth, all is well—and thus the devil cheateth their souls, and leadeth them away carefully down to hell.
>
> And behold, others he flattereth away, and telleth them there is no hell; and he saith unto them: I am no devil, for there is none—and thus he whispereth in their ears, until he grasps them with his awful chains, from whence there is no deliverance. [2 Nephi 28:19, 21–22]

Several years ago, in a large city, my wife and I saw a sign in front of a church with this notice on the bulletin board: "Sunday Worship Services, 10:00 a.m." And below that, "Sunday Sermon Topic: Nice Sins for Good People." Though I did not attend these services, I have wondered ever since about the flattering and the pacifying and the lulling and the ear tickling that must have taken place in that setting.

Do not be deceived! There are no niceties, no goodnesses associated with sin, however small or large the transgression may appear.

King David's flaxen-thread glance at Bathsheba resulted in the strong cords of adultery and death. The little murmurs of Laman and Lemuel led to the big breakup of a family and the splitting of a nation. Moreover, the little errors that you and I commit can become very binding if not checked. It is written,

> His own iniquities shall take the wicked himself, and he shall be holden with the cords of his sins. [Proverbs 5:22]

I suggest that you make a careful assessment of your life and determine your own state of affairs. Are you encumbered with so-called "nice" sins? Do you lie a little? Are you reckless with the truth? Are you perfectly honest with others? Do you gossip, do you dig verbal pits for your friends? Can you see any evidences of flaxen cords in your young lives? If so, be very careful.

I would also suggest to you, in the spirit of helpfulness, that the process of repentance is the means of escape from the clutches of sin and is not unlike the process of cultivating a desirable habit. Permit me to make the comparison:

Step one in habit formation, I said, was to define the habit. Equivalent action in repentance is *recognition of error.*

Step two in habit formation is to bind yourself to action. This step in repentance is *resolve to do better.*

Step three in habit formation is to put the new conduct into operation. In repenting, we *reform our living pattern.*

Step four in habit formation is to bolster will or desire. In repenting, *we reflect seriously upon the forgiving nature of God and Christ's atonement.*

Step five in habit formation is do not look back. In repentance, *we refrain from committing the error again.*

Step six in habit formation is to plunge wholeheartedly into the new conduct. This action in repentance is *complete faith and reliance in the new direction one is taking.*

One Church leader describes repentance as

> the process whereby a mortal soul—unclean and stained with the guilt of sin—is enabled to cast off the burden of guilt, wash away

> the filth of iniquity, and become clean every whit, entirely free from the bondage of sin. [*MD*, p. 630]

Without the hopes and prospects embodied in the principle of repentance, it is doubtful that many of us would be able to retain our balance and sanity. We do err frequently; we do fall short of the mark; we often disappoint ourselves and those around us. If a means of escape and relief through repentance were not extended us, we would probably not be strong enough to cope with life.

One sagging spirit, fettered by remorse for sin, cried out:

> I wish that there were some wonderful place
> Called the Land of Beginning Again,
> Where all our mistakes and all our heartaches
> And all of our poor selfish grief
> Could be dropped like a shabby old coat at the door,
> And never be put on again.
> [Louisa Fletcher, "The Land of Beginning Again," *Best Loved Poems of the American People,* selected by Hazel Felleman (Garden City, NY: Garden City Publishing, 1936), p. 101]

How blessed we are to know that there is a "Land of Beginning Again"! This land is the gospel of Jesus Christ, and the door to it is that blessed principle of repentance. When we apply this principle in the Lord's way, cords and chains are removed, and we are freed from the enemies of our souls.

Some years ago, on this very campus, Elder Robert L. Simpson, one of my beloved quorum associates, spoke about new beginnings and the principle of repentance. I would like to share with you just a portion of his inspired message. He said, speaking to a group much like you:

> I can almost hear some of you saying at this very moment, "It's all so futile. Here I am only [38 days into the new year], and already I've goofed twice."
>
> Young people, I want to assure you that you're not too far from par for the course. Just about everybody has had a bad start sometime or another. As I was watching the Rose Bowl game on

> television the other day, I had a flashback of something that happened to me many years ago on a high school football field not too far from that Rose Bowl. Speaking of getting off to a bad start, I think I hold the record. It was my first year in high school football. I'd been playing second string all through the practice games, and this was the first big league game. Six thousand cheering people were in the stands. As we were breaking after our halftime pep talk, the coach suddenly said, "Simpson, you start the second half."
>
> The old adrenalin came rushing, and I went charging out onto the field. This was my chance. Just about that time the coach said, "Oh, and by the way, I want you to kick off, Simpson."
>
> I determined right then and there that I was going to kick that ball farther than any football had ever been kicked in history. I really wanted to make a good showing on my first chance on the first string. Well, the referee waved his arm and blew his whistle. I could hear those six thousand people. I looked at that ball and came charging down the field. I felt everything tingling in my body; the excitement was so high.
>
> Well, you have probably already guessed it. I missed the ball. . . . But that isn't the half of it. This was back in the days when the quarterback held the ball with his finger. I broke the quarterback's finger.
>
> Now, if you think that you're off to a bad start, I just want to set your mind at ease and let you know that it could be worse. I also want you to know that I had a coach that had confidence [in me] because he left me in. I don't know why, but he did, and I played the rest of the game. If I weren't so modest, I might also tell you that I made all-league that year. ["Your 1975 Game Plan," *BYU Speeches of the Year* 1975 (Provo, Utah: Brigham Young University Press, 1976), pp. 319–20; also *Ensign*, January 1977, p. 83]

I love the lesson that is taught in Elder Simpson's experience. A young man of less determination might have been bound to failure by missing that ball. And, if not by that, certainly by breaking the quarterback's finger. However, Elder Simpson had "plasticity" and confidence and resolve, and he repented of his error and made all-league.

Just one week ago I heard a young man in California at a stake conference talk about repentance, or the Land of Beginning Again.

He shared with us the sequence of actions that, over the course of years, has taught him to respect the advice and direction of his parents. This is the way he outlined it: one, Dan decides to do something; two, Dan talks to his parents; three, parents suggest to Dan that he not do it and explain why; four, Dan does it anyway; five, Dan winds up in trouble; six, Dan doesn't do that any more. Well, that's the spirit of repentance. That's the spirit of the Land of Beginning Again, that glorious principle of repentance which is afforded to all of us.

As you give further thought to what I have said about bad habits and sin, I would hope that you would retain foremost in your minds a scene which Enoch was privileged to see. He saw in his vision the coming of the Son of Man, the restoration of the gospel, and many other things. He may even have seen in vision this institution. Then he heard a voice saying,

> Wo, wo be unto the inhabitants of the earth.
>
> And he beheld Satan; and he had a great chain in his hand, and it veiled the whole face of the earth with darkness; and he looked up and laughed, and his angels rejoiced. [Moses 7:25–26]

The chain held by Satan is referred to in the scriptures as "the chains of hell" (Alma 12:11), "the bands of iniquity" (Mosiah 23:12), "chains of darkness" (2 Peter 2:4), and "the everlasting chains of death" (Alma 36:18). Such chains are used in making us captives of the evil one. Normally, they are not thrown over a man or a woman suddenly or in one single act. They start as flaxen threads and encumber a person habit by habit, sin by sin, and strand by strand. And if not cut and cast off through the process of repentance, they can become heavy chains and the awful "snare of the devil" (2 Timothy 2:26).

So, be very careful. While you are here at this institution, while you are in your "plastic" years, identify your weaknesses, replace bad habits with good ones, and avoid any and every appearance of evil. I have one desire for all of you, and that desire is that you will succeed in your academic and religious lives. Please be careful. Do not allow the chains of Satan to fall upon you. Do not allow those little threads to encircle you about. Throw them off. Cut them loose. Do not allow him to make you his. Satan is very uncomfortable, he is very miserable, and he seeks to make you and me miserable like unto himself.

God bless you, my friends. I bear testimony to you that the gospel of Jesus Christ has been restored to the earth. I have perfect confidence in the principle of repentance. I know that Christ did atone for your sins and mine, if we will but repent. May we take advantage of that which he has provided us and use his grace in moving ourselves forward on the important path that leads to eternal life. This is my prayer this evening, in the name of the Lord Jesus Christ. Amen.

Carlos E. Asay was a member of the Presidency of the First Quorum of the Seventy when this fireside address was given in the Marriott Center on 7 February 1982.

Fourteen Fundamentals in Following the Prophet

EZRA TAFT BENSON

MY BELOVED brothers and sisters, I am honored to be in your presence today. You students are a part of a choice young generation—a generation that might well witness the return of our Lord.

Not only is the Church growing in numbers today, it is growing in faithfulness, and, even more important, our young generation, as a group, is even more faithful than the older generation. God has reserved you for the eleventh hour—the great and dreadful day of the Lord. It will be your responsibility not only to help bear off the kingdom of God triumphantly but to save your own soul and strive to save those of your family and to honor the principles of our inspired Constitution.

To help you pass the crucial tests that lie ahead, I am going to give you today several facets of a grand key that, if you will honor them, will crown you with God's glory and bring you out victorious in spite of Satan's fury.

Soon we will be honoring our prophet on his eighty-fifth birthday. As a church we sing the song, "We Thank Thee, O God, for a Prophet." Here then is the grand key: Follow the prophet. And here are fourteen fundamentals in following the prophet, the president of The Church of Jesus Christ of Latter-day Saints.

First: *The prophet is the only man who speaks for the Lord in everything.*

In section 132, verse 7, of the Doctrine and Covenants the Lord speaks of the prophet—the president—and says: "There is never but one on the earth at a time on whom this power and the keys of this priesthood are conferred."

Then, in section 21, verses 4–6, the Lord states:

> Wherefore, meaning the church, thou shalt give heed unto all his words and commandments which he shall give unto you as he receiveth them, walking in all holiness before me;
>
> For his word ye shall receive, as if from mine own mouth, in all patience and faith.
>
> For by doing these things the gates of hell shall not prevail against you.

Did you hear what the Lord said about the words of the prophet? We are to "give heed unto all his words"—as if from the Lord's "own mouth."

Second: *The living prophet is more vital to us than the standard works.*

President Wilford Woodruff tells of an interesting incident that occurred in the days of the Prophet Joseph Smith:

> I will refer to a certain meeting I attended in the town of Kirtland in my early days. At that meeting some remarks were made that have been made here today, with regard to the living oracles and with regard to the written word of God. The same principle was presented, although not as extensively as it has been here, when a leading man in the Church got up and talked upon the subject, and said: "You have got the word of God before you here in the Bible, Book of Mormon, and Doctrine and Covenants; you have the written word of God, and you who give revelations should give revelations according to those books, as what is written

in those books is the word of God. We should confine ourselves to them."

When he concluded, Brother Joseph turned to Brother Brigham Young and said, "Brother Brigham, I want you to take the stand and tell us your views with regard to the living oracles and the written word of God." Brother Brigham took the stand, and he took the Bible, and laid it down; he took the Book of Mormon, and laid it down; and he took the Book of Doctrine and Covenants, and laid it down before him, and he said: "There is the written word of God to us, concerning the work of God from the beginning of the world, almost, to our day. And now," said he, "when compared with the living oracles those books are nothing to me; those books do not convey the word of God direct to us now, as do the words of a Prophet or a man bearing the Holy Priesthood in our day and generation. I would rather have the living oracles than all the writing in the books." That was the course he pursued. When he was through, Brother Joseph said to the congregation: "Brother Brigham has told you the word of the Lord, and he has told you the truth." [*CR*, October 1897, pp. 18–19]

Third: *The living prophet is more important to us than a dead prophet.*

The living prophet has the power of TNT. By that I mean "Today's News Today." God's revelations to Adam did not instruct Noah how to build the ark. Noah needed his own revelation. Therefore, the most important prophet, so far as you and I are concerned, is the one living in our day and age to whom the Lord is currently revealing his will for us. Therefore, the most important reading we can do is that of any of the words of the prophet contained each week in the Church section of the *Deseret News* and any words of the prophet contained each month in our Church magazines. Our marching orders for each six months are found in the general conference addresses, which are printed in the *Ensign* magazine.

I am so grateful that the current conference report is studied as part of one of your religion classes—the course entitled "Teachings of the Living Prophets," number 333. May I commend that class to you and suggest that you get a copy of the class manual at your bookstore whether you're able to take the class or not. The manual is entitled "Living Prophets for a Living Church."

Beware of those who would pit the dead prophets against the living prophets, for the living prophets always take precedence.

Fourth: *The prophet will never lead the Church astray.*

President Wilford Woodruff stated: "I say to Israel, the Lord will never permit me or any other man who stands as president of this Church to lead you astray. It is not in the program. It is not in the mind of God" (*The Discourses of Wilford Woodruff,* selected by G. Homer Durham [Salt Lake City: Bookcraft, 1946], p. 212).

President Marion G. Romney tells of this incident that happened to him:

> I remember years ago when I was a Bishop I had President [Heber J.] Grant talk to our ward. After the meeting I drove him home. . . . Standing by me, he put his arm over my shoulder and said: "My boy, you always keep your eye on the president of the Church, and if he ever tells you to do anything, and it is wrong, and you do it, the Lord will bless you for it." Then with a twinkle in his eye, he said, "But you don't need to worry. The Lord will never let his mouthpiece lead the people astray." [*CR,* October 1960, p. 78]

Fifth: *The prophet is not required to have any particular earthly training or credentials to speak on any subject or act on any matter at any time.*

Sometimes there are those who feel their earthly knowledge on a certain subject is superior to the heavenly knowledge God gives to his prophet on the same subject. They feel the prophet must have the same earthly credentials or training that they have had before they will accept anything the prophet has to say that might contradict their earthly schooling. How much earthly schooling did Joseph Smith have? Yet he gave revelations on all kinds of subjects. We haven't yet had a prophet who earned a doctorate in any subject, but as someone said, "A prophet may not have his Ph.D., but he certainly has his LDS." We encourage earthly knowledge in many areas, but remember, if there is ever a conflict between earthly knowledge and the words of the prophet, you stand with the prophet, and you'll be blessed and time will vindicate you.

Sixth: *The prophet does not have to say "Thus saith the Lord" to give us scripture.*

Sometimes there are those who haggle over words. They might say the prophet gave us counsel but that we are not obligated to follow it unless he says it is a commandment. But the Lord says of the Prophet Joseph, "Thou shalt give heed unto all his *words and commandments* which he shall give unto you" (D&C 21:4; emphasis added).

And speaking of taking counsel from the prophet, in D&C 108:1, the Lord states: "Verily thus saith the Lord unto you, my servant Lyman: Your sins are forgiven you, because you have obeyed my voice in coming up hither this morning to receive *counsel* of him whom I have appointed" (emphasis added).

Said Brigham Young, "I have never yet preached a sermon and sent it out to the children of men, that they may not call Scripture" (*JD* 13:95).

Seventh: *The prophet tells us what we need to know, not always what we want to know.*

"Thou hast declared unto us hard things, more than we are able to bear," complained Nephi's brethren. But Nephi answered by saying, "The guilty taketh the truth to be hard, for it cutteth them to the very center" (1 Nephi 16:1–2). Or, to put it in another prophet's words, "Hit pigeons flutter."

Said President Harold B. Lee:

> You may not like what comes from the authority of the Church. It may contradict your political views. It may contradict your social views. It may interfere with some of your social life. . . . Your safety and ours depends upon whether or not we follow. . . . Let's keep our eye on the president of the Church. [*CR*, October 1970, p. 152–53]

But it is the living prophet who really upsets the world. "Even in the Church," said President Kimball, "many are prone to garnish the sepulchres of yesterday's prophets and mentally stone the living ones" ("To His Servants the Prophets," *Instructor* 95 [August 1960], p. 257).

Why? Because the living prophet gets at what we need to know now, and the world prefers that prophets either be dead or mind their own business. Some so-called experts of political science want the prophet to keep still on politics. Some would-be authorities on evolution want the prophet to keep still on evolution. And so the list goes on and on.

How we respond to the words of a living prophet when he tells us what we need to know, but would rather not hear, is a test of our faithfulness.

Said President Marion G. Romney, "It is an easy thing to believe in the dead prophets." And then he gives this illustration:

> One day when President Grant was living, I sat in my office across the street following a general conference. A man came over to see me, an elderly man. He was very upset about what had been said in this conference by some of the Brethren, including myself. I could tell from his speech that he came from a foreign land. After I had quieted him enough so he would listen, I said, "Why did you come to America?"
>
> "I am here because a prophet of God told me to come."
>
> "Who was the prophet?" I continued.
>
> "Wilford Woodruff."
>
> "Do you believe Wilford Woodruff was a prophet of God?"
>
> "Yes," said he.
>
> "Do you believe that President Joseph F. Smith was a prophet of God?"
>
> "Yes, sir."
>
> Then came the "sixty-four dollar question." "Do you believe that Heber J. Grant is a prophet of God?"
>
> His answer: "I think he ought to keep his mouth shut about old age assistance."
>
> Now I tell you that a man in his position is on the way to apostasy. He is forfeiting his chances for eternal life. So is everyone who cannot follow the living prophet of God. [*CR*, April 1953, p. 125]

Eighth: *The prophet is not limited by men's reasoning.*

There will be times when you will have to choose between the revelations of God and the reasoning of men—between the prophet and the politician or professor. Said the Prophet Joseph Smith, "Whatever God requires is right, no matter what it is, although we may not see the *reason* thereof until long after the events transpire" (*Scrapbook of Mormon Literature,* vol. 2, p. 173).

Would it seem reasonable to an eye doctor to be told to heal a blind man by spitting in the dirt, making clay, and applying it to the man's eyes and then telling him to wash in a contaminated pool? Yet this is precisely the course that Jesus took with one man, and he was healed (see John 9:6–7). Does it seem reasonable to cure leprosy by telling a man to wash seven times in a particular river? Yet this is precisely what the prophet Elisha told a leper to do, and he was healed (see 2 Kings 5).

> For my thoughts are not your thoughts, neither are your ways my ways, saith the Lord.
>
> For as the heavens are higher than the earth, so are my ways higher than your ways, and my thoughts than your thoughts. [Isaiah 55:8–9]

Ninth: *The prophet can receive revelation on any matter—temporal or spiritual.*

Said Brigham Young:

> Some of the leading men in Kirtland were much opposed to Joseph the Prophet, meddling with temporal affairs. . . . In a public meeting of the Saints, I said "Ye Elders of Israel, . . . will some of you draw the line of demarcation, between the spiritual and the temporal in the Kingdom of God, so that I may understand it?" Not one of them could do it. . . .
>
> I defy any man on earth to point out the path a Prophet of God should walk in, or point out his duty, and just how far he must go, in dictating temporal or spiritual things. Temporal and spiritual things are inseperably [*sic*] connected, and ever will be. [*JD* 10:363–64]

Tenth: *The prophet may be involved in civic matters.*

When a people are righteous they want the best to lead them in government. Alma was the head of the Church and of the government in the Book of Mormon, Joseph Smith was mayor of Nauvoo, and Brigham Young was governor of Utah. Isaiah was deeply involved in giving counsel on political matters, and of his words the Lord himself said, "Great are the words of Isaiah" (3 Nephi 23:1). Those who would remove prophets from politics would take God out of government.

Eleventh: *The two groups who have the greatest difficulty in following the prophet are the proud who are learned and the proud who are rich.*

The learned may feel the prophet is only inspired when he agrees with them; otherwise, the prophet is just giving his opinion—speaking as a man. The rich may feel they have no need to take counsel of a lowly prophet.

In the Book of Mormon we read:

> O that cunning plan of the evil one! O the vainness, and the frailties, and the foolishness of men! When they are learned they think they are wise, and they hearken not unto the counsel of God, for they set it aside, supposing they know of themselves, wherefore, their wisdom is foolishness and it profiteth them not. And they shall perish.
>
> But to be learned is good *if* they hearken unto the counsels of God.
>
> And whoso knocketh, to him will he open; and the wise, and the learned, and they that are rich, who are puffed up because of their learning, and their wisdom, and their riches—yea, they are they whom he despiseth; and save they shall cast these things away, and consider themselves fools before God, and come down in the depths of humility, he will not open unto them. [2 Nephi 9:28–29, 42; emphasis added]

Twelfth: *The prophet will not necessarily be popular with the world or the worldly.*

As a prophet reveals the truth, it divides the people. The honest in heart heed his words, but the unrighteous either ignore the prophet or fight him. When the prophet points out the sins of the world, the worldly either want to close the mouth of the prophet or else act as if the prophet does not exist, rather than repent of their sins. Popularity is never a test of truth. Many a prophet has been killed or cast out. As we come closer to the Lord's second coming, you can expect that as the people of the world become more wicked, the prophet will be less popular with them.

Thirteenth: *The prophet and his counselors make up the First Presidency—the highest quorum in the Church.*

In the Doctrine and Covenants, the Lord refers to the First Presidency as "the highest council of the church" (107:80) and says, "Whosoever receiveth me, receiveth those, the First Presidency, whom I have sent" (112:20).

Fourteenth: *The prophet and the presidency—the living prophet and the First Presidency—follow them and be blessed; reject them and suffer.*

President Harold B. Lee relates this incident from Church history:

> The story is told in the early days of the Church—particularly, I think, at Kirtland—where some of the leading brethren in the presiding councils of the Church met secretly and tried to scheme as to how they could get rid of the Prophet Joseph's leadership. They made the mistake of inviting Brigham Young to one of these secret meetings. He rebuked them, after he had heard the purpose of their meeting. This is part of what he said: "You cannot destroy the appointment of a prophet of God, but you can cut the thread that binds you to the prophet of God and sink yourselves to hell." [*CR*, April 1963, p. 81]

In a general conference of the Church, President N. Eldon Tanner stated:

> The Prophet spoke out clearly on Friday morning, telling us what our responsibilities are. . . .
>
> A man said to me after that, *"You know, there are people in our state who believe in following the Prophet in everything they think is right, but when it is something they think isn't right, and it doesn't*

> *appeal to them, then that's different."* He said, "Then they become their own prophet. They decide what the Lord wants and what the Lord doesn't want."
>
> I thought how true, and how serious when we begin to choose which of the covenants, which of the commandments we will keep and follow. When we decide that there are some of them that we will not keep or follow, we are taking the law of the Lord into our own hands and become our own prophets, and believe me, we will be led astray, *because we are false prophets to ourselves when we do not follow the Prophet of God.* No, we should never discriminate between these commandments, as to those we should and should not keep. [*CR,* October 1966, p. 98; emphasis added]

"Look to the Presidency and receive instruction," said the Prophet Joseph Smith (*Teachings,* p. 161). But Almon Babbitt didn't, and in the Doctrine and Covenants, section 124, verse 84, the Lord states: "And with my servant Almon Babbitt, there are many things with which I am not pleased; behold, he aspireth to establish his counsel instead of the counsel which I have ordained, even that of the Presidency of my Church."

In conclusion, let us summarize this grand key, these "Fourteen Fundamentals in Following the Prophet," for our salvation hangs on them.

First: The prophet is the only man who speaks for the Lord in everything.

Second: The living prophet is more vital to us than the standard works.

Third: The living prophet is more important to us than a dead prophet.

Fourth: The prophet will never lead the Church astray.

Fifth: The prophet is not required to have any particular earthly training or credentials to speak on any subject or act on any matter at any time.

Sixth: The prophet does not have to say "Thus saith the Lord" to give us scripture.

Seventh: The prophet tells us what we need to know, not always what we want to know.

Eighth: The prophet is not limited by men's reasoning.

Ninth: The prophet can receive revelation on any matter—temporal or spiritual.

Tenth: The prophet may be involved in civic matters.

Eleventh: The two groups who have the greatest difficulty in following the prophet are the proud who are learned and the proud who are rich.

Twelfth: The prophet will not necessarily be popular with the world or the worldly.

Thirteenth: The prophet and his counselors make up the First Presidency—the highest quorum in the Church.

Fourteenth: The prophet and the presidency—the living prophet and the First Presidency—follow them and be blessed; reject them and suffer.

I testify that these fourteen fundamentals in following the living prophet are true. If we want to know how well we stand with the Lord, then let us ask ourselves how well we stand with his mortal captain. How closely do our lives harmonize with the words of the Lord's anointed—the living prophet, the president of the Church, and with the Quorum of the First Presidency?

May God bless us all to look to the prophet and the presidency in the critical and crucial days ahead is my prayer, in the name of Jesus Christ. Amen.

Ezra Taft Benson was the president of the Council of the Twelve Apostles of The Church of Jesus Christ of Latter-day Saints when this devotional address was given in the Marriott Center on 26 February 1980.

Gifts of Love

HENRY B. EYRING

I AM DELIGHTED to be here with you. I pray that I may have the blessings of the Spirit so that I can say something useful to you.

A father asked me yesterday to advise him about giving a Christmas gift to his daughter. He just can't decide whether or not to give this gift, or how to give it. His daughter is a college student; she may even be listening today. Her hectic life of school activities is made even harder because she doesn't have a car. She begs rides, and she sometimes misses appointments. Her dad doesn't have enough money for another car, at least not without some real sacrifice by his family. But he's found a used car he might buy for her if he cuts enough corners on the family budget. And now he's wondering. He asked me, "Will that car really be good for her, or will it be a problem? I love her, and she really could use it, but do you think it will help her or spoil her?" Let me guess. I can hear you rooting for the car: "Go for it! Go for it!"

I didn't try to answer his question then, but I could sense his worry and sympathize with him. You ought to have sympathy for both givers and getters at Christmastime. Last night my sons, Matthew and John, and I spent time at a toy store. Above us a red Santa Claus spun slowly as the sound of a mother whispering with clenched teeth floated over the stacks of toys to our aisle:

"Don't tell me what your brother did to you. I saw *everything.* Do you want me to hit you right here in the store? Now you go outside and sit on that bench. And you stay there. And if you don't I won't get you a thing." John and I shrugged and smiled at each other as we moved on, and I hummed inwardly, " 'Tis the season to be jolly."

Gift giving isn't easy. It's *hard* to give a gift with confidence. There are so many things that can go wrong. You wonder if the person on the other end will want it. My batting average on that is low. At least I think it is. You can't really tell what gets returned after Christmas, but I am cautious enough that I always wrap the gift in the box from the store where I bought it.

I've always daydreamed of being a great gift giver. I picture people opening my gifts and showing with tears of joy and a smile that the giving, not just the gift, has touched their hearts. You must have that daydream, too. Many of you are probably already experts in gift giving. But even the experts may share some of my curiosity about what makes a gift great. I've been surrounded by expert gift givers all my life. None of them has ever told me how to do it, but I've been watching and I've been building a theory. I think it's finally ready to be shared, at least among friends at this university. Here it is: The Eyring Theory of Gift Giving and Receiving. I call it a theory because it is surely incomplete. And calling it a theory means I expect you will change and improve it. I hope so, because then it will be yours. But at least I can help your theory building along.

My theory comes from thinking about many gifts and many holidays, but one day and one gift can illustrate it. The day was not Christmas nor even close to it. It was a summer day. My mother had died in the early afternoon. My father, my brother, and I had been at the hospital. As we walked out, my brother and I went to the car together, smiled, and looked up at the mountains. We remembered how Mother had always said she loved the mountains so much. He and I laughed and guessed that if the celestial worlds are really flat, like a sea of glass, she would be eager to get away to build her own worlds, and the first thing she'd build would be mountains. With that we smiled and got into the car and drove home. We went to the family home, and Dad met us there. There were just the three of us.

Friends and family came and went. In a lull, we fixed ourselves a snack. Then we visited with more callers. It grew late and dusk fell; I remember we still had not turned on the lights.

Then Dad answered the doorbell again. It was Aunt Catherine and Uncle Bill. When they'd walked just a few feet past the vestibule, Uncle Bill extended his hand, and I could see that he was holding a bottle of cherries. I can still see the deep red, almost purple, cherries and the shining gold cap on the mason jar. He said, "You might enjoy these. You probably haven't had dessert."

We hadn't. The three of us sat around the kitchen table and put some cherries in bowls and ate them as Uncle Bill and Aunt Catherine cleared some dishes. Uncle Bill then asked, "Are there people you haven't had time to call? Just give me some names, and I'll do it." We mentioned a few relatives who would want to know of Mother's death. And then Aunt Catherine and Uncle Bill were gone. They could not have been with us more than twenty minutes.

Now, you can understand my theory best if you focus on one gift: the bottle of cherries. And let me explain this theory from the point of view of one person who received the gift: me. As we'll see, that is crucial. What matters in what the giver does is what the receiver feels. You may not believe that yet, but trust me for the moment. So let's start from inside me and with the gift of the bottle of cherries.

As near as I can tell, the giving and receiving of a great gift always has three parts. Here they are, illustrated by that gift on a summer evening.

First, I knew that Uncle Bill and Aunt Catherine had felt what I was feeling and had been touched. I'm not over the thrill of that yet. They must have felt we'd be too tired to fix much food. They must have felt that a bowl of home-canned cherries would make us, for a moment, feel like a family again. And not only did they feel what I felt, they were touched by it. Just knowing that someone had understood meant far more to me than the cherries themselves.

I can't remember the taste of the cherries, but I remember that someone knew my heart and cared.

Second, I felt the gift was free. I knew Uncle Bill and Aunt Catherine had chosen freely to bring a gift. I knew they weren't doing so to compel a response from us. The gift seemed, at least to me, to provide them with joy just by their giving it.

And third, there was sacrifice. Now you might say, "Wait. How could they give for the joy of it and yet make a sacrifice?" Well, I could see the sacrifice because the cherries were home bottled. That meant Aunt Catherine had prepared them for her family. They must have liked cherries. But she took that possible pleasure from them and gave it to us. That's sacrifice. However, I have realized since then this marvelous fact: It must have seemed to Uncle Bill and Aunt Catherine that they would have more pleasure if we had the cherries than if they did. There was sacrifice, but they made it for a greater return: our happiness. Most people feel deprived as they sacrifice to give another person a gift, and then they let that person know it. But only expert givers let the receiver sense that their sacrifice brings them joy.

Well, there it is—a simple theory. When you're on the receiving end, you will discover three things in great gift givers: (1) they felt what you felt and were touched, (2) they gave freely, and (3) they counted sacrifice a bargain.

Now you can see it won't be easy to use this theory to make big strides in your gift giving this Christmas. I don't expect you'll all rush out now and buy gifts brilliantly. It will take some practice—more than one holiday—to learn how to feel and be touched by what is inside someone else. And giving freely and counting sacrifice as joy will take a while. But you could start this Christmas being a good receiver. You might notice and you might appreciate. My theory suggests that you have the power to make others great gift givers by what you notice. You could make any gift better by what you choose to see, and you could, by failing to notice, make any gift a failure.

You can guess the advice I might have given my friend—the one with the car-less daughter. Would a car be a good gift? Of course it could be, but something very special must happen in the eyes of that daughter. On Christmas morning, her eyes would need to see past the car to Dad and to the family. If she saw that he had read her heart and really cared, if she saw that she'd not wheedled the car from the family nor that they had given it to extract some performance, and if she really saw the sacrifice and the joy with which it was made for her, then the gift would be more than wheels. In fact, the gift would still be carrying her long after the wheels no longer turned. (And from the dad's description of the car's age, that time could come fairly soon.) Her appreciation, if it lasts, will make a great gift of whatever awaits her on Christmas morning.

Gift giving requires a sensitive giver and receiver. I hope we will use this little theory not to criticize the gifts that come our way this year, but to see how often our hearts are understood and gifts are given joyfully, even with sacrifice.

There is something you could do this Christmas to start becoming a better gift giver yourself. In fact, as students, you have some special chances. You could begin to put some gifts—great gifts—on layaway for future Christmases. Let me tell you about them.

You could start back in your room today. Is there an unfinished paper somewhere in the stacks? (I assume there are stacks there; I think I know your room.) Perhaps it is typed and apparently ready to turn in. Why bother more with it? I learned why during a religion class I taught once at Ricks College. I was teaching from section 25 of the Doctrine and Covenants. In that section Emma Smith is told that she should give her time to "writing, and to learning much" (verse 8). About three rows back sat a blonde girl whose brow wrinkled as I urged the class to be diligent in developing writing skills. She raised her hand and said, "That doesn't seem reasonable to me. All I'll ever write are letters to my children." That brought laughter all around the class. I felt chagrined to have applied that scripture to her. Just looking at her I could imagine a full quiver of children around her, and I could even see the letters she'd write in purple ink, with handwriting slanting backwards, neat round loops, and circles for the tops of the *i*'s. Maybe writing powerfully wouldn't matter to her.

Then a young man stood up, near the back. He'd said little during the term; I'm not sure he'd ever spoken before. He was older than the other students, and he was shy. He asked if he could speak. He told in a quiet voice of having been a soldier in Vietnam. One day, in what he thought would be a lull, he had left his rifle and walked across his fortified compound to mail call. Just as he got a letter in his hand, he heard a bugle blowing and shouts and mortar and rifle fire coming ahead of the swarming enemy. He fought his way back to his rifle, using his hands as weapons. With the men who survived, he drove the enemy out. The wounded were evacuated. Then he sat down among the living, and some of the dead, and he opened his letter. It was from his mother. She wrote that she'd had a spiritual experience that assured her that he would live to come home if he were righteous. In my class, the boy said quietly, "That letter was scripture to me. I kept it." And he sat down.

You may have a child someday, perhaps a son. Can you see his face? Can you see him somewhere, sometime, in mortal danger? Can you feel the fear in his heart? Does it touch you? Would you like to give freely? What sacrifice will it take to write the letter your heart will want to send? You won't do it in the hour before the postman comes. Nor will it be possible in a day or even in a week. It may take years. Start the practice this afternoon. Go back to your room and write and read and rewrite that paper again and again. It won't seem like sacrifice if you picture that boy, feel his heart, and think of the letters he'll need someday.

Now, some of you may not have a paper waiting for you. It may be a textbook with a math problem hidden in it. (They hide them these days; the math is often tucked away in a special section that you can skip. And so many of you do.) Let me tell you about a Christmas in your future. You'll have a teenage son or daughter who'll say, "I hate school." After some careful listening, you'll find it is not school or even mathematics he or she hates—it's the feeling of failure.

You'll correctly discern those feelings and you'll be touched; you'll want to freely give. So you'll open the text and say, "Let's look at one of the problems together." Think of the shock you will feel when you see that the same rowboat is still going downstream in two hours and back in five hours, and the questions are still how fast the current is and how far the boat traveled. Just think what a shock it will be when you remember you've seen that problem before. Why, that rowboat has been in the water for generations! You might think, "Well, I'll make my children feel better by showing them that I can't do math either." Let me give you some advice: They will see that as a poor gift.

There is a better gift, but it will take effort now. My dad, when he was a boy, must have tackled the rowboat problem and lots of others. That was part of the equipment he needed to become a scientist who would make a difference to chemistry. But he also made a difference to me. Our family room didn't look as elegant as some. It had one kind of furniture—chairs—and one wall decoration—a green chalkboard. I came to the age your boy or girl will reach. I didn't wonder if I could work the math problems; I'd proved to my satisfaction that I couldn't. And some of my teachers were satisfied that that was true, too.

But Dad wasn't satisfied. He thought I could do it. So we took turns at that chalkboard. I can't remember the gifts my dad wrapped and helped put under a tree. But I remember the chalkboard and his quiet voice. In fact, there were some times when his voice was not quiet at all—he did shout, I'll have to admit in his presence—but he built up my mathematics, and he built up me. To do this took more than knowing what I needed and caring. It took more than being willing to give his time then, precious as it was. It took time he had spent earlier when he had the chances you have now. Because he had spent time then, he and I could have that time at the chalkboard and he could help me. And because he gave me that, I've got a boy who has let me sit down with him this year. We've rowed that same boat up and down. And his teacher wrote "much improved" on his report card. But I'll tell you what's improved most: the feelings of a fine boy about himself. Nothing

I will put under the tree for Stuart this year has half the chance of becoming a family heirloom that his pride of accomplishment does.

Now I see some art (or are they music?) majors smiling. They're thinking, "He surely can't convince me there's a gift hidden in my unfinished assignments." Let me try. Last week I went to an Eagle Scout court of honor. I've been to dozens, but this one had something I won't forget. Before the Eagle badge was given, there was a slide and sound show. The lights went down, and I recognized two voices on the tape. One was a famous singer in the background, and the other, the narrator, was the father of the new Eagle Scout. The slides were of eagles soaring and of mountains and of moon landings. I don't know if the Eagle Scout had a lump in his throat quite the size of mine, but I know he'll remember the gift. His dad must have spent hours preparing slides, writing words that soared, and then somehow getting music and words coordinated for the right volume and timing. You'll have a boy someday who will be honored at such an event, with all his cousins and aunts and uncles looking on. And with your whole heart, you'll want to tell him what he is and what he can be. Whether you can give that gift then depends on whether you feel his heart now and are touched and start building the creative skills you'll need. And it will mean more than you now can dream, I promise you.

There is yet another gift some of you may want to give that takes starting early. I saw it started once when I was a bishop. A student sat across my desk from me. He talked about mistakes he had made. And he talked about how much he wanted the children he might have someday to have a dad who could use his priesthood and to whom they could be sealed forever. He said he knew that the price and pain of repentance might be great. And then he said something I will not forget: "Bishop, I am coming back. I will do whatever it takes. I am coming back." He felt sorrow. And he had faith in Christ. And still it took months of painful effort. Finally, he asked if it were enough. And he said he didn't want me to guess; he wanted to be sure.

About that time a kind priesthood leader took me aside and asked me if I had any questions. I said that I did, and I asked how I could know when a person has done what it takes to be forgiven. To my surprise, he didn't give me a lecture on repentance or on revelation. He just asked some questions. They weren't what I had expected. They were questions like these: "Does he attend all his meetings?"

"Yes."

"Does he come on time?"

"Yes."

"Does he do what he is asked?"

"Yes."

"Does he do it promptly?"

"Yes."

The questions went on that way for a few minutes. And all the answers were the same. Then he said, "Do you have your answer?"

And I said, "Yes."

And so somewhere this Christmas there is a family with a righteous priesthood bearer at its head. They have eternal hopes and peace on earth. He'll probably give his family all sorts of gifts wrapped brightly, but nothing will matter quite so much as the one he started a long time ago in my office and has never stopped giving. He felt then the needs of children he'd only dreamed of, and he gave early and freely. He sacrificed his pride and sloth and numbed feelings. I am sure it doesn't seem like sacrifice now.

He could give that gift because of another one given long ago. God, the Father, gave his Son, and Jesus Christ gave us the Atonement, the greatest of all gifts and all giving. They somehow felt all the pain and sorrow of sin that would fall on all of us and everyone else who would ever live. I testify that what Paul said is true:

> We have a great high priest, that is passed into the heavens, Jesus the Son of God. . . .

> For we have not an high priest which cannot be touched with the feeling of our infirmities; but was in all points tempted like as we are, yet without sin.
>
> Let us therefore come boldly unto the throne of grace, that we may obtain mercy, and find grace to help in time of need. [Hebrews 4:14–16]

I bear you my testimony that Jesus gave the gift freely, willingly, to us all. He said, "Therefore doth my Father love me, because I lay down my life, that I might take it again. No man taketh it from me, but I lay it down of myself" (John 10:17–18). All men and women come into this life with that gift. They will live again, and if they will, they may live with him.

And I bear you testimony that as you accept that gift, given through infinite sacrifice, it brings joy to the giver. Jesus taught, "I say unto you, that likewise joy shall be in heaven over one sinner that repenteth, more than over ninety and nine just persons, which need no repentance" (Luke 15:7).

If that warms you as it does me, you may well want to give a gift to the Savior. Others did at his birth. Knowing what we do, how much more do we want to give him something. But he seems to have everything. Well, not quite. He doesn't have you with him again forever, not yet. I hope you are touched by the feelings of his heart enough to sense how much he wants to know you are coming home to him. You can't give that gift to him in one day, or one Christmas, but you could show him today that you are on the way. You could pray. You could read a page of scripture. You could keep a commandment.

If you have already done these things, there is still something left to give. All around you are people he loves and can only help through you and me. One of the sure signs that a person has accepted the gift of the Savior's atonement is gift giving. The process of cleansing seems to make us more sensitive, more gracious, more pleased to share what means so much to us. I suppose that's why the Savior spoke of giving in describing who would finally come home.

> Then shall the King say unto them on his right hand, Come, ye blessed of my Father, inherit the kingdom prepared for you from the foundation of the world:
>
> For I was an hungred, and ye gave me meat: I was thirsty, and ye gave me drink: I was a stranger, and ye took me in:
>
> Naked, and ye clothed me: I was sick, and ye visited me: I was in prison, and ye came unto me.
>
> Then shall the righteous answer him, saying, Lord, when saw we thee an hungred, and fed thee? or thirsty, and gave thee drink?
>
> When saw we thee a stranger, and took thee in? or naked, and clothed thee?
>
> Or when saw we thee sick, or in prison, and came unto thee?
>
> And the King shall answer and say unto them, Verily I say unto you, Inasmuch as ye have done it unto one of the least of these my brethren, ye have done it unto me. [Matthew 25:34–40]

And that, I suppose, is the nicest effect of receiving great gifts. It makes us want to give, and give well. I've been blessed all my life by such gifts. I acknowledge that. I'm sure you do, too. Many of those gifts were given long ago. We're near the birthday of the Prophet Joseph Smith. He gave his great talent, and his life, that the gospel of Jesus Christ might be restored for me and for you. Ancestors of mine from Switzerland and Germany and Yorkshire and Wales left home and familiar ways to embrace the restored gospel, as much for me as for them, perhaps more. It was ten years after the Saints came into these mountains before my great-grandfather's journal shows one reference to so much as a Christmas meal. One entry reads, in its entirety: "December 25, 1855: Fixed a shed and went to the cedars. Four sheep died last night. Froze." I acknowledge such gifts, which I only hope I am capable of sending along to people I have not yet seen.

And so shall we do what we can to appreciate and to give a merry Christmas?

"Freely ye have received, freely give" (Matthew 10:8). I pray that we will freely give. I pray that we will be touched by the feelings of others, that we will give without feelings of compulsion or expectation of gain, and that we will know that sacrifice is made sweet to us when we treasure the joy it brings to another heart. For this I pray, in the name of Jesus Christ. Amen.

Henry B. Eyring was commissioner of education for the Church Educational System when this devotional address was given in the Marriott Center on 16 December 1980.

The Blessings of Adversity

JAMES E. FAUST

IT IS ALWAYS a special thrill and blessing to come upon this campus. My message today is simple, but one that you may not wish to hear. I have chosen to speak concerning the blessings of adversity. The theme was best expressed by the Lord when he said, "Be patient in afflictions, for thou shalt have many; but endure them, for, lo, I am with thee, even unto the end of thy days" (D&C 24:8).

During the past two years, and indeed for about five years of my life, I have lived in countries where most of the people are far below the poverty level of the United States. During this last period of time, as President Oaks indicated, we made our home in São Paulo, Brazil. During most of that time our neighbor to the north was constructing a new home. The carpenters, the tile setters, the plumbers, and the cabinetmakers on that house received far below what we know as the minimum wage. In fact, some lived in a shack on the site. There was cold running water available from the end of a hose, but no warm or hot water. Their work day was from 6:00 A.M. till about 5:30 P.M. This meant that at about 5:00 in the morning they would begin to prepare their meals and get ready for work.

My college-age daughter, Lisa, could not help complaining that she was awakened almost every morning by their clarion-voiced singing. They sang, they laughed, they chattered—only occasionally unpleasantly—the whole day through. When I explained to Lisa how little money they made and how little they had, she made an interesting observation, "But Dad, they seem so happy." And happy they were. Not one owned an automobile, nor even a bicycle—just the clothes on their backs—but they found life pleasant and fulfilling. We were reminded again how little it takes to make some people happy.

Many years ago when I was practicing law, I organized a company for one of the new car dealers in this area. I served as his legal counsel and a corporate officer for many years, and one of my sons has taken over my responsibilities as legal counsel. Recently we were both at his place of business. I noticed the rows and rows of beautiful, shiny, gleaming, expensive new cars. Out of concern I mentioned to the proprietor that if he did not get those cars sold, the finance charges would be exorbitant and eat up the profits. My son said, "Dad, don't look at it that way. Look at all the profit those cars will bring."

While I think he was more right than I, it suddenly occurred to me that my son had never been through a depression. We looked at the problem through different eyes because I am a child of the Great Depression. I cannot forget what a merciless taskmaster debt is.

For some years we lived by a very skilled mechanic and his choice family. He was a specialist. He and his wife resolved never again to go into debt. This resolution was born of a bitter memory: when they were newly married and had their small family, the depression came along, and skilled as he was he could not find a job. His home, along with the homes of many others, was foreclosed; and they lived through the depression in a chicken coop made reasonably comfortable through his mechanical skills.

We now have a generation many of whom perhaps have not fully known nor appreciated the refining blessings of adversity. Many have never been hungry because of want. Few have been forced not to do things because they did not have the money. Yet

I am persuaded that there can be a necessary refining process in adversity that increases our understanding, enhances our sensitivity, and makes us more Christlike. Lord Byron said, "Adversity is the first path to truth" (*Don Juan,* canto xii, stanza 50 [1823]). The lives of the Savior and his prophets clearly and simply teach how necessary adversity is to achieve a measure of greatness.

Edmund Burke defined it well when he said:

> Adversity is a severe instructor, set over us by one who knows us better than we do ourselves, as he loves us better too. He that wrestles with us strengthens our nerves and sharpens our skill. Our antagonist is our helper. This conflict with difficulty makes us acquainted with our object, and compels us to consider it in all its relations. It will not suffer us to be superficial. [*The International Dictionary of Thoughts* (Chicago: J. G. Ferguson Publishing Company, 1969), p. 11]

I would suppose that many of you students are having a difficult time making ends meet. Indeed, it may be very painful. It would, from your standpoint, be unkind to say that this experience may be good for you and may be remembered in more affluent times warmly and even with some fondness. One of my more successful cousins went through law school using much candlelight because he and his bride could not afford electricity to light the rooms.

The present general counsel of General Motors is a black man. Without question he holds one of the most lucrative and prestigious positions for lawyers in all of the world. He was a poor boy and was required to obtain his education through heroic efforts and under circumstances that were difficult in the extreme. He was required to work one and two jobs regularly and, if I am not mistaken, occasionally three. He was asked if he felt uncomfortable among the highest-paid executives of the world; his answer was no. He said that most of them had been poor boys like him who had worked their way up, being tested, challenged, threatened, and discouraged. Adversity is the refiner's fire that bends iron but tempers steel.

It would appear that the shortage of energy will change our lifestyles. The president of Texaco, Mr. John McKinley, some time ago explained to a group in which I was present that in the United States, and even in the world, there are abundant sources of energy. But it will require that these be harnessed, and it will be more expensive because of the capital it takes to convert that energy into usable forms. This means that we will not be able in the future to be so profligate and wasteful of energy.

Hopefully, the quality of life will improve. It may mean that to be happy we are not going to be able to rely upon physical comforts or to satisfy our whims, but must learn to draw upon inner strengths and inner resources. It will likely mean that we will find our entertainment and pleasure in simpler things that do not cost money and are closer to home. Hopefully, it will mean the development of untapped inner strengths and resources that will bring an inner peace and a self-understanding so articulately explained by Anwar Sadat in a recent essay that no doubt many of you read in *Time* magazine. He related his experience of being confined in a British jail. Like Sadat, hopefully we will find ourselves and like ourselves better, be more at peace with our surroundings, and appreciate more our fellowmen. We will become less sated with the material and the mechanical and learn to cultivate a taste for bread and milk.

President David O. McKay said:

> Today there are those who have met disaster, which almost seems defeat, who have become somewhat soured in their natures; but if they stop to think, even the adversity which has come to them may prove a means of spiritual uplift. Adversity itself may lead toward and not away from God and spiritual enlightenment; and privation may prove a source of strength if we can but keep the sweetness of mind and spirit. [David O. McKay, *Treasures of Life* (Salt Lake City: Deseret Book Company, 1962), pp. 107–8]

May I suggest a few things that might be done to prepare us for a time when we are less affluent and possibly happier.

1. Wean ourselves away from dependence for our happiness upon mere material and physical things. This could mean a bicycle instead of a car, and walking instead of a bicycle. It may mean skim milk instead of cream.

2. Learn to do without many things and have some reserve to fall back on. A recent article in Indiana concerning the present coal crisis and telling of a member of the Church there, a coal miner with a year's supply, brought much publicity and attention in the newspapers.

3. Develop an appreciation for the great gifts of God as found in nature, in the beauty of the seasons: the eloquent testimony of God in the sunrise and the sunsets, the leaves, the flowers, the birds, and the animals.

4. Engage in more physical activity that does not employ the use of hydrocarbons, including walking, jogging, swimming, and bicycling.

5. Have a hobby that involves your mind and your heart and can be done at home.

6. Pay your tithes and offerings. The keeping of this commandment will not insure riches—indeed, there is no assurance of being free from economic problems—but it will smooth out the rough spots, give the resolution and faith to understand and accept, and create a communion with the Savior that will enhance the inner core of strength and stability. "Who hath not known ill fortune, never knew himself, or his own virtue," said David Mallett (*The International Dictionary of Thoughts,* p. 12).

7. Develop the habit of singing or, if this is not pleasant, whistling. Singing to oneself will bring less comment and question than talking to oneself. My father one time came home from a deer hunt empty-handed, but his heart was renewed and his spirit lifted. He recounted with great appreciation that one of his companions had frightened the deer away because he was always singing trumpet-voiced to himself as he walked through the pines and the quaking aspen. Father was more enriched by the mirth of the song than by the meat of the venison.

In life we all have our Gethsemanes. A Gethsemane is a necessary experience, a growth experience. A Gethsemane is a time to draw near to God, a time of deep anguish and suffering. The Gethsemane of the Savior was without question the greatest suffering that has ever come to mankind, yet out of it came the greatest good in the promise of eternal life. One of the lessons learned by the Savior in his Gethsemane was declared by Paul to the Hebrews:

> Though he were a Son, yet learned he obedience by the things which he suffered:
>
> And being made perfect, he became the author of eternal salvation unto all them that obey him;
>
> Called of God an high priest after the order of Melchizedek. [Hebrews 5:8–10]

The image of the Savior to many from a public relations standpoint was described by Isaiah: "He is despised and rejected of men; a man of sorrows, and acquainted with grief: and we hid as it were our faces from him; he was despised, and we esteemed him not" (Isaiah 53:3).

Perhaps in all literature, sacred or profane, there is none more eloquent than sections 121, 122, and 123 of the Doctrine and Covenants, received and written by Joseph Smith the Prophet while in the Liberty Jail in the spring of 1839.

> O God, where art thou? And where is the pavilion that covereth thy hiding place?
>
> How long shall thy hand be stayed, and thine eye, yea thy pure eye, behold from the eternal heavens the wrongs of thy people and of thy servants, and thine ear be penetrated with their cries?
>
> Yea, O Lord, how long shall they suffer these wrongs and unlawful oppressions, before thine heart shall be softened toward them, and thy bowels be moved with compassion toward them?
>
> [Then comes the promised relief:] My son, peace be unto thy soul; thine adversity and thine afflictions shall be but a small moment;
>
> And then, if thou endure it well, God shall exalt thee on high; thou shalt triumph over all thy foes.

> Thy friends do stand by thee, and they shall hail thee again with warm hearts and friendly hands.
>
> Thou art not yet as Job; thy friends do not contend against thee, neither charge thee with transgression, as they did Job. [D&C 121:1–3, 7–10]

Out of these circumstances also came the great promise of verse 26 in this same section: "God shall give unto you knowledge by his Holy Spirit, yea, by the unspeakable gift of the Holy Ghost, that has not been revealed since the world was until now." But the Prophet Joseph Smith was warned:

> The ends of the earth shall inquire after thy name, and fools shall have thee in derision, and hell shall rage against thee;
>
> While the pure in heart, and the wise, and the noble, and the virtuous, shall seek counsel, and authority, and blessings constantly from under thy hand.
>
> And thy people shall never be turned against thee by the testimony of traitors. [D&C 122:1–3]

In this adversity also came these great truths recorded in section 121:

> Hence many are called, but few are chosen.
>
> No power or influence can or ought to be maintained by virtue of the priesthood, only by persuasion, by long-suffering, by gentleness and meekness, and by love unfeigned;
>
> By kindness, and pure knowledge, which shall greatly enlarge the soul without hypocrisy, and without guile—
>
> Reproving betimes with sharpness, when moved upon by the Holy Ghost [I am not always able to determine when I am "moved upon by the Holy Ghost"]; and then showing forth afterwards an increase of love toward him whom thou hast reproved, lest he esteem thee to be his enemy;
>
> That he may know that thy faithfulness is stronger than the cords of death.
>
> Let thy bowels also be full of charity towards all men, and to the household of faith, and let virtue garnish thy thoughts unceasingly; then shall thy confidence wax strong in the presence of

> God; and the doctrine of the priesthood shall distil upon thy soul as the dews from heaven.
>
> The Holy Ghost shall be thy constant companion, and thy scepter an unchanging scepter of righteousness and truth; and thy dominion shall be an everlasting dominion, and without compulsory means it shall flow unto thee forever and ever. [D&C 121:40–46]

Why is adversity often such a good schoolmaster? Is it because adversity teaches so many things? Through difficult circumstances we are often forced to learn discipline and how to work. In often unpleasant circumstances we may also be subjected to a buffeting, honing, and polishing that can come in no other way. Most of your leaders in the General Authorities are familiar with adversity. They have not been and are not exempt. Allow me to illustrate by telling you something of three that I have selected only because of their great familiarity with difficulty.

Early in life, President Kimball learned the necessity of work. He had many painful experiences in his early years preparatory to his great ministry. As a young boy he nearly drowned once, suffered Bell's palsy, lost his mother through death, while still a young man lost his beloved sister Ruth, and shortly after marriage contracted smallpox, at which time Sister Kimball counted 125 pustules on his face.

He learned early about financial reverses and lost some investments. Like Job, he suffered from boils that continued for many years, and on one occasion came onto his nose and lips. Once he suffered 24 boils at one time; and not long thereafter he began to suffer the excruciating pain of heart attacks that recurred for many years and finally resulted in open-heart surgery. He became bothered by a hoarseness in his voice; it was relieved through a blessing of the Brethren, but it later returned along with the boils. A serious cancer in the vocal cords, it required surgery and thereafter voice training and cobalt treatments. Also, the Bell's palsy returned temporarily and skin cancers had to be removed.

The result of this refiner's fire was that he came forward with a refined spirit, a sensitive and understanding heart, and a kindness and humility that are unparalleled. President Kimball can be described in the words that the Lord spoke concerning Job. May I read in the book of Job, substituting the name Spencer for Job: "Hast thou considered my servant [Spencer], that there is none like him in the earth, a perfect and an upright man, one that feareth God, and escheweth evil? and still he holdeth fast his integrity, although thou movedest me against him, to destroy him without cause" (Job 2:3).

I have always been interested in the background of President Nathan Eldon Tanner. At this university some years ago, President Tanner recalled his humble and difficult beginnings. Speaking of his parents, he said,

> When they arrived in Southern Alberta, Father had no money, and he had to sell his team in order to finance. But the thing I have always been pleased about was that Father never thought of calling on the government. He went and worked for his neighbor, and he broke horses so they would have horses to use. He lived in a dugout on a homestead, where I lived the first part of my life. He often said, "I bet ten dollars against a quarter section of land of the Dominion Government that I could make a go of it. I nearly succeeded." He also said, "You know, when I came to this country [referring to Canada], I didn't have a rag to my back. Now I am all rags."
>
> We lived after that in a little hamlet. I don't suppose this would be of interest to you, but in that little hamlet we didn't even have a telephone. We didn't have a daily paper; we didn't have a weekly paper—regularly. We had no running water—hot or cold water. So you can imagine other things we didn't have and some things we did have! We had no central heating, you can be sure of that. In fact, I often wondered if we had any heating in the house. [President Nathan Eldon Tanner, "My Experiences and Observations," speech given at Brigham Young University, May 17, 1966, p. 6]

From these difficult beginnings came the giant we know as Nathan Eldon Tanner. He was a speaker of the Alberta Legislature, Minister of Mines and Lands in the province, president of the Trans-Canadian Pipeline, branch president, bishop, stake president,

Assistant to the Council of the Twelve, apostle, and counselor to four presidents of the Church.

I should like to share with you an incident or two in the early life of President Marion G. Romney, best told in his own words:

> I'm a Mexican by birth. I was born in Colonia Juarez, Chihuahua, Mexico. My parents happened to be down there at the time. I was raised there until I was about fifteen years old. During the last two or three of those years, the Madero Revolution was in progress. The rebels and the federalists were chasing each other through the country; each taking everything we colonists had, by way of arms and ammunition and by way of supplies. Finally we were forced to leave. I came out of Mexico with the Mormon refugees in 1912.
>
> I remember I had a very thrilling experience on the way from where we lived to the railroad station about eight miles south of Colonia Juarez. We went in a wagon. . . . I was riding with my mother and her seven children and my uncle (her brother) and his family of about five or six children. . . . We had one trunk—that was all we were able to bring. I was seated on the trunk in the back of the wagon. . . . The Mexican rebel army was coming up the valley from the railroad station toward our town. They were not in formation. They were riding their saddle horses. Their guns were in the scabbards. Two of them stopped us and searched us. They said they were looking for guns. We didn't have any guns or ammunition. They did find $20 on my uncle—pesos, not dollars. . . . They took that and then waved us on. They went up the road about as far as from here to the back of this room, stopped, turned around, drew their guns from their scabbards, and pointed them down the road at me. As I looked up the barrels of those guns, they looked like cannons to me. They didn't pull their triggers, however, as evidenced by the fact that I am here to tell the story. That was a very thrilling experience! One of my maturing experiences.
>
> [President Romney continues,] The rebels blew up the railroad track after the train we were on passed over it. Later, Father and the rest of the men came out to El Paso, Texas, on horseback. We never returned nor did we recover any of our property while my father lived.

> Father and I went to work to earn a living for his large family. There were no welfare programs then. We had a difficult time making a living. We had to "root hog" or die. [Marion G. Romney, speech at Salt Lake Institute of Religion, 18 October 1974]

I had the opportunity to see how well President Romney handles a trowel when he laid the cornerstone for the São Paulo Temple. President Romney said, "Going to school but part-time, it took me from 1918 to 1932 to get through college."

After he was married and his family was started, he worked full-time at the post office in order to provide for his family while he went through law school. In these difficult conditions his marks were so high and his scholarship so excellent that he was later admitted to the Order of the Coif. The Order of the Coif admits only the most distinguished law scholars. I was never invited to join that organization.

Someone has said that among the law students the "A" students make the professors, the "B" students make the judges, and the "C" students make the money. President Romney and I both proved that adage wrong because President Romney did not become a law professor and I did not make a fortune. He practiced law and became a bishop, stake president, one of the first Assistants to the Twelve, a member of the Council of the Twelve, and, as we know, has given great service as a counselor in the First Presidency to two presidents. He has demonstrated his great love and compassion for people through his many years of guidance in the welfare program of the Church.

Indeed, the difficult and adverse experiences of these three Brethren are comparable to experiences in the lives of many others of your leaders, and I have mentioned only these three because it seemed to me that their familiarity with adversity was more than ample.

Thomas Paine wrote:

> I love the man who can smile in trouble, who can gather strength in distress and grow brave by reaction. 'Tis the business of little

> minds to shrink, but he whose heart is firm, and whose conscience approves his conduct, will pursue his principles to the death.

I wish to invoke the blessings of Almighty God upon you choice and chosen young people who are held in such high esteem. Much is expected of you. Do not presume, because the way is at times difficult and challenging, that our Heavenly Father is not mindful of you. He is rubbing off the rough edges and sensitizing you for your great responsibilities ahead. I ask his blessings to be upon you spiritually, and pray that your footsteps might be guided along the paths of truth and righteousness. I promise you the rich and rewarding blessings of selfless service, and wish you to know that by the personal gift of the Holy Ghost I have come to know that Jesus is the Christ, the Son of God, and that he was crucified for the sins of the world.

I wish to conclude as I began, "Be patient in afflictions, for thou shalt have many; but endure them, for, lo, I am with thee, even unto the end of thy days." In the name of Jesus Christ. Amen.

Elder James E. Faust was a member of the First Council of the Seventy when this devotional address was given in the Marriott Center on 21 February 1978.

No Other Talent Exceeds Spirituality

VAUGHN J. FEATHERSTONE

ON THE WAY over here I thought of a fellow up in Idaho who moved into a ward. He had a wooden leg from the knee down. No one ever found out how he got this wooden leg or what happened to his own leg. The Saints talked about it a lot, but never to him. Finally, after about three weeks, two or three of the sisters were talking together, and one of them said, "My curiosity just won't let me rest. I've got to ask him how he got his wooden leg. I'm just going to go over and ask him."

So when he came through the door in the foyer, she walked up and said, "Do you mind if I ask you a question?"

And he said, "No, if you promise to ask only one."

She said, "Very well, then. How did you lose your leg?"

And he said, "It was chewed off." Life is full of surprising answers.

Some time back, a fellow who collected chime clocks happened to pick up one to go along with the rest of his collection. He had many chime clocks that were distributed throughout his house. Each night after he got a new clock he would put it in the bedroom, and then he would listen to the chimes going off during the night.

After he and his wife had settled down and the clock began to chime, he remembered counting up to ten, eleven, twelve, thirteen, fourteen. He shook his wife and said, "Wake up, Ma, it's later than I've ever known it to be."

I think I would like to talk to you about a subject that is relative to "it's later than I've ever known it to be."

I attended a conference with Elder Bruce McConkie up in Grace, Idaho, in 1967, where I had the privilege of speaking. As I finished speaking, he stood up and took the remainder of the time. He said something like this—and I'm not exactly sure of the words, but the thought is the same—"No other talent exceeds spirituality." So I'd like to talk to you and use that as my theme this evening: No other talent exceeds spirituality.

Now, if that is true, how then do we gain spirituality? Tonight we heard this lovely soloist and the accompanist. It takes talent to produce the kind of music that they rendered. We hear great orators, we view tremendous paintings, and we see great drama productions—all demanding great talent. And yet, no other talent exceeds spirituality. How do you gain spirituality?

During the past almost nine years since I heard that statement, there has hardly been a day go by that I haven't thought of the talent of spirituality. There are several subjects I believe I think of every single day. One is purity of heart. Another one came in the form of a question from President Romney, who said to me at a conference one time: "Brother Featherstone, do you think the brethren of the priesthood will ever come to understand that they were born to serve their fellowmen?" And the other thought I think of daily is that no other talent exceeds spirituality. I believe that hardly a day goes by that I don't think of these three statements.

I have several suggestions for gaining spirituality. I'd like to start first with service. I believe if you really want to be spiritual, you must first make a commitment and a decision to serve the Lord's children. If you cannot make that commitment, I don't believe you will be able to gain the level of spirituality that is necessary in this life to achieve all that we want to achieve. I attended a conference over in Hawaii, and after the conference several young people came up to shake hands. One young man came up to me and asked, "Bishop Featherstone, would you tell me how I can gain humility?" Well, you know, we take an entire life studying about humility. How do you gain humility?

I said, "Well, I have some ideas on it. But it would take longer than we've got here. But maybe in a sentence or two, I could say this: When you think you've got it, you've lost it." Then I said, "Think of the most humble person on the face of the earth. Who is that?"

He said, "I suppose it's President Kimball."

And I said, "I think you're right. What do you think he does more than any other person on the face of the earth?"

He thought for a minute, then said, "I don't know."

Then I said, "I believe it's service. I believe President Kimball is totally committed to service. If you want to be humble, you serve with every particle of your being."

I believe humility and spirituality go hand in hand, and I believe service has to be part of it. While I served in Boise, Idaho, in the high council, I was called to be a home teacher to a man by the name of Archie; so we went to see Archie. He was a member of the Church, but I doubt he had been in the Church since he was baptized. His wife wasn't a member of the Church. My son Scott, who had not been a home teacher before, went with me to his home. I remember knocking on the door. The man came to the door with a can of beer in one hand and a cigarette in the other, and he said, "Yes? Can I help you?"

I said, "We're your new home teachers. My name is Vaughn Featherstone, and this is my son, Scott."

And he said, "Yes?"

And I said, "We realize it is inopportune to come at this time without an appointment, but we just wanted to visit long enough to make an appointment, and we'll try not to overstay our welcome. We'll be courteous and considerate of your time. But have you got a few minutes?"

And he said, "Come in."

And so we went inside, but he didn't invite us to sit down. So we stood there for about five or ten minutes, and I said, "We'd like to visit you at least once a month and see how everything is going. Then, if you need anything, we'll give you our phone number so you can call us." So I left that instruction for him, and I said, "What would be a good night to come?"

He said, "Normally, Thursdays I'm home. I don't have union meetings or other things on Thursday, so I'd normally be home if you want to come."

I said, "We'll plan on coming the first Thursday of each month."

He said, "Very good, then."

So we shook hands and we left. When we got outside, I said to Scott, "I hope you got a chance to look around the house while you were in there to see if he had any hobbies or anything from which we might gain a common ground of interest."

Scott said, "Dad, I didn't even dare look."

I said, "All right, we'll be back on the first Thursday, and when we go in I'll give a little discussion and you be looking around the house."

So, on the first Thursday of the month, we prepared, we had a prayer, and then we drove down and parked in front of his home. We knocked on the door. Just before we had come to the door, I said, "Now, Scott, you look around, and if you see something which might be a hobby, give me a signal with your eyes and I'll know that you've seen something. I'll look in that direction to see what his hobby is." So we got inside and sat down, and the television was behind me. He had me sit with my back to the television and he sat facing it. He could look over my shoulder at the television. He didn't turn it down very much—just one-nineteenth of a turn, and so the sound was still pretty loud. Finally his wife got up and walked over and turned it down. I could see that he was just a little annoyed. I gave a little discussion that I didn't think would be offensive, then I looked over at Scott to see if he could give me a signal that he had seen some indication of a hobby. He just shrugged his shoulders. So I got the signal that Scott could not get a clue as to whether he had a hobby or not.

I said, "Well, fine, Archie, we'll be back to see you and your wife again on the first Thursday—unless you need me, and then give me a call. I'll tell the bishop everything is all right at your home."

We got up to leave, and when we got to the door, right by the door was a big picture of a sheriff's posse. As we walked out I said, "Archie, are you a member of that sheriff's posse?"

And he said, "No, I'm not a member of that posse. If you'll look closely, you'll see that that's the Ada County Junior Sheriff's Posse. They're all teenagers."

And I looked closely.

"In fact," he said, "this little gal here, Sandy Thompson, is in your seminary class."

I said, "She certainly is."

And we looked at the picture and talked for a minute. I said, "How did you know that I taught seminary?"

He said, "I was down to the arena where we do our training with the horses and they do their routines. I happened to mention to a friend that we had a new home teacher from the Mormon church named Featherstone. That's kind of a funny name." Then Archie told us that Sandy Thompson happened to hear it and said, "Did you say Featherstone, Vaughn Featherstone?"

Archie said, "Yes."

"And he's your home teacher now?"

"Yes."

"Well, I think you'll like him. He's my seminary teacher. He teaches early morning seminary, and we like him."

And so I guess that helped the next time to give us a little better footing as we got into Archie's home. Anyway, we'd broken the ice with him. He started to talk about the junior sheriff's posse. He got more and more excited, and after about ten minutes of telling us all about the sheriff's posse, I said, "Archie, we'd love to come watch you do your routines sometime. Where do you do your training?" And he told me. I said, "I'd like to talk to you more about it, but we shouldn't overstay our welcome tonight."

He said, "Hold on, before you leave I want to tell you something. Do you know what we're going to do? We're going to buy black lighting. Can you imagine what it would be like to have all these horseback riders in the posse in iridescent shirts and hats, with the horses' hooves and bridles painted with iridescent paint? Then we will turn off all the lights in the stadium and turn on the black lighting. You won't even see the horses except their hooves. And you won't even see anything of the riders except their shirts or blouses, or a hat. It would really be impressive. It would be the finest thing done in western Idaho!"

You know, I got a little excited just listening to him. I said, "You know, that's a great idea. Have you got your black lighting?"

And his chin dropped an inch. He said, "Not yet, but we're going to get it."

I said, "How much have you saved for it? How much money have you earned?"

He said, after his chin dropped a little bit more, "Well, actually, we haven't earned anything yet, but we're going to earn it."

I said, "How are you going to raise the money?"

And his chin dropped again. I was really hitting him in the right places. He said, "Actually, we don't know. We don't know how to raise the money."

I said, "How much do you have to raise?"

He said, "Twelve hundred dollars is what it will cost."

"You don't know how to raise the money but you have to raise twelve hundred dollars? You want black lighting for next year and you don't know what to do?"

"No."

I said, "How would you like me to volunteer to be the Ada County Junior Sheriff's Posse finance chairman?"

And he said, "Oh, you don't want to do that, do you?"

I lied and said, "Yes."

He said, "All right. You decide how you want us to help you."

I said, "I'll go home and work out a program and come back. You have all of your committee there, and we'll expose them to a plan to raise the money."

So I went home and sat up late that night. I figured out a way to raise the money. Next Wednesday I called him up and said, "Archie, we've got a plan. Can you have all the committee down there on Thursday night? If they like the plan, we'll raise the money this way."

So Thursday night came, and Scott and I went down. Here were about fifteen people milling around—and I guess we were the only two Mormons except Archie in the entire group. There was a card table with coffee cups, two big urns of coffee, and two glasses of milk. I tell you, Scott and I got there quick in case one of the coffee drinkers might change his mind and decide the milk looked good.

Anyway, we milled around and talked for a minute. Then Archie said, "I have my home teacher from the Mormon church. He's volunteered to be our finance chairman to raise the money for our black lighting. He's got a program here to present to us." Archie turned the time over to me, and I had the plan on large paper cards. I went through my presentation. Then I said, "Well, what do you think?"

He said, "That's great! That's the way we ought to raise the money. But we made a mistake. You know, I told you it was twelve hundred dollars?"

"Yes."

"It isn't twelve hundred dollars. It's actually eighteen hundred dollars. I called Idaho Power, and they said it would cost us about eighteen hundred dollars for the lighting materials we want."

I said, "Well, that doesn't make any difference. It only changes one figure, and we can do that. It won't create any more work. You see, we were going to go to four of the large corporations and ask each one of them for $300, and four times $300 is $1,200. So we'll just change that $300 to $450. But I do have one request that I'll need if we are going to raise the money this way. I'd like Archie to go with me to these four large corporations to help raise the money in case someone asks technical questions that I can't answer."

He said, "I'd be glad to go."

So, having been employed by Albertson's, I thought, "They're a large corporation with their national headquarters in Boise." At that time Bob Bolinder, a member of the Church on the high council in the neighboring stake, was the executive vice president. I made an appointment with him, and then I called Archie. I put on the best suit I had that morning, and we got ready to go meet with Bob Bolinder at eight o'clock.

At eight o'clock Archie came in, and he had on his painting uniform—he was a painter.

I said, "Archie, let's go."

So we went in, and Bob was very kind. We sat down in his office and went through our presentation. I could see the mental wheels turning. The company normally wouldn't give to this kind of a charity. I could see him trying to figure out how to turn us down.

I said, "Bob, before you make a decision, I just want you to know I home teach this man."

Bob said, "You'll get your money." So we got $450 there.

Then we went to Boise Cascade and made an appointment with Robert Hansburger, at that time the chief executive officer for Boise Cascade. His office was on the very top floor of the Idaho Bank Building. The office provided a view over the whole north part of the community. We went up, and again I dressed in the best clothing I had, and Archie came in his painting uniform. We went up to the plush executive offices, and in a minute we were welcomed in. We sat down in front of a large black desk; the room was furnished in huge overstuffed black leather chairs and matching furniture. Robert Hansburger said, "You gentlemen want to make a presentation to me?"

I said, "That's right."

So I went through this presentation, and when we finished, he said, "I want you to know that's an excellent presentation. Go down to our personnel department and ask them for the money. If they won't give it to you, I'll write out a personal check for $450."

Well, that provided a lot of confidence as we went downstairs to the personnel department. I knew the personnel director. I said,

"Mike, we've been asked by Mr. Hansburger to make this presentation to you." When we finished, I said, "Mike, before you make up your mind whether you can give us the money or not, I want you to know Mr. Hansburger said if you wouldn't give us the money he would write us out a personal check."

He said, "You can have your $450."

Then we went to Morrison Knudsen, and they were very kind. We talked to Mr. Perkins, the president of the company. He gave us $450.

Then we went to the Jack Simplot Company. Jack was tremendous. I can't tell you what kind of language he used, but he was great. So Jack Simplot gave us the money, and we had eighteen hundred dollars.

A while later the Ada County Junior Sheriff's Posse had a fall banquet at the conclusion of their season. Since I was a member of the committee, I was invited to the banquet. After they finished the dinner, one of the girls, who was chairman of the evening's affair, stood up and said, "We'd like to make a special award tonight." She reached down and grabbed a beautifully wrapped package from underneath the table. She said, "Archie, would you come up here?"

So Archie stood up and went to the podium and stood there by her. She handed him a gift and said, "Would you please unwrap it?"

So he unwrapped it, and there was this beautiful plaque: "To our good friend Archie, chairman of the Ada County Junior Sheriff's Posse." I saw this hard, crusty Archie begin to weep. Tears streamed down his cheeks. I got a little emotional as I sat there.

Pretty soon someone at the dinner said, "Speech! Speech!"

Well, Archie couldn't have spoken if his life had depended on it. He just came and sat down by me.

So then the emcee said, "Now we've got another award we want to give." She reached down under the pulpit again for a smaller package. She said, "Vaughn Featherstone, would you come up here?" I went over and unwrapped a little shield with a horse's head projecting from it. The shield was inscribed with a thanks for my being chairman of the finance committee. I started to weep. I'd never been given an award for home teaching before.

Then probably the same person called out, "Speech! Speech!" Well, I usually can say something, but that night I was so filled with emotion I couldn't say anything. I just sat down by Archie.

I gained a spiritual experience from serving Archie Turner. I had an experience that I'll never forget in my life. It's as though it happened yesterday. I know how close I felt we had to be as we went to each of those organizations. I prayed, and I prayed fervently that everything would go right. And it seemed to go all right. So I know if you're going to have increased spirituality you must give of yourself through service.

Some time back I also had the privilege of touring the Hawaiian Mission. We asked a particular person to make an itinerary for us. As I looked at the itinerary, I said, "Well, you don't have us scheduled to go to Kaulapapa, the leper colony on Molokai."

The person said, "Well, Bishop Featherstone, there are only thirteen members in the leper colony, and we haven't had a General Authority there for about seven years. Really, we don't have time. The only way you can get down is to walk down a steep three-hour trail—or we can charter a plane."

I said, "I believe if the Savior came to tour this mission, the first place he would go would be to the leper colony. You get us into the leper colony."

He said, "I'll do my best."

I said, "No, not your best. Just do it. We want to go."

So he made the arrangements, and on Friday morning the mission president, and President Ruth Funk and her husband, and I met out at the airport. The mission had chartered a little plane. I remember climbing aboard the airplane, and, as I recall, there were no seats in it. We sat on duffel bags in the back. I think they wired the door closed. Of course, there was no concern on our part; we were on the Lord's errand. The plane lifted off, and we flew across the ocean to the island of Molokai. We came around the Kaulapapa peninsula. We landed on a little dirt landing field where the weeds had grown high. As we taxied in, all thirteen lepers who were members of the Church were standing there waiting to meet us. I guess it was one of the most humbling experiences I've ever had in my life. We climbed off the plane and went over to them. Most wore large glasses so you couldn't see their faces. Some had the appearance that they had been mutilated where the skin had sloughed away due to the disease. They held their hands back under their arms so we couldn't see them, and they wore heavy coats.

As we walked up to them, we didn't know whether or not the disease was arrested. That really wasn't important to us. I remember reaching out to shake hands; they acted as if they didn't want to shake hands. Maybe they were afraid for us to touch them. But we insisted. Each one of us, Sister Funk and her husband, myself, and the mission president, cupped their little mutilated hands in our hands, walked down the line, and shook hands with each one of them.

We got to the very end man, and his name was Jack Sing. He's the branch president. He had come to pick us up in his 1951 Cadillac. He had bought it new, it had five thousand miles on it, and it was absolutely immaculate, inside and outside. I guess the only place they drive it is out to the airport once every seven years or so. We climbed in, and he took us to the chapel. On the way I said, "Jack, how long have you been branch president?"

He said, "Well, I've been in the colony fifty-two years. My wife came after I'd been here thirty years. She's been here twenty-two years."

I asked, "What proportion of that time have you served as branch president?"

He thought and he thought, and then said, "I don't remember."

I said, "Think. It's really important to me."

And again he thought. Finally he said, "I just can't remember."

I doubt there are many bishops or branch presidents who wouldn't remember how long they'd been serving.

Anyway, we got to the chapel and climbed out of the car. Here was this little LDS church for the leper colony, a quaint little peaked chapel, very simple. On the grounds it looked as if they'd taken scissors and clipped the edge of the lawn around the cobblestones and the little sidewalk. It looked as if they'd taken the dirt and crumbled it in their hands. Every single flower bed was sweet and fresh. It looked as if they'd even picked the dead leaves off each of the tropical plants. Then we went inside. There was a clean, immaculate chapel with a large row of pews down one side with a pulpit at the front, then a large wide aisle down the middle, and then another row of pews with a pulpit at the back on the other side. The lepers would sit on one side and conduct their services, and those who were not leprous would sit on the other side and conduct services. It was very interesting.

As we entered, I thought about lepers in the Savior's time. I suppose even now in some parts of the world, if one has leprosy, he has to cry out, "Unclean! Unclean!" Inside my heart something started welling forth, and I thought, "What a travesty of life! Why isn't it that the peddler of pornography, the adulterer, and the fornicator have to cry out, 'Unclean! Unclean!' instead of some of the sweetest and purest Saints I have ever met in my life?"

We drove back out to the airport and boarded the plane. As we lifted off the landing strip, I believe all thirteen members were there to see us off. It had been a great spiritual experience. But again, I believe it was simple in service, and, I believe, if we want to be spiritual, we'd better learn to serve.

I think another thing we've got to have if we're going to have spirituality is charity. You remember that "charity covereth a multitude of sins." Over at the Sweden area conference, Elder Howard W. Hunter told a story that impressed me greatly. He said that up in British Columbia the police department had collected many bikes over a period of time. Every six months they had an auction and auctioned off all these bikes. At one of these auctions, the auctioneer started auctioning off the bikes. Have you ever noticed how something all of a sudden starts making a pattern in your mind? Well, the auctioneer noticed that every time they'd bring a bike out and he would say, "Who will start the bidding?" a little boy on the front row would say, "I bid one dollar, sir." And then the bidding would go up beyond that. He noticed that the little boy would be the first one to bid. He'd bid one dollar. He noticed the little boy's eyes would particularly sparkle and all the hope would well up within him when a racer bike would be brought out. He said the bikes were purchased, one by one, and each time the little boy would bid, and each time the bikes were sold for much more. Finally, the auctioneer looked over at the last racer bike being brought forth. An assistant helped him display the racer bike in front of the group, and then the auctioneer said, "This is the last racer bike we have. How much am I bid?" This little boy's hopes were waning, but he cried out, "I bid one dollar, sir." Then the bidding went to two and three and five and seven-fifty and finally eight-fifty. And the auctioneer said, "Going once, going twice, going, and gone for nine dollars to this little boy over on the front row!" Then he reached in his pocket and he pulled out eight dollars and laid them on the counter. The little boy came up and put his one dollar in nickels and dimes and pennies alongside it, picked up his racer bike, and started out the door. And then he laid the bike down and ran back to the auctioneer and threw his arms around the auctioneer's neck and cried.

My question: There must have been at least a hundred at the auction, probably two or three hundred. Why was it that only one person could see the plight and the need of a little fellow? It really didn't make any difference if one of them didn't get a bike, but it was very vital that this little boy have a bike. He'd earned all he could, and he was there to buy a bike. Only one person had the charity, the pure love of the Savior, and saw the need. Now, my question: What would you have done had you been there? Would you have been aware of the little boy's needs? Are we sometimes so concerned about our own needs that we forget just how vital charity is?

I brought along a letter that I'm almost embarrassed to share with you, but I think it is essential to make a point. In the Saturday afternoon session of every stake conference that I go to, I talk about families and the relationship between husbands and wives and their children: the need for a father, particularly, to understand the needs of his sons and daughters in the home. When that session of a particular conference was over, a father came up to me and said, "I'm going to write to you and tell you something that I'm not very proud of." So he wrote this letter:

> Dear Bishop Featherstone:
>
> You probably don't recall the brief conversation we had on the stand at the stake center last Saturday night. I told you I had a seventeen-year-old son to whom I hadn't spoken a kind word in nine years. I was going home to tell him how much I love him. He has caused his mother and me many hours of heartbreak, especially in the last two years. He and I haven't had a father-son relationship in over half his life. Isn't that a frightening thought? The little unhappiness he has caused us is nothing compared to the lonely hours he must have spent because of me all those years—the many nights he went to bed feeling so unloved and unwanted by me, his father. I used to react so violently to the slightest misstep. I had reached the point where he could do nothing right even when he tried. I have even uttered the words, "I detest you." Can you imagine? When he got home Saturday night I sat him on the couch and told him how sorry I was, that I loved him dearly, because he is my son and not for the kind of person he may be, that someday he will discover the value of the precious gift of the priesthood, and I will ordain him an elder with love and pride. Wherever he may go, whatever he may do, though his actions cost me what little I have in worldly goods, all I will be able to say to him now is, "I love you, my precious son." For nine years I have never said one kind thing to my son.

There is more in the letter, but I think that makes the point. I believe, finally, in a moment, this father discovered what charity is.

I believe you have to have understanding. Understanding is critical if you're going to have spirituality.

I picked up something I'd like to share with you that I think is very outstanding. Marv Abrams, who works in the grocery business in Boise, had a large frame with a message inside hanging on his office wall. I stood in his office and read it and asked, "Can I get a copy of that?" He sent it to me, and this is what is in it. It's called "A Legacy." (I guess President Dallin Oaks might be familiar with it.)

In the pocket of a ragged old coat belonging to one of the insane patients of the Chicago poorhouse, a will was found after the man's death. According to Barbara Boyd of the *Washington Law Reporter,* the man had been a lawyer. Written in a firm hand on a few scraps of paper, the will was so unusual that it was sent to another attorney, who was so impressed with its contents that he read it before the Chicago Bar Association. (That's why I mentioned that President Oaks might be familiar with it.) A resolution was passed ordering the will probated, and it is now on the records of Cook County, Illinois.

My Last Will and Testament

I, Charles Lownsberry, being of sound and disposing mind and memory, do hereby make and publish this, my last will and testament, in order as justly may be to distribute any interest in the world among succeeding men that part of my interest which is known in law and recognized in the sheepbound volumes. As my property being inconsiderable and of none account, I make no disposition of in my will. My right to live, being but a life estate, is not at my disposal. But these things excepted, all else in the world I now proceed to devise and bequeath.

ITEM: I give to good fathers and mothers in trust for their children all good little words of praise and encouragement and all quaint pet names and endearments, and I charge said parents to use them justly but generously as the deeds of their children shall require.

ITEM: I leave to children, inclusively, but only for the term of their childhood, all and every the flowers, the fields, and the blossoms and the woods, with the right to play among them freely according to the customs of children, warning them at the same time against thistles and thorns. And I devise to children the banks of the brooks, and the golden sands beneath the waters thereof, and the odors of the willows that dip therein, and the white clouds that float high over the giant trees. And I leave the children the long, long days to be merry in a thousand ways and the night and the train of the Milky Way to wonder at—but subject, nevertheless, to the right hereinafter given to lovers.

> ITEM: I devise to boys jointly all the useful idle fields and commons where ball may be played, all pleasant waters where one may swim, all snow-clad hills where one may coast, and all streams and ponds where one may fish or where, when grim winter comes, one may escape—to hold the same for the period of their boyhood—and all meadows with the clover blossoms and butterflies thereof, the woods with their appurtenances, the squirrels and the birds and echoes and strange noises and all distant places which may be visited together with the adventure there found. And I give to said boys each his own place at the fireside at night with all pictures that may be seen in the burning wood and to enjoy without let or hindrance or without any encumbrance or care.
>
> ITEM: To lovers I devise their imaginary world with whatever they may need as the stars of the sky, the red roses by the wall, the bloom of the hawthorn, the sweet strains of music, and all else they may desire to figure to each other the lastingness and beauty of their love.
>
> ITEM: To young men jointly I devise and bequeath all the boisterous, inspiring sports of rivalry, and I give to them the disdain of weakness and undaunted confidence in their own strength. Though they are rude, I leave to them the power to make lasting friendships and possessing companions, and to them exclusively, I give all merry songs and grave choruses to sing with lusty voices.
>
> ITEM: And to those who are no longer children or youths or lovers I leave memory and bequeath to them the volumes of the poems of Burns and Shakespeare and of other poets, if there be others, to the end that they may live the old days over again freely and fully without tittle or diminution.
>
> ITEM: To our loved ones with snowy crowns, I bequeath the happiness of old age, the love and gratitude of their children until they fall asleep.

Finally, someone said about this man, "After all, was he so poor and insane? If that was the world in which he lived, was he not richer than are some who go about freely and who have money in the bank? At any rate, to each of us he bequeathed something. Let us not fail to get our legacy."

Yes, I think understanding is very critical, and as you can see from this article, this man had great understanding.

I once had an experience in Denver when I heard a great man, John Sloan, a vice president of the Boy Scouts of America, tell about Bobby and his birthday. Bobby lived in a community much like the television show *The Waltons*. It was a backwoods kind of place where things weren't going too well for the entire community.

Little Bobby came down from his bedroom early on his birthday and burst into the kitchen. His mother had to immediately tell him, "Bobby, we haven't bought you a birthday gift this year. It's not that we don't have the money for it. We've been saving money, but we put the money away. We're going to give it to you now. We want you to learn a lesson. Instead of us buying something we think you'd like, we've saved the money, and we're going to let you take it and buy something you would like." So with this she reached up on the shelf and pulled down a pint bottle with money in it. She poured the contents out on the table, and then she let Bobby count it. He quickly pulled aside the dollar, the quarters, and dimes. He had a total of four dollars and eighty cents. As he scooped this up and put it into his pocket, she said, "Now remember, Bobby, you can buy something that will seem glamorous and it will just fade as a bubble in an instant and be gone, or you can buy something that will have lasting value to you. It's your decision to make, but make it wisely." With this instruction, Bobby burst through the open front door and down the sidewalk. Then he ran down the road about two and a half blocks as fast as his legs would carry him. He came to a large two-story house, and the sign was still out on the front lawn: "Purebred puppies for sale." He walked up to the door and knocked on it. In a moment a handsome, middle-aged woman came to the door. She looked around and couldn't see anyone. Then she looked down, and there was Bobby. She said, "Yes, young man, can I help you?"

He said, "You have purebred puppies for sale?"

She said, "We do."

"I'd like to see them, please."

The woman looked at him, and she looked at his meager clothing and thought, "Well, he surely can't afford one of *my* puppies." She was about to turn him away, but Bobby stared at her with a steel gray glare. So she let him in. He sat down in the hallway, and she went downstairs and brought one of the puppies up. She laid it on the floor in front of Bobby. You know how puppies are at that age. He jumped up into Bobby's lap and was kissing and bouncing all around.

Bobby was trying to hold him still, and he said, "How much is this puppy?"

The woman said, "They are twenty-five dollars apiece."

He said, "That's a lot more than $4.80, isn't it?"

"Yes, it's quite a lot more, Bobby."

"Do you have any other puppies for sale?"

"Well, yes, we have one other puppy, but he is not for sale. We promised the veterinarian that we'd have him put away."

Bobby said, "Can I please see him?"

"No, Bobby, he's not for sale. We promised the vet we'd have him put away."

Then Bobby stared at her with his steel gray glare a second time and said, "I want to see the other puppy."

The woman buckled under the pressure, went downstairs, and got the second puppy. She put the first one back and brought the second one up. When she brought it up and laid it in front of Bobby, he saw it had two crippled front legs. Bobby picked the puppy up, held it close to him, and said, "Please sell me this puppy. I want this puppy more than I've ever wanted a puppy in my life. I want this one more than any other puppy in the whole world. Please sell him to me."

But the woman said, "I'm very sorry, Bobby. He's not for sale."

Bobby said, "If you sell him to me, I promise to give him more understanding than anyone in the whole world could."

Then he put the puppy down on the floor and stood up and lifted up his pant legs and showed her the metal braces on his crippled legs. If we're going to be spiritual, we need to have understanding. Bobby had understanding.

Repentance is also vital. I think if we're going to be spiritual, or pure in heart, or if we're going to have humility, we need to repent. Repentance ought to be part of our lives every single day.

Major things ought to be taken care of, of course, but also other minor things. Repentance ought to be just part of us and part of our being.

I recently had a sweet couple come to my office. They'd driven sixteen hours all the way from a distant city. As they came to my office, they wanted a half-hour appointment; then they were going to turn around and drive the sixteen hours home without doing one other bit of business. So I said to my secretary, "Work them in. Whatever it takes, you work them in." So she pushed back the schedule and worked this couple in.

The man came in first and said, "You came to our stake conference, and you talked about repentance. After you left, on Monday night, my wife and I were sitting together in our family home evening. All of our children are raised, and my wife said, 'I think you're thinking what I am.' And I said, 'I think I am. We need to go see Bishop Featherstone, don't we?' She said, 'Yes, that's what I've been thinking. We'd better go see him.' " So they drove all those hours to see me.

Well, let me stop right here and say that they didn't need to do that. They have local ecclesiastical leaders, a bishop and a stake president who can handle transgression confessions. I suppose they wanted to see me because I had been the one who had triggered some thoughts about repentance in their minds.

The man came in and said, "Bishop, forty-three years ago, the week before my wife and I got married, we had sexual relations—once. We went to get our temple recommends from the bishop. He wasn't there, and he had just left them lying on the credenza. His wife handed them to us. There was no question, nothing; he had already signed them. We went to the stake president and, seeing the bishop's signature, he didn't bother to question us. He just signed them and handed them to us. We went to the temple unworthily. While we were on our honeymoon we decided we would make that up to the Lord. We both felt so bad about it. We came back from our honeymoon, and we always paid more than a 10-percent tithing. We paid more than our share of building fund and budget and welfare and have through all these years.

We've accepted every assignment that has come to us in the Church. But for forty-three years we've carried a transgression burden on our hearts. We've prayed about it and worried about it. We feel we've been forgiven, but we realize now that every major transgression must be confessed. We've known it all along, I guess. We just haven't had enough courage before, and so now we want to confess. Now I want my wife to come in because she needs to tell you the same thing. She has the right to confess." So his wife came in and confessed the same thing.

Well, we, as General Authorities, are common judges to a degree. We interview bishops and stake presidents, and we interview missionaries before they go out in the mission field to determine worthiness. I guess I was thinking that we would normally send this couple back to their bishop or to the stake president, but I couldn't bear the thought of having this lovely couple have to carry that burden one more step in this life. So I said, "I think I'll call President Kimball and see how he'd respond. If he feels all right, I can close this for you." So I called President Kimball on the phone and said, "President, I've got this lovely couple in my office. They've driven sixteen hours to get here. They have a half-hour appointment, and they're leaving and going back home. Do I have the right in this case, as a common judge, to close this matter for them?"

He said, "Are they in your office?"

I said, "Yes."

"Have them come up."

I said, "All right." I hung up the phone, turned to this couple, and said, "President Kimball would like to see you." Their faces went white. I took them out in the lobby. We took the elevator up to the twenty-fifth floor and back into Arthur Haycock's office. When President Kimball heard our voices, he got up and came over to the door. I introduced him to this couple.

I said, "Now, President, I'll just turn them over to you and I'll see you later."

I started leaving, and he said, "Bishop, I'd like you to come in, too."

"Yes, sir."

So I went in and we sat down beside his desk. Now here is this man with stacks and stacks of work, I guess, that only the prophet can do: sealing cancellation approvals, cases concerning those who have committed other kinds of transgressions, etc., work he himself must do to make a determination as to the disposition of the case. But you would have thought that he didn't have one other care in the world except this couple. He said to this couple, "You don't have to tell me the problem because Bishop Featherstone explained it on the phone. But I have a couple of questions to ask. Have you suffered equal to the transgression? It was a major transgression. Have you suffered equal to the transgression?"

The man started to cry, and he said, "President, we've suffered many times more than the transgression."

President Kimball said, "Have you prayed for forgiveness?"

Together, tears streamed down their cheeks, and they said, "We haven't offered a prayer since we've been married that we haven't asked for forgiveness."

Then he asked them some other questions in the tenderest, sweetest way, and then he said, "Do you mind if I come over and kneel and have a prayer with you?" He came out from behind his desk and knelt down with us.

I should stop here and tell you this: Do you know that General Authorities and bishops and stake presidents have the right to forgive on behalf of the Church, but only one man on the face of the earth has the right to forgive on behalf of the Lord?

President Kimball said, "I use that right very carefully and sparingly and only when I have absolute certainty and absolute knowledge as to what I should do." Anyway, he knelt down, and we all knelt around him. Then he said these words, and I'll never forget the feeling I had. I wish I could in some way give you the spiritual experience I had in that instant.

He said, "Heavenly Father, we love thee." I've said that to the Lord, but I have never felt the same influence. I felt he really was saying it in a way I'd never heard it expressed before. The tears came to my eyes and streamed down my cheeks. During the rest of the prayer he pleaded on behalf of this couple.

In section 45 of the Doctrine and Covenants the scripture teaches about the Savior, his being our advocate with the Father. I know now even more clearly than I ever have before what an advocate is. President Kimball pleaded on behalf of this couple. Finally, as he finished his prayer and we stood up, he walked over and he put his arm through my arm and pulled me close and asked me a question. Do you know, I don't even remember the question. I didn't answer it. I just remember turning to him, and I said, "President Kimball, I love you." I was deeply touched. It was about all I could say. I couldn't have said anything else. Then he let go of my arm and walked over to this man. The man put his arms around President Kimball and laid his head down on President Kimball's shoulder and sobbed. President Kimball embraced him for a moment and then went to the woman. The woman reached out, took hold of President Kimball's hands, and then tenderly reached up and kissed him on the cheek.

Then President Kimball said this to the man, "I want you to forgive yourself, and I want you to forgive your wife. I don't ever want you to mention it again. It's closed."

Then he said to the wife, "I want you to forgive yourself, and I want you to forgive your husband. I don't want you to ever mention this again. It's closed."

As we left President Kimball's office, I was filled with a compassionate spirit as though the Savior had been there in President Kimball's place. The woman was overcome. We literally had to hold her up. We got out in the hallway and she said, "Please, can you take me somewhere where I can sit down?" We took her and sat her down on one of the large couches up in that area and she regained her strength. In 3 Nephi we read that the Saints were overcome. What a precious experience, and what a purging, uplifting experience repentance is. I believe we have to have repentance to be spiritual.

I believe it's going to take some kind of sacrifice on your part if you really want to have spirituality. In the mid-1830s this great man, Joseph the Prophet, sent two missionaries back to Massachusetts. When they arrived there, they started preaching, and they came across a man by the name of Orson Spencer. Orson was converted and believed. His fiancée believed, and so they went to her parents to tell them that they were going to be baptized in the Church before they got married. (By the way, she came from one of the fine families in Massachusetts.) As their petite, delicate little daughter and her fiancé explained what was going to take place, the father said to her, "If you choose to marry Orson, and if you join this Church, you are no longer welcome in our home, we never want to see you again, we disown you, and we disinherit you." That was about the summary of the total conversation.

Orson and his fiancée left together. The young couple went outside, and she said, "Well, Orson, I know only one thing. I know I want to marry you, and so we'll do whatever you say." So they joined the Church, they were married, and they had five children back in Massachusetts.

She was a frail little soul, and I guess having five children fairly close together was just too much for her. She became somewhat ill. They decided they would go westward where the Saints were. So they made their trek westward to Nauvoo, where the Saints had gathered. As they got to Nauvoo, the frontier life was just too much for little Kathryn Spencer. She became progressively worse. Finally, Brigham Young announced they were going farther westward.

As they prepared to go, Orson feared for his wife's life. He wrote back to her parents and said, "Please let Kathryn come home and nurse her back to health. She's been sick. I despair for her life. I don't believe she'll make it across the plains, and we're going to leave soon. Please let me know." He also said this, "I'll do anything you ask." Then he sent the letter off.

Weeks passed and a month more, and still no word. It was time to move westward. They prepared the covered wagons, and they took this frail little soul, put her on a stretcher, and lifted her up into Orson's wagon. Then they rolled westward. As you recall, during those bitter cold winter months the plains would freeze as hard as granite at night, and the wagons could easily roll across the plains in the morning. Then the midmorning sun would come out and thaw the earth, turning it into a giant sea of mud. The wheels would sink in up to their axles, and they would make only a few yards every hour.

Finally, eighteen days out, they made an encirclement for the night. Orson was outside doing a few chores just before retiring. Orrin Porter Rockwell rode into the camp with mail and distributed it around the camp. He came to Orson and handed him a letter from his wife's parents. He quickly read, "Yes, we would love to have our daughter home. We'd love to see her again, but only on the condition that she'll leave you and leave her newfound church. Then we'll nurse her back to health. We'd love to see her again, but only on those conditions. If not, we never want to see her again, we disown her, we disinherit her, and she's not welcome in our home."

Orson felt terrible. He climbed up into the wagon, and he told his wife what he had done—that he'd written to her parents. She had not known until this very moment. He said, "I told them I would do anything, and this is their answer."

He handed her the letter, and she read it. Then she put it down and said, "Orson, would you hand me the Bible?"

He reached over and handed her the Bible, and she opened it up to a particular scripture and said, "Now would you read that to me, Orson?"

In the little covered wagon, as the evening shadows were fleeting across the sky, he read to her, "Intreat me not to leave thee, or to return from following after thee: for whither thou goest, I will go; and where thou lodgest, I will lodge: thy people shall be my people, and thy God my God" (Ruth 1:16).

"No, Orson, I won't leave you." He sat by her at the head of the bed, and they had a very tender moment. They talked, and then her eyes closed. He touched her pallid face, but her eyes never again opened in this life. The next morning they had a brief graveside service by a shallow grave. The only music was the lowing of the cattle. Then Orson Spencer climbed up on the covered wagon and prepared to roll westward. His oldest daughter climbed up on the seat next to him. Who was the oldest daughter? Aurelia Spencer Rogers, the founder of the Primary. I'll love Aurelia Spencer Rogers as long as I live because she's influenced my life, my children's lives, and my children's children's lives. I'll love her for the great contribution she made to our family. But even more than Aurelia Spencer Rogers, I'll love this Kathryn, who sacrificed and raised up an Aurelia Spencer Rogers. We must have sacrifice to be spiritual.

We lived in Garden Grove, California, for a period of time, and I remember there was a sister in our ward I heard about. She was somewhat considering joining the Jehovah's Witnesses, so the bishop asked if I would go visit with the family to see if I couldn't give them a spiritual experience and tie them back to the foundation of the gospel. I went over to visit them, and I learned this story on my very first visit.

They had lost a little baby, and it had happened in the neighbor's swimming pool. The little baby, under two, had crawled out through the backyard and somehow had made its way through an open gate into the pool area and had fallen into the pool. The mother in just a moment missed her child. She ran into her backyard, and, of course, the first place you always go when you have children that age is to the most treacherous area—either to the street or to the pool. She ran immediately to the pool and saw her baby lying on the bottom. She couldn't swim. She plunged in, and her husband explained to me, "She would not come up. She didn't know how to get to the bottom of the pool to get her baby, and she would not come up without the baby."

Someone inside the neighbor's home heard the splashing and went outside. Two people had to pull her out of the pool physically or she would have drowned trying to get her baby off of the bottom of the pool. Someone else dove in and retrieved the baby, but the baby was drowned.

Now, I believe, as I've thought about this, that there is a practicality to having spirituality. Why didn't someone many, many years back teach a little girl how to swim? We never know what might take place later. The mother would have given anything to have known how to swim—in fact, she almost gave her life. If only someone had taught her how to swim.

I don't know all the obstacles you'll have in your life, but be practical as you gain spirituality. Don't be afraid to get out into the business world and learn all that you can. Be practical.

Of course, you also have to have faith if you're going to have the kind of spiritual experience we're talking about. Dr. Gustov Eckstein, one of the world's most renowned ornithologists, for twenty-five years had made an intense study of birds. He had hybrids and had crossbred birds that no other human being had ever produced. He had also kept meticulous records on the birds. For twenty-five years, each day, as per habit, he would walk into his laboratory and down the two or three steps over to the stereo. He would turn the classical music on very loud, the birds would begin to sing, and he would hum along. Then he would do his work during the eight-hour day. At 5:30 or so he'd walk over, turn the stereo off, walk out of his laboratory, and that was his day.

One day, after twenty-five years, he hired a new custodian. The custodian watched Dr. Eckstein leave. He thought the laboratory needed to be aired out, so he lifted all the windows, and during the night the birds all flew out through the windows. The next morning when Dr. Eckstein came, he walked into his laboratory and there wasn't one single bird there. He saw the open windows and felt devastated and heartsick. Out of habit he walked over to the stereo and turned the music up very loud—classical music. He went and sat down on the steps, put his head down in his hands, and wept.

"Twenty-five years, my lifetime's work. Must I start over again?" All of these thoughts were going through his mind as tears streamed down his cheeks.

All of a sudden he heard a fluttering of wings. Dr. Eckstein looked up. The birds were flying back through the windows! The music had gone out through the open windows and through the trees and down the street, and the birds were coming back. Dr. Eckstein said, "Every bird came back."

I have faith that, if you'll live the kind of life you ought to live, if you have faith and keep the classical music of the gospel of Jesus Christ playing in the ears of those who once were exposed to the gospel, the music will go out through the open windows and down through the streets and the trees, and one day every single one of your parents or brothers or sisters who may be inactive (or someday your children who may be inactive) will come back. You should have hope and have faith and believe that.

In conclusion, you need to study the scriptures. (Of course, there are a hundred other subjects I could have mentioned regarding how to gain spirituality, but these are a few for your consideration.) I believe you need to love the scriptures and study them. One of my very favorite books, just for sheer pleasure reading, is the Pearl of Great Price. I just love to sit down and read it. I feel as if I'm carried away in the spirit with Enoch. I can stand and see Enoch weep and see the heavens weep. I can hear him cry to the Lord,

> How is it that thou canst weep, seeing thou art holy, and from all eternity to all eternity?
>
> And were it possible that man could number the particles of the earth, yea, millions of earths like this, it would not be a beginning to the number of thy creations. [Moses 7:29–30]

Then it goes on to tell in those scriptures how the Lord answers Enoch, "Behold these thy brethren," and Enoch then beholds that all of the myriad of beings who would ever live upon the earth "are the workmanship of mine own hands, and . . . in the day I created them . . . gave I unto man his agency" (Moses 7:32). Then he talked about their wickedness and their misery. Enoch saw the wickedness and misery of men. I can see this just as clearly as if I were there: "Enoch . . . stretched forth his arms, and his heart swelled wide as eternity; and his bowels yearned; and all eternity shook" (Moses 7:41). You know, I wouldn't know that any more than if I had been there.

I believe, as you study the scriptures, you'll come to really know, not *of* the Savior, but really know *him.* And you will know our

Heavenly Father. Now, God bless you. If we can achieve anything in this life, let us achieve spirituality. There is no greater talent in the world than spirituality, in the name of Jesus Christ. Amen.

Vaughn J. Featherstone was a member of the First Quorum of the Seventy when this fireside address was given in the Smith Fieldhouse on 1 August 1976.

The Gospel and Romantic Love

BRUCE C. HAFEN

I ONCE HEARD President Holland tell about a conversation he overheard between two freshman women talking about their favorite subject. One of them said, "Do you believe in college marriage?" The other replied, "Well, yeah, if the colleges really love each other." I would like to believe that there are no two colleges anywhere who "love each other" more than BYU and Ricks. I am in love with both places and consider both as my home. I must admit I think it is a blessing to the BYU campus to have several thousand former Ricks students here. The blessings also flow the other way, as we at Ricks are continually assisted in many ways by our BYU friends. When you catch cold in Provo, we sneeze in Rexburg. When you itch, we scratch. Indeed, when your able academic vice president, Jae Ballif, was given the title of "Provost" at the BYU campus, we immediately began to consider if our academic vice president should be called our "Rexburgst."

I'd like to say just a word about President Holland. For all his abundant gifts of personality and intellect, I think the core of Jeff Holland's soul is essentially spiritual. I believe the Lord has brought him here for a mission that is primarily spiritual in nature.

He and Pat will bless this campus now and for years to come with their own unique blend of spiritual courage, insight, and devotion. Happily, the Lord has prepared the two of them in such a way that the intellectual life of this campus will only be made richer by the abundant brand of spiritual life the Hollands inspire.

Today's audience includes a few students who were at Ricks College earlier this year when I talked about "The Gospel and Romantic Love." I apologize to them because I am talking on that subject again today. I would add, however, that it is primarily because of the response of the Ricks students that I feel impressed to give this talk here. As I do so, I pray for inspiration, not only because of the importance and sensitivity of the subject, but also because of my great love and respect for the students of Brigham Young University.

Elder Boyd K. Packer once said to a group of students on this campus:

> The powers awakened earlier in your life have been growing. You have been responding to them, probably clumsily, but they now form themselves into a restlessness that cannot be ignored. You are old enough now to fall in love—not the puppy love of the elementary years, not the confused love of the teens, but the full-blown love of eligible men and women, newly matured, ready for life. I mean romantic love, with all the full intense meaning of the word, with all of the power and turbulence and frustration, the yearning, the restraining, and all of the peace and beauty and sublimity of love. No experience can be more beautiful, no power more compelling, more exquisite. Or if misused, no suffering is more excruciating than that connected with love. ["Eternal Love," BYU Fireside, 3 November 1963]

In approaching this topic, I feel I am walking on holy ground. This subject, delicate as it is, inspires my deepest reverence. The idea of romantic love, so commonplace that it is touched upon in virtually every book or movie or magazine, is also at the very center of the gospel of Jesus Christ. It is one of the greatest of God's laws that a man shall "leave his father and his mother, and shall cleave unto his wife: and they shall be one flesh" (Genesis 2:24). As Elder

Packer put it, "Romantic love is not only a part of life, but literally a dominating influence of it. It is deeply and significantly religious. There is no abundant life without it. Indeed, the highest degree of the celestial kingdom is unobtainable in the absence of it."

The other side of this coin, of course, is represented by what Alma told his wayward son, Corianton, who had gone after the Lamanite harlot Isabel. He said to his son: "Know ye not . . . that these things are an abomination in the sight of the Lord; yea, most abominable above all sins save it be the shedding of innocent blood or denying the Holy Ghost?" (Alma 39:5).

I once saw, at close range, the face of a faithful father who had just learned that his handsome and promising young son had violated the law of chastity and that the boy's immature young girlfriend was pregnant. I'll never forget the look in that man's eyes as it dawned on him that his child of promise had willfully rejected what his parents had taught and what they wanted him to be. The father just sat in stunned silence, staring sadly at the rain outside his window in a grief that knew no comfort. As the tears ran freely down his face, he asked himself out loud: "Why? Why would he turn his back on all he knows to be right?" There came no answer but the gentle sound of the falling rain.

Why indeed? Why such a commandment? Sometimes we give as reasons for the law of chastity the risk of pregnancy or abortion, the possibility of an unwanted or embarrassing marriage, or the chance of a terrible venereal disease. With adultery, we talk about the damage of destroying an existing marriage or family. As serious as these things are, I'm not sure they are the fundamental reason for the Lord's having placed this commandment ahead of armed robbery, fraud, and kidnapping in the seriousness of sins. Think of it—unchastity is second only to murder. Perhaps there is a common element in those two things—unchastity and murder. Both have to do with *life,* which touches upon the highest of divine powers. Murder involves the wrongful *taking* of life; sexual transgression may involve the wrongful *giving* of life, or the wrongful tampering with the sacred fountains of life-giving power. Perhaps we should not expect the reasons for this commandment to be fully understandable to our finite minds. So often with our deepest feelings of joy or testimony or gratitude, we may attempt to describe their meaning with words, but our words fail us when we try to plumb the depths of those precious things that are too sacred, too significant, and even too mysterious to be susceptible to quickly understood explanations. Why is nature so exquisitely beautiful and full of harmony? Why do our hearts respond to the sight of little children laughing? Why, especially, do our hearts respond to overflowing when those little children we see laughing before us are our very own children? All we know is that God himself has said, time after time, over all the generations of man, "Thou shalt love thy wife with all thy heart, and shalt cleave unto her and none else" (D&C 42:22), "Thou shalt not . . . commit adultery, . . . nor do anything like unto it" (D&C 59:6).

I have been around enough to know that this is not the first time you have ever heard this subject mentioned from the pulpit. But I have also been around enough to know, especially recently, that no matter what you have heard and no matter how often, today we live in a world so completely soaked through with tragically wrong and evil ideas about sex that you must be *warned*—in love and kindness, but warned—lest the moral sleeping sickness that has overcome this nation's atmosphere claim you into deadly slumber. There have always been violators of the moral code, but the last few years have witnessed in this country a staggering revolution in sexual attitudes. Our social norms apparently began to unravel during the unrest of the 1960s, among students to start with. Research shows that in the period from 1970 to 1975, the number of college students who accepted the practice of premarital sex grew from about 50 percent to nearly 90 percent (Katz and Cronin, "Sexuality and College Life," *Change,* February–March 1980, p. 44). College students are the most permissive of all groups, and they are *your* peer group. You cannot help being influenced by their general attitudes.

It would be of no help to you, by the way, to seek counsel about sexual norms in America from a typical professional therapist. The American Psychiatric Association recently voted to remove homosexuality from its list of disorders, even though one study pointed out by our own Allen Bergin showed that 50 percent of the male homosexuals surveyed in one American city had at least 500 sexual partners and 28 percent of them had had 1,000 partners (see "Bringing the Restoration to the Academic World: Clinical Psychology As a Test Case," *BYU Studies* 19 [1979]: 449, 464). If that is normal behavior, we've got problems. A representative of today's mainstream attitude among psychotherapists recently wrote in a professional journal that most people in his field believe "that human disturbance is largely associated with and springs from absolutistic thinking—from dogmatism, inflexibility, and that [being extremely religious] is essentially emotional disturbance" (Ellis, "Psychotherapy and Religious Values," *Journal of Consulting and Clinical Psychology* 48 [1980]: 635). In other words, the way to relieve one's guilt about an immoral life is to begin believing there is no such thing as an immoral life. Whatever you want to do is moral if you want to do it. This same psychologist expressed his concern about the mental stability of people who commit themselves to "unequivocal loyalty to any interpersonal commitments, especially marriage." You can imagine what this man and his professional associates would think of temple marriage. The same attitudes are springing up everywhere in other fields. I've done a lot of reading in my own field of law; I've read widely in the social sciences. It's now simply a fact that most of those who write and most of those who produce today's movies, TV programs, and popular music, as well as those who set the editorial policies of many national magazines, believe that sex outside of marriage is really quite harmless, if not rather healthy. I recently heard Mormon filmmaker Kieth Merrill express his opinion that today's movie producers have no more hesitation about showing sexual acts on the screen than they do about showing people eating dinner.

Something deep within our national soul has gone wrong, brothers and sisters, and it cannot help but influence our attitudes and dull our normal senses in frightening ways. Twenty years ago there was much public support for the things you and I believe in, despite some occasional straying from those principles. All that is different now. Now we are almost suffocated by a dense fog of sensuality. Kenneth Kolson has described this basic change in national attitude in talking about *Playboy* magazine:

> While *Playboy* is much the same thing that it was during the 1950's, it is not *exactly* the same thing, and the difference is crucial. During the 50's, there was, of course, pornography. We used to get it at the newsstand from the old man with the black cigar who would produce it, literally, from "under-the-counter." Sometimes it would circulate through the boys' locker room—usually pictures of fat [women] with missing teeth. It was available, all right, but one came by it ["out behind the barn," so to speak]. But now that the *Playboy* philosophy has been declared innocent by the grand jury of public opinion, now that it "is involved in the mainstream of our culture and values," it is acquired, and consumed, as thoughtlessly as a pound of bologna. You pack Mildred and the kids in the station wagon, buzz down to the local drugstore, plunk your two bucks down on the counter, and bring home artful pictures of young women who have straight teeth, deep suntans, and college educations. Every one of them is a former cheerleader, a current jogger, concerned about ecology. Middle class. When you get home, you throw your copy on the coffee table promiscuously [alongside *Time* and *Newsweek*], a public pronouncement that *you* buy *Playboy* for the literature. It's true: the difference between the 50's and [today] is that we don't give pornography a second thought any more. [*Chronicles of Culture,* September–October 1979, p. 18]

And that is exactly what has gone wrong. We don't give it a second thought. The attitude of acceptance here and what I've seen in Europe is so widespread that there is nothing to compare with it in the last several centuries, in any civilized society; not since Rome, not since Sodom and Gomorrah.

The enormous scope of the drift is what makes it so treacherous. Even as we are surrounded by abnormality, everything somehow seems so normal. As written by Pascal:

> When everything is moving at once, nothing appears to be moving, as on board ship. When everyone is moving towards

> depravity, no one seems to be moving, but if someone stops, he shows up the others who are rushing on, by acting as a fixed point. [Blaise Pascal, *Pensées,* vol. 33 (Chicago: Encyclopaedia Britannica, Great Books of the Western World, 1952)]

We—you and I—must be that fixed point.

I want you to know that it isn't easy for me to paint such an extreme picture. I am usually a pretty calm and reasonable guy. But on this particular subject of sexual morality, I honestly believe our society is within the grip of the evil one, even in the moment when so many Americans feel more "free" than ever before. There is a reason why the scriptures record the word *devilish* after the words *carnal* and *sensual.* We read in the Pearl of Great Price that "Satan came among them, . . . and they loved Satan more than God. And men began from that time forth to be carnal, sensual, and devilish" (Moses 5:13). And then when Cain slew Abel, he said, "I am free" (Moses 5:33). Cain was never more in bondage than when he said, "I am free." In exactly the same way, the American people have never been in greater moral bondage than in this time when they glory in being "free" to pursue pleasure in any form they fancy as if there will never be any tomorrow.

Can you see why the Brethren tell us to stay away from X- and R-rated movies? Can you see why they plead with us to avoid drugs, alcohol, vulgar music, and the other products of the carnal environment that now surrounds us almost as water surrounds the fish of the sea? These aren't trivial things, brothers and sisters. This isn't just a modern version of a fussy Victorian concern about bobby sox, social dancing, and driving over twenty miles an hour. This is not just Coke and makeup and nylons for twelve-year-olds. If the H-bomb symbolizes our age, we are playing now not just with fire, but with nuclear power. The prince of darkness has dragged out the heavy artillery. He is no longer limited to arrows and swords and BB guns. Now he is Darth Vader, with laser guns, light speeds, and the Death Star. We are near the end of a fight to the finish, and no holds are barred.

Let me talk now, on the other hand, about the more positive aspects of the law of chastity, because that part of the law is fundamental and important. Elder Packer said,

> Oh, youth, the requirements of the Church are the highway to love, with guardrails securely in place, with help along the way. How foolish is the youth who feels the Church is a fence around love to keep him out. How fortunate is the young person who follows the standards of the Church, even if just from sheer obedience or habit, for he will find rapture and a joy fulfilled.

I'd like to read a provocative statement about the positive side of the law of chastity from an English writer:

> Never was an age more sentimental, more devoid of real feeling, more exaggerated in false feeling, than our own. . . . The [TV] and the film are mere counterfeit emotion all the time, the current press and literature the same. People wallow in emotion: counterfeit emotion. They lap it up: they live in it and on it. . . .
>
> . . . A young couple fall in counterfeit love, and fool themselves and each other completely. But, alas, counterfeit love is good cake but bad bread. It produces a fearful emotional indigestion. . . .
>
> . . . The peculiar hatred of people who have not loved one another, but who have pretended to, . . . is one of the phenomena of our time. . . .
>
> . . . [But there is a] profound instinct of fidelity in a man, which is, as shown by world-history, just a little deeper and more powerful than his instinct of faithless sexual promiscuity. . . . The instinct of fidelity is perhaps the deepest instinct in the great complex we call sex. Where there is real sex there is the underlying passion for fidelity. And the prostitute knows this, because she is up against it. She can only keep men who [want the counterfeit: and these men] she despises. . . .
>
> . . . The [Chief Thinkers of our generation know] nothing of [this]. To [them,] all sex is infidelity and only infidelity is sex. Marriage is sexless, null. Sex is only manifested in infidelity, and the queen of sex is the chief prostitute. . . .
>
> This is the teaching of the . . . Chief Thinkers of our generation. And the vulgar public agrees with them entirely. Sex is a

> thing you don't have except to be naughty with. Apart from . . . infidelity and fornication, sex doesn't exist. . . .
>
> [However, the truth is that the Christian] Church created marriage by making it a sacrament, a sacrament of man and woman united in . . . communion, . . . and never to be separated, except by death. And even when separated by death, still not freed from the marriage. . . . Marriage, making one complete body out of two incomplete ones, and providing for the complex development of the man's soul and the woman's soul in unison, throughout a life-time. Marriage sacred and inviolable, the great way of earthly fulfilment for man and woman, in unison. . . .
>
> . . . And this, this oneness gradually accomplished throughout a life-time in twoness, is the highest achievement of time or eternity. From it all things human spring, children and beauty and well-made things; all the true creations of humanity. . . . The will of God is that He wishes this, this oneness, to take place, fulfilled over a lifetime. . . .
>
> . . . The oneness of . . . man and woman in marriage completes the universe, as far as humanity is concerned, completes the streaming of the sun and the flowing of the stars. [D. H. Lawrence, *Essays on Sex, Literature and Censorship* (New York: Twayne, 1953), pp. 96–111]

Properly understood, then, the scriptures counsel us to be virtuous not because romantic love is bad, but precisely because romantic love is so good. It is not only good; it is pure, precious, even sacred and holy. For that reason, one of Satan's cheapest and dirtiest tricks is to make profane that which is sacred. Building on a metaphor from President Harold B. Lee, it is as though Satan holds up to the world a degraded image of sexual love suggested by imagining the drunken, boisterous laughter of filthy men in a brothel, located on some crowded, dusty highway of life, where the flower of fair womanhood is jeered at, dirtied, brutalized, and ultimately crushed with unclean hands. Meanwhile, far, far away from the madding crowd, high up in the cool protected valleys of tall mountains, grows the priceless flower of virtue—untarnished, pure, and unsullied. It waits as a noble prize for those valiant few who are willing to climb to its heights by paying the price of patience, obedience, and a lifetime of devotion—an endless, unselfish loyalty to spouse and children.

May I suggest now eight brief, practical steps for those who would one day be true sweethearts, based on a foundation of righteous living.

First, have reverence for the human body and the life-giving powers of that body. That basic attitude is what I have hoped to convey in most of what I have said today. Your body is a temple. It is sacred and holy. Have the same reverence for it that you have for any temple that seeks to be the dwelling place for the Spirit of the Lord. It is also the dwelling place of the seeds of human life, the nurturing of which, with your chosen companion, within the bounds set by God himself, is lovely, of good report, and praiseworthy.

Second, during the time of courtship, please be emotionally honest in the expression of affection. Sometimes you are not as careful as you might be about when, how, and to whom you express your feelings of affection. You must realize that the desire to express affection can be motivated by other things than true love. As Erich Fromm put it,

> Desire can be stimulated by the anxiety of aloneness, by the wish to conquer or be conquered, by vanity, by the wish to hurt and even to destroy, as much as it can be stimulated by love. It seems that sexual desire can easily blend with and be stimulated by any strong emotion, of which love is only one. Because sexual desire is in the minds of most people coupled with the idea of love, they are easily misled to conclude that they love each other when they want each other physically. . . . [But] if [this] desire . . . is not stimulated by love, . . . it . . . leaves strangers as far apart as they were before—sometimes it makes them ashamed of each other, or even makes them hate each other, because when the illusion has gone they feel their estrangement even more markedly than before. [*The Art of Loving* (New York: Harper and Row, 1956), pp. 45–46]

In short, save your kisses—you might need them someday. And when any of you—men or women—are given entrance to the heart of a trusting young friend, you stand on holy ground. In such a place you must be honest with yourself—and with your friend—about love and the expression of its symbols.

Third, be friends first and sweethearts second. Lowell Bennion once said that relationships between young men and young women should be built like a pyramid. The base of the pyramid is friendship. And the ascending layers are built of things like time, understanding, respect, and restraint. Right at the top of the pyramid is a glittering little mystery called romance. And when weary travelers in the desert see that glitter on top of the pyramid from far off, they don't see what underlies the jewel to give it such prominence and hold it so high. Now, you don't have to be very smart to know that a pyramid won't stand up very long if you stand it on its point instead of its base. In other words, be friends first and sweethearts later, not the other way around. Otherwise, people who think they are sweethearts may discover they can't be very good friends, and by then it may be too late.

Fourth, develop the power of self-discipline and self-restraint. Please remember that nobody ever fell off a cliff who never went near one. You've got to be like Joseph, not like David. When Potiphar's wife tried to seduce him, the scripture says, Joseph "fled, and got him out" (Genesis 39:12). Joseph knew that it is wiser to avoid temptation than to resist it. King David, by contrast, somehow developed too much confidence in his own ability to handle temptation. He was tragically willing to flirt—to flirt with evil, and it ultimately destroyed him. In your courtships, even when you feel there is a growing foundation of true love, show your profound respect for that love and the possibilities of your life together by restraining your passions. Please don't be deceived by the false notion that anything short of the sex act itself is acceptable conduct. That is a lie, not only because one step overpoweringly leads to another, but also because the handling of another's body is in an important sense part of the sexual act that is kept holy by the sanctuary of chastity. If ever you are in doubt about where the line is between love and lust, draw the line toward the side of love. Nobody ever fell off a cliff who never went near one.

Fifth, in your searching for the fulfillment of your romantic longings, live for the presence of the Holy Spirit, that you may have it as your constant guide. Don't date someone you already know you would not ever want to marry. If you should fall in love with someone you shouldn't marry, you can't expect the Lord to guide you away from that person after you are already emotionally committed. It is difficult enough to tune your spiritual receiver to the whisperings of heaven without jamming up the channel with the loud thunder of romantic emotion. The key to spiritual guidance is found in one word: worthiness. I won't take time to discuss it now but would urge you, if you want to do a little scripture study, to compare Doctrine and Covenants 63:16–17 with Doctrine and Covenants 121:45–46. You'll find something interesting there. Those who garnish their thoughts with virtue have the Spirit and have confidence in God's presence. Those who have lust in their hearts can't have the Spirit.

Sixth, avoid the habit of feeling sorry for yourself, and don't worry excessively about those times when you feel socially unsuccessful. Everybody in the world doesn't have to marry you—it only takes one. I remember the experience of a choice young woman who had been very popular and successful in many ways in her hometown. She passed up two or three chances to get serious with young men because she planned to attend college at a Church school, where she expected to find more promising opportunities. After she had been at that school for about six months without a date, however, she began to wonder if she had some loathsome disease. Seeing that experience through her eyes was very sobering for me about the risks we take in any large population center for LDS students, because sheer size and numbers can so easily cause people to make incredibly superficial judgments about others in ways that emphasize appearance above far more important but less obvious factors.

The opportunities for developing friendships (as sometimes distinguished from having "dates") with members of the opposite sex are very plentiful at a place like BYU and Ricks. Often these relationships lead to more promising possibilities than does the big social whirl. It's also less expensive. In approaching these opportunities, remember: "Worry not that you are not well known. Seek to be worth knowing." The college-age years are a wonderful time in which to experience a variety of human relationships, to go places and do things, to read widely, to find yourself, to develop the roots of spiritual and emotional maturity. To gain this kind of ripeness and growth simply takes time, experience, and effort.

The discouragement you may feel as another empty Friday night rolls by is often a form of the insecurity we all encounter as we try to find ourselves. Without the apparent approval of your self-worth that comes through social success, you may begin to doubt whether your life is really worthwhile. That kind of self-doubt is only part of a larger problem that accompanies most of us, married or single, all the days of our lives. There are times when we wonder if the Lord loves us; we wonder if other people love us. And so we mistakenly seek the symbols of success—whether that is being popular or being rich or being famous within our own sphere. Sometimes you may let someone take improper liberties with you, or you may indulge yourself in some practice that seems to bring temporary relief but only makes you feel worse in the long run. Some even make poor marriage choices, just to show the world that *somebody* will have them.

Ultimately, however, only the Lord's approval of our lives really matters. If you seek to be worth knowing and seek to do his will, all the rest will take care of itself. Never forget that all things work together for good to them who love God (see Romans 8:28). Your time for marriage may not come until the autumn of your life and then, in Elder Packer's phrase: "be more precious for the waiting." Even if your time should not come in this life, the promises of eternal love are still yours in the Lord's view of time if only you are faithful.

Seventh, avoid at all costs, no matter what the circumstances, abortion and homosexuality. As serious as is fornication or adultery, you must understand that abortion and homosexuality are equally wrong and may be worse. Even persons who only assist others, much less pressure them, to have an abortion are in jeopardy of being denied the privilege of missionary service. They may also be called upon to face a Church court, at the peril of their membership in the Church.

Eighth, if, through some unfortunate experience in your past, you have committed a moral transgression of the kind we have been talking about today, there is a way by which you may receive full forgiveness. There is no more glorious language in all scripture than the words of Isaiah, speaking as if it were by the voice of the Lord himself:

> Though your sins be as scarlet, they shall be white as snow; though they be red like crimson, they shall be as wool.
>
> If ye be willing and obedient, ye shall eat the good of the land. [Isaiah 1:18–19]

The steps for the process of repentance are outlined in President Kimball's masterful book *The Miracle of Forgiveness.* If your transgressions are of the serious kind, you will need to see your bishop and voluntarily offer a full and complete confession. As frightening as that experience may seem to you, by this means you will find purpose and a peace of mind more hopeful and uplifting than you can now imagine. As you wonder how you might stand in the eyes of the Lord after such an experience, I commend to you the counsel of Elder Vaughn Featherstone, who talked in the October 1980 general conference about the repentance process for serious transgressions. The most memorable part of that candid and loving sermon was Elder Featherstone's expression of his attitude toward those who have had the courage and the faith to confess their sins and even face Church discipline, if necessary. Because I so much share Elder Featherstone's feelings, I would like to quote a portion of his remarks:

> In Exodus 32, Moses had gone up to the mountain. The children of Israel had fashioned a golden calf with a graving tool. The people offered burnt offerings, and they sat down to eat, drink, and play; and there was great wickedness when Moses came down out of the mountain. He cast the tablets out of his hands,

> and they were broken; he burned the golden calf and caused the idolaters to be slain.
>
> Then, when the people had repented (and that is the key), Moses went back before the Lord and prayed, "Yet now, if thou wilt forgive their sin—; and if not, blot me, I pray thee, out of thy book which thou hast written" (Exodus 32:32).
>
> I have listened to possibly a thousand major transgressions; and each time after a truly repentant transgressor has left my office, I have either knelt behind the desk or bowed my head in prayer and said, "Lord, forgive him or her, I pray thee. If not, blot my name also out of thy book. I do not want to be where they aren't, for they are some of the most Christlike people I have ever met."
>
> Though their sins be as scarlet, they may become white as the driven snow (see Isaiah 1:18), and the Lord has promised he would remember their sins no more (see D&C 58:42). ["Forgive Them, I Pray Thee," *Ensign,* November 1980, p. 31]

I guess one reason I appreciate Elder Featherstone's feelings so much is that those are also my feelings about you. That's why I am willing to take the risk today that maybe you think I'm being too serious. I'm willing to take that chance because I don't want to be where the students of Ricks College and Brigham Young University are not.

For all that I have said by way of warning about the social conditions of the day or the limits we must place on ourselves, I'd like you to remember that the teachings of the gospel about romantic love are full of hope and peace and joy of the most uplifting and everlasting kind. I will always remember my straight-arrow friend that I met here in Provo who told me he took his fiancée to the bishop for a recommend to be married before they had ever experienced *any* physical dimension to their relationship—and I mean any!

After the regular interview, the wise bishop asked them, "Well, do you feel the spark when you hold each other close?"

My friend was perplexed. "The spark?"

The bishop tried to explain, but my friend was having trouble catching on. So the bishop *assigned* them to take one week to see if they had "the spark" in their relationship. He knew they'd figure it out and still remain worthy.

As my friend told me this story, I couldn't help asking, "Well, what did you find out?"

He blushed a little bit, and then he said, "Well, we finally fulfilled the assignment."

They learned the same thing that I have learned, about being sweethearts on the foundation of everlasting friendship and love. I testify to you with all my heart that the commandments of God are designed for our ultimate happiness, and that being sweethearts in the way the Lord intended it is worth waiting for, in the name of Jesus Christ. Amen.

Bruce C. Hafen was the president of Ricks College in Rexburg, Idaho, when this devotional address was given in the Marriott Center on 28 September 1982.

The Widow's Mite

GORDON B. HINCKLEY

IT IS A GREAT opportunity and a great privilege to be with you this beautiful morning. I appreciate the effort you have made to gather here. It has been the custom, reaching back many years, for a member of the First Presidency to speak to you at the beginning of a new school year. I would very much like to say something that will be helpful to all, and to this end I have prayed for the direction of the Holy Spirit.

I bring you the love and greetings of President Kimball and President Romney. President Kimball serves not only as president of the Church but also as chairman of the board of trustees of this university, and President Romney serves as a vice chairman. I am confident they would have enjoyed being with you this morning, had circumstances permitted. As you are aware, President Kimball is now in his ninetieth year, and, because of the infirmities of age, he is unable to get out and speak as he once did with such vigor. President Romney is similarly handicapped.

I wish to share with you some of my concerns in the responsibility that has been thrust upon me. I want you to bear some of that responsibility. If you are a member of the Church, you too have a challenge to be concerned with its strength and growth.

I remember many years ago when a man, both prominent and well-to-do, came to see Stephen L Richards, who was then a member of the First Presidency. The man had a son who was denied a missionary call because of his moral misbehavior. The man was very forceful, almost demanding, in his request that the son be permitted to go. At the time I had responsibility for the missionary program of the Church and was in the room when the conversation took place. After the man had finished his lengthy and demanding argument, President Richards said, "Brother, I have some responsibility for the affairs of this Church. You do also. If you were seated where I sit, knowing the circumstances that I know, you would feel exactly as I do. Now, in your position as a member of this Church, as one who holds the priesthood, you too have responsibility for its growth and program, and for its discipline. My heart goes out to you, for I know that what you say comes of love for your son. However, I am asking you, as a man with a responsibility for the progress of the Church, to look at the larger affairs of the kingdom. Then you make the decision in that light." After a thoughtful silence, it was the father who made the decision that his son should not go.

It has now been more than four years since I was called into the Presidency. For two and a half of those four years, not of my own wish, I have had thrust upon me the burden of the day-to-day work of the office of the Presidency. Please do not misunderstand me. I am not complaining. I have been blessed by the Lord in a marvelous and wonderful way. I have been blessed with the confidence of his chosen servants, Presidents Kimball and Romney. I have been blessed with the loyalty, the unflagging devotion, and the help of the Council of the Twelve, of each member of the First Quorum of the Seventy, of the Presiding Bishopric, and of the membership of the Church across the world. I have been remembered in many prayers, and I am grateful beyond power of expression.

Incident to the responsibility that I have, I have chaired the meetings of the board of trustees of this university. For many years I have served as chairman of the executive committee of the board.

I also chair the meetings of the Budget and Appropriations Committee of the Church. This is a very serious responsibility.

As you are aware, on July 8, 1838, the Lord revealed to the Prophet Joseph Smith the law of tithing as it applies to the members of the Church in this dispensation.

On that same day, he gave a revelation in which he said that the tithing funds of the Church should be "disposed of by a council, composed of the First Presidency of my Church, and of the bishop and his council, and by my high council" (D&C 120).

Based on that revelation, we have in the Church what we call the Council on the Disposition of the Tithes. This council is composed of the First Presidency, the Council of the Twelve, and the Presiding Bishopric. Theirs is the ultimate responsibility for all Church expenditures.

Serving, in effect, as an executive committee of that council, we have what we designate the Budget and Appropriations Committee. This committee meets weekly to consider for approval all items of Church expenditure. These might include a score or more of new chapels in various places throughout the world, or a building or renovation project on the BYU campus, a new temple somewhere, or any number of things. I need not tell you that with hundreds of buildings under construction (more than 900 at this time), the number of dollars involved is enormous. Again, it is my responsibility to chair these meetings and to sign the approvals for the expenditures. It is a worrisome responsibility.

Where does the money come from? There are many who look upon the Church as an organization of great wealth. We have been classified as being equal to many institutions of the Fortune 500. Our assets are spoken of glibly by those who either do not know the facts, or with gross distortion for purposes of sensationalism.

The fact, of course, is that we do have tremendous assets when the value of all Church buildings and facilities is included. But these assets are not income producing. They are consumers. They consist of thousands of meetinghouses across the world, many temples, seminaries and institutes, and, of course, Brigham Young University. They have cost millions in investments, and they produce scarcely anything in the way of a direct dollar return on those investments. There is only one reason for their existence, and that is to serve the needs of *people* as sons and daughters of God who have a peculiar and important relationship with him.

I repeat that the Church is frequently spoken of as an institution of great wealth. When all is said and done, the Church is wealthy only in the faith of its people. One of the expressions of that faith is the payment of tithing. The Church is spoken of as an institution with great business interests. The income from those business properties would keep the Church going for only a very short time. The fact is that tithing is the Lord's law of finance. It came of revelation from him. It is a divine law with a great and beautiful promise. It is applicable to every member of the Church who has income. It is applicable to the widow in her poverty as well as to the wealthy man in his riches. It is simple of understanding. One need only compare it with the income tax to recognize the simplicity that comes of the wisdom of God in contrast with the complexity that comes of the wisdom of men.

I hold in my hand a widow's mite. It was given me in Jerusalem many years ago, and I was told that it is genuine. I have it framed, and I keep it in my office as a constant reminder of the fearsome responsibility of spending that which comes of the consecrations of the members of the Church. Most of the wonderful, faithful Latter-day Saints who pay their tithing are men and women of modest means. They not only pay their tithing, but they also make many other contributions for the strengthening of this work.

Some time back a small, bent, elderly woman came to my office. For the purpose of this talk I shall call her Mary Olsen, although that is not her name and she would not wish her identity disclosed. She said she had just come over from the temple. She took from her purse her checkbook. She said that she had been a widow for many years, that life had not been easy for her. She had a great love for the Lord and his Church. She had faithfully paid her tithing all her life. She felt she would not live much longer. Now, she said, she felt she ought to be doing more to help than she had done. In a hand shaky with age, she wrote a check for $5,000. She handed it to me. I noted the address where she lived. It was in a poor neighborhood. I confess that as I looked at that check tears came into my eyes. I have held many larger checks than that in my hands. But as I held the check of this widow, I was almost overcome by her faith and the seriousness of the trust that was mine in the expenditure of her consecrated contribution.

My dear young friends, we—you and I—are trustees of that which has been given to the Lord by Mary Olsen and thousands like her whose devotion is as great and whose sacrifice is as certain. This beautiful campus, with its many programs, is a consumer of a very substantial portion of the widow's contribution. She gives her offering to the Lord, and she is then released from responsibility. The responsibility then becomes mine—*and yours!*

What might she expect of you? I am going to talk quickly of four or five things that I think she might appropriately expect.

First, I think she might expect on your part a deep sense of gratitude and appreciation. I recognize that the fees you spend to attend BYU are high and sometimes difficult to pay. But you should know that several times the amount you pay comes from the sacred funds of the Church to cover the actual cost of your presence on this campus. That applies to every one of you who is here. You are truly privileged. There are approximately 26,000 of you. There are literally legions of other worthy young men and women who are members of the Church who would do almost anything to be here. Why should you be so treated when a beautiful and brilliant girl in the British Isles, or that qualified young man in Argentina, or that able and faithful girl in Japan, are just as worthy and just as eligible as you?

Gratitude is among the greatest of virtues. I hope there is not a day that passes that you do not get on your knees and thank the Lord for the marvelous privileges you have in attending this university. Where in the world is there a more beautiful campus than this? Where are there better facilities? Where is there a better-qualified faculty of men and women not only of learning, but also of faith? Where will you find better associations than here? (I might add, parenthetically, where will you find a football team more worthy of cheering about?)

I know the academic grind is hard. I know you sometimes get discouraged as you face it. I know that for many of you there is acute loneliness even with so many around you. I may say, however, that you would have these problems and more at any other university. Be thankful. Be appreciative of the marvelous opportunity you have to study at this magnificent university.

Second, the widow who brought to me her offering—which has become a portion of the funding of this university—would expect you to save, protect, and do all you can to preserve these remarkable facilities that have cost so much. We constantly receive requests from people across the world to establish another university in one place or another. It would be a wonderful thing if we could do so. However, we must face the fact that it would be too expensive, more than we could afford, to build and maintain such a plant and faculty. It is your home while you are here. Take good care of it. I am appalled when I see property defaced, or vandalized, or damaged through carelessness, or resources wasted. There must never be such on this campus. It was built to its present state in large measure by money from the tithes of the Church. It is maintained in large measure by such funds. Take care of it. A sacred trust is placed in you to do so.

Third, the widow of whom I speak expects that while you are here you will experience an increase in faith and a strengthened knowledge of the things of God, and, more particularly, of the restored gospel of Jesus Christ.

Each of you is expected to take courses in religion. Some may resent that. I hope not. These courses, taught by qualified instructors, represent one of the major differences between this and other universities. You have opportunities here that you would not have in any other school in quite the same measure. Do not resent these studies. Dig in and drink up that which is offered for your enlightenment and the strengthening of your testimony. Most of you will never again have such an opportunity as you will have here to learn the gospel in an environment of scholarship. Drink deeply of eternal truths.

Fourth, another great expectation is that many of you will find your companions here. Generally speaking there is no better place to find one of your own kind, with the same standards, the same ambitions, the same desire and willingness to serve the Lord as you go forward with your lives. It is expected that a marriage arising out of associations on this campus will be a marriage based on love, appreciation, and mutual respect, with an understanding of the heavy responsibilities as well as the potential for happiness in time and throughout eternity, through the exercise of the priesthood in the house of the Lord.

In anticipation of that, you can never be immoral. You cannot be dishonest in courting or in marriage without violating the great trust that is placed in you as a student of Brigham Young University.

Fifth, the final great expectation in terms of your presence here is that you will better qualify yourselves to fill positions of responsibility in the world of which you will become a part. All of us are tremendously proud of BYU's great football accomplishments. They redound to the honor of the school. They reflect good to the Church. We are proud of the team and wish for them continued success.

However, the primary purpose of BYU is not football. The primary purpose of BYU is to provide a first-class education in the disciplines and skills that will qualify you for productive lives while at the same time inculcating within you a solid foundation of spiritual values.

You will violate a sacred trust with the widow I mentioned, and with all of us, if you fail to take advantage of the great opportunity that is yours here to learn in order that you might go forth to serve.

That service must be given with integrity. There can be no cheating in the halls of learning without consequent impact on one's fitness to serve in the world of work. If we turn out lawyers with smart techniques and shallow honesty, then we have broken a trust. If we turn out teachers whose only objective is to get a job rather than to serve the needs of boys and girls, then again we have failed. If we turn out business graduates whose only objective is to grow rich regardless of principle, again the sacrifices of our people to maintain this school have been in vain.

Yours must be a higher vision and a higher mission. Yours is the responsibility to study and learn, to qualify yourselves in an exceptional way for positions of responsibility in the professions, in the business world, and for life in general. And over and beyond this, yours is a most sacred and binding responsibility to do so while observing every element of moral behavior and while employing the principle of the Golden Rule as taught by the Son of God.

We have great expectations for you. We are entitled to those expectations. The widow of whom I spoke, and the hundreds of thousands like her who bring their tithes to the storehouse of the Lord, count on you to do something in a very exceptional and worthy way.

Let the beginning of this new school year be marked with the resolution to stand a little taller, to work a little harder, to keep your lives square with the principles of morality and integrity that are of the very essence of the gospel of Jesus Christ. Be humble. Be prayerful. Be studious. Have a wonderful time. Enjoy life. But know also that it is serious and that there will flow from your time and efforts marvelous results both temporal and eternal if you will live the gospel of Jesus Christ while here, and prepare to live it when you leave here.

If you do this, we who have a sacred trusteeship will know that that which is provided here will not have been in vain, but that the funds to build and maintain this institution will bear marvelous and rewarding dividends for the present as well as for generations yet to come. We pray for you. We hope that you will pray for yourselves. We ask the Lord to bless you and sustain you, to give you strength and the capacity to understand and assimilate that which you are taught so that, when you have completed your work here, you may go forward into the world as men and women of faith, of great learning, and of tremendous integrity.

God bless you so to do, I humbly pray in the name of Jesus Christ. Amen.

Gordon B. Hinckley was second counselor in the First Presidency of The Church of Jesus Christ of Latter-day Saints when this devotional address was delivered in the Marriott Center on 17 September 1985.

For Times of Trouble

JEFFREY R. HOLLAND

I WOULD LIKE to be quite personal this morning—personal about you and personal about myself. I have thought about you a great deal over the past few weeks and have prayed to know what might be helpful to you. In doing so I have been drawn back to my own days as a student and some of the challenges I faced then. While such experiences now border on primitive history, fit only for a geology lecture, I'm nevertheless going ahead. I have wondered if some of your experiences and feelings might even now be very much the same.

I come this morning knowing the semester is nearly over and that what suggestions I offer were perhaps needed months ago. Furthermore, the year is nearly over and maybe for some an entire college career. But part of what I want to stress is that every day counts—including these remaining few in the semester—and that you have thousands of days thereafter. I will speak of you as you are right now and will hope it matters as much to the graduating senior as to the first-semester freshman.

I wish to speak today of a problem that is universal and that can, at any given hour, strike anywhere on campus—faculty, staff, administration, and especially students. I believe it is a form of evil. At least I know it can have damaging effects that block our growth, dampen our spirit, diminish our hope, and leave us vulnerable to other more conspicuous evils. I address it here this morning because I know of nothing Satan uses quite so cunningly or cleverly in his work on a young man or woman in your present circumstances. I speak of doubt—especially self-doubt—of discouragement, and of despair.

In doing so I don't wish to suggest that there aren't plenty of things in the world to be troubled by. In our lives, individually and collectively, there surely are serious threats to our happiness. I watch an early-morning news broadcast while I shave and then read a daily newspaper. That is enough to ruin anyone's day, and by then it's only 6:30 in the morning. Iran, Afghanistan, inflation, energy, jogging, mass murders, kidnapping, unemployment, floods—with all of this waiting for us we are tempted, as W. C. Fields once said, to "smile first thing in the morning and get it over with." But my concerns for you today are not the national and international ones. I wish to speak a little more personally of those matters that do not make headlines in the *New York Times* but that may be important in your personal journal. I'm anxious this morning about your problems with school and love and finances and the future, about your troubles concerning a place in life and the value of your contribution, about your private fears regarding where you are going and whether you think you will ever get there. Against a backdrop of hostages and high prices I wish to speak more personally of you and fortify you, if I am able, against doubt—especially self-doubt—and discouragement and despair. This morning I want to attack double-digit depression.

In doing so, however, I wish at the outset to make a distinction F. Scott Fitzgerald once made, that "trouble has no necessary connection with discouragement—discouragement has a germ of its own, as different from trouble as arthritis is different from a stiff joint" (*The Crack-Up*, 1945). Troubles we all have, but the "germ" of discouragement, to use Fitzgerald's word, is not in the trouble, it is in us. Or to be more precise, I believe it is in Satan, the prince of darkness, the father of lies. And he would have it be in us. It's frequently a small germ, hardly worth going to the Health Center for, but it will work and it will grow and it will spread. In fact, it can become almost a habit, a way of living and thinking, and there the greatest damage is done. Then it takes an increasingly severe toll on our spirit, for it erodes the deepest religious commitments we can make—those of faith, and hope, and charity. We turn inward and look downward, and these greatest of Christlike virtues are damaged or at the very least impaired. We become unhappy and soon make others unhappy, and before long Lucifer laughs.

As with any other germ, a little preventive medicine ought to be practiced in terms of those things that get us down. There is a line from Dante that says, "The arrow seen before cometh less rudely" (*The Divine Comedy*). President John F. Kennedy put the same thought into one of his state of the union messages this way: "The time to repair the roof is when the sun is shining." The Boy Scouts say it best of all: "Be prepared." That isn't just cracker-barrel wisdom with us; it is theology. "And angels shall fly through the midst of heaven, crying with a loud voice . . . Prepare ye, prepare ye" (D&C 88:92). "But if ye are prepared ye shall not fear" (D&C 38:30). And fear is part of what I wish to oppose this morning. The scriptures teach that preparation, if you will, is perhaps the major weapon in your arsenal against discouragement and self-defeat.

For example, if as a student you are the way I was, you may be discouraged over money matters—and almost everyone is, at least some of the time. A recent study indicated that financially related problems outranked all other factors in marital difficulty by a margin of three to one. And the pressure can be about that great on single students as well. If shared misery provides any consolation for you, take heart—you have friends. From the day I walked into my first college class until I staggered out the exit of my last—a period of time stretching over twelve years and four degrees—I was responsible for every cent of my education. I know that many in this audience are getting through school exactly the same way—part-time jobs, loans, working spouses, an almost desperate plea for scholarships, postponed personal comforts, and all the rest.

These things can be troublesome, but you have an obligation—to yourself, if to no one else—to see that they are not destructive. Prepare. "The arrow seen before cometh less rudely." Take advantage of this tender age to learn to use a budget, to sit down at a table spread out with your debts and come to grips with the economic facts of life. It's none too soon if you've made it to college and still have not had to establish personal fiscal priorities to decide what you will have at the expense of some things you will not have. Get it down on paper and deal with it there. That is the counsel given to husbands and wives, and the same solution works for others. The alternative is to leave it churning in your stomach and head and heart, all of which are susceptible to their own forms of ulcer.

I see the Brethren labor over the wise use of the Church's resources. I see President Oaks labor over it for the university. I hope soon to see someone labor over it for our nation. You can consider it part of a very valuable education to labor over it in your own life. Plan. Prepare. Budget. Work. Save. Sacrifice. Spend cheerfully on things that matter. Smile at an old pair of shoes. Pay your tithing. Cherish a used book. Though some of you may be living in almost desperate financial straits, I promise you there is a way. Such times may be burdensome. Such sacrifice may be hard. But it does not have to lead—for you it must not lead—to despair and destruction and defeat. In the words of Henry David Thoreau:

> Most of the luxuries, and many of the so-called comforts of life, are not only not indispensable, but positive hindrances to the elevation of mankind. [*Walden* (1854), 1, "Economy"]

> Love your life, poor as it is. . . . The setting sun is reflected from the windows of the almshouse as brightly as from the rich man's abode. [*Walden* (1854), 18, "Conclusion"]

Now no one here need be so dramatic as to peer out of an almshouse, but you may be going without some things, you may even consider yourself poor. Well, "Love your life, poor as it is." "If God so clothe the grass of the field, which to day is, and to morrow is cast into the oven, shall he not much more clothe you, O ye of little faith?" (Matthew 6:30).

Quite apart from the financial challenge, schoolwork itself can be quite a drag. (Hold your applause.) I suppose it's fair to say that math and English and economics and zoology can be discouraging on certain days, especially as finals approach. But a little preparation can work wonders here as well. Otherwise, it's the night before the paper is due or the morning before the afternoon exam, and despair distills upon us as the dews from heaven. I plead with you, in making your university experience a pleasant and rewarding one, work conscientiously in the early weeks, and you'll work more cheerfully at the end.

I remember handing in a paper to Dean Bruce B. Clark, who was at the time the teacher of an English literature class I was taking. I loved the class and knew from the first day of instruction that three short papers would be due on clearly stated dates during the term. Yet I left those papers—in every case, I think—until the night before they were due. I remember Dean Clark handing one of them back to me, saying something like, "You had the makings of a good paper here. It's too bad you didn't spend more time on it." I was devastated. Here was the chairman of my major department, teaching only one class a semester that year, the very symbol of my academic hopes and dreams for the B.A., saying, "You didn't work very hard." Oh, I had worked hard all right—from 9:00 the night before until 3:00 that morning, without stopping, without breathing.

Now, my young brothers and sisters, I *deserved* to be devastated. I should have been devastated. And it *could* have been a good paper. Perhaps that discouraged me more than anything. You see, *I* discouraged me. I discouraged *myself.* Remember, dear Brutus, "The fault . . . is not in our stars, but in ourselves" (William Shakespeare, *Julius Caesar*). And that's the worst kind of despair, the kind of self-despising that eats at our image and crushes our hopes. It isn't the class or the teacher or the paper. It never is. I simply should have done better. I should have been at work much sooner. I should have written a draft or two and then left it alone for a time. I should have gone back to it in freshness and strength. I might even have asked for some suggestions. I should have reworked it and shaped it and fine-tuned it over several rewritings. At the end I should have been working with a scalpel; as it was, I delivered one butchered idea, the meat axe still dripping as I walked into class. And furthermore, you don't type very well at 3:00 in the morning. The point is the same with school as with money or marriage or profession or any hope and dream. Prepare. Plan. Work. Sacrifice. Rework. Spend cheerfully on matters of worth. Carry the calm, and wear the assurance of having done the best you could with what you had. If you work hard and prepare earnestly, it will be very difficult for you to give in or give up or wear down. If you labor with faith in God and in yourself and in your future, you will have built upon a rock. Then, when the winds blow and the rains come—as surely they will—you shall not fall.

Of course, some things are not under your control. Some disappointments come regardless of your effort and preparation, for God wishes us to be strong as well as good. There, too, I say, "Love your life, poor as it is." Drive even these experiences into the corner, painful though they may be, and learn from them. In this, too, you have friends through the ages in whom you can take comfort and with whom you can form timeless bonds.

Thomas Edison devoted ten years and all of his money to developing the nickel-alkaline storage battery at a time when he was almost penniless. Through that period of time, his record and film production was supporting the storage battery effort. Then one night the terrifying cry of fire echoed through the film plant. Spontaneous combustion had ignited some chemicals. Within moments all of the packing compounds, celluloids for records, film, and other flammable goods had gone up with a roar. Fire companies from eight towns arrived, but the fire and heat were so intense and the water pressure so low that the fire hoses had no effect. Edison was sixty-seven years old—no age to begin anew. His daughter was frantic, wondering if he was safe, if his spirits were broken, how he would handle a crisis such as this at his age. She saw him running toward her. He spoke first.

He said, "Where's your mother? Go get her. Tell her to get her friends. They'll never see another fire like this as long as they live."

At 5:30 the next morning, with the fire barely under control, he called his employees together and announced, "We're rebuilding." One man was told to lease all the machine shops in the area, another to obtain a wrecking crane from the Erie Railroad Company. Then, almost as an afterthought, he added, "Oh, by the way. Anybody know where we can get some money?"

Virtually everything you now recognize as a Thomas Edison contribution to your life came *after* that disaster. Remember, "Trouble has no necessary connection with discouragement—discouragement has a germ of its own."

If you are trying hard and living right and things still seem burdensome and diffcult, take heart. Others have walked that way before you.

Do you feel unpopular and different, or outside the inside of things? Read about Noah again. Go out there and take a few whacks on the side of your ark and see what popularity was like in 2500 B.C.

Does the wilderness stretch before you in a never-ending sequence of semesters? Read about Moses again. Calculate the burden of fighting with the pharaohs and then a forty-year assignment in Sinai. Some tasks take time. Accept that. But as the scripture says, "They come to pass." They do end. We will cross over Jordan eventually. Others have proven it. I stand before you as a living symbol that anyone can make it through school, fill a mission, and find a job.

Are you afraid people don't like you? The Prophet Joseph Smith could share a few thoughts with you on that subject. Has health been a problem? Surely you will find comfort in the fact that a veritable Job has led this Church into one of the most exciting and revelatory decades of this entire dispensation. President Kimball has known few days in the last thirty years that were not filled with pain or discomfort or disease. Is it wrong to wonder if President Kimball has in some sense become what he is not only *in spite* of the physical burdens but also in part *because* of them? Can you take courage from your shared sacrifice with that giant of a man who has defied disease and death, has shaken his fist at the forces of darkness and cried when there was hardly strength to walk, "Oh, Lord, I am yet strong. Give me one more mountain" (see Joshua 14:11–12).

Do you ever feel untalented or incapable or inferior? Would it help you to know that everyone feels that way, too, including the prophets of God? Moses initially resisted his destiny, pleading that he was not eloquent in language. Jeremiah thought himself a child and was afraid of the faces he would meet.

And Enoch? I ask all of you to remember Enoch as long as you live. This is the young man who, when called to a seemingly impossible task, said, "Why is it that I have found favor in thy sight, and am but a lad, and all the people hate me; for I am slow of speech?" (Moses 6:31).

Enoch was a believer. He stiffened his spine and squared his shoulders and went stutteringly on his way. Plain old, ungifted, inferior Enoch. And this is what the angels would come to write of him:

> And so great was the faith of Enoch that he led the people of God, and their enemies came to battle against them; and he spake the word of the Lord, and the earth trembled, and the mountains fled, even according to his command; and the rivers of water were turned out of their course; and the roar of the lions was heard out of the wilderness; and all nations feared greatly, so powerful was the word of Enoch, and so great was the power of the language which God had given him. [Moses 7:13]

Plain old, inadequate Enoch—whose name is now synonymous with transcendent righteousness. The next time you are tempted to paint your self-portrait dismal gray, highlighted with lackluster beige, just remember that in like manner have this kingdom's most splendid men and women been tempted. I say to you as Joshua said to the tribes of Israel as they faced one of their most diffcult tasks, "Sanctify yourselves: for to morrow the Lord will do wonders among you" (Joshua 3:5).

There is, of course, one source of despair more serious than all the rest. It is linked with poor preparation of a far more serious order. It is the opposite of sanctification. It is the most destructive discouragement in time or eternity. It is transgression against God. It is depression embedded in sin.

Here your most crucial challenge, once you have recognized the seriousness of your mistakes, will be to believe that you can change, that there can be a different you. To disbelieve that is clearly a satanic device designed to discourage and defeat you. When you get home tonight, you fall on your knees and thank your Father in Heaven that you belong to the Church and have grasped a gospel that promises repentance to those who will pay the price. *Repentance* is not a foreboding word. It follows *faith,* the most encouraging word in the Christian vocabulary. Repentance is simply the scriptural invitation for growth and improvement and progress and renewal. You can change! You can be anything you want to be in righteousness.

If there is one lament I cannot abide—and I hear it from adults as well as from students—it is the poor, pitiful, withered cry, "Well, that's just the way I am." If you want to talk about discouragement, that phrase is one that discourages me. Though not a swearing man, I am always sorely tempted to try my hand when I hear that. Please spare me your speeches about "That's just the way I am." I've heard that from too many people who wanted to sin and call it psychology. And I use the word *sin* again to cover a vast range of habits, some seemingly innocent enough, that nevertheless bring discouragement and doubt and despair.

You can change anything you want to change, and you can do it very fast. That's another satanic suckerpunch—that it takes years and years and eons of eternity to repent. It takes exactly as long to repent as it takes you to say, "I'll change"—and mean it. Of course there will be problems to work out and restitutions to make. You may well spend—indeed, you had better spend—the rest of your life proving your repentance by its permanence. But change, growth, renewal, and repentance can come for you as instantaneously as for Alma and the sons of Mosiah. Even if you have serious amends to make, it is not likely that you would qualify for the term "the vilest of sinners," which is the phrase Mormon uses in describing these young men. Yet as Alma recounts his own experience in the thirty-sixth chapter of the book that bears his name, his repentance appears to have been as instantaneous as it was stunning.

Do not misunderstand. Repentance is not easy or painless or convenient. It is a bitter cup from Hell. But only Satan, who dwells there, would have you think that a necessary and required acknowledgment is more distasteful than permanent residence. Only he would say, "You can't change. You won't change. It's too long and too hard to change. Give up. Give in. Don't repent. You are just the way you are." That, my friends, is a lie born of desperation. Don't fall for it.

As you know, the Brethren used to announce in general conference the names of those who had been called on missions. Not only was this the way friends and neighbors learned of the call, more often than not it was the way the missionary learned of it as well. One such prospect was Eli H. Pierce. A railroad man by trade, he had not been very faithful in Church meetings—"Even had my inclinations led in that direction, which I frankly confess they did not," he admitted. His mind had been given totally to what he demurely calls "temporalities." He said he had never read more than a few pages of scripture in his life and that he had spoken to only one public gathering (an effort that he says was no credit to himself or to those who heard him). He used the vernacular of the railroad and the barroom with a finesse born of long practice. He bought cigars wholesale—a thousand at a time—and he regularly lost his paycheck playing pool. Then this classic understatement: "Nature never endowed me with a superabundance of religious sentiment; my spirituality was not high and probably even a little below average."

Well, the Lord knew what Eli Pierce was, and he knew something else. He knew what I'm pleading for today. He knew what Eli Pierce could become. When the call came that October 5 in 1875, Eli wasn't even in the Tabernacle. He was out working on one of the railroad lines. A fellow employee, once recovered from the shock of it all, ran out to telegraph the startling news. Brother Pierce writes, "At the very moment this intelligence was being flashed over the wires, I was sitting lazily thrown back in an office rocking chair, my feet on the desk, reading a novel and simultaneously sucking on an old Dutch pipe just to vary the monotony of cigar smoking." (For my friends in the English Department I would just hasten to add that the novel reading was probably a more serious transgression than the pipe smoking.)

He goes on. "As soon as I had been informed of what had taken place, I threw the novel in the waste basket, the pipe in a corner [and have never touched either to this hour]. I sent in my resignation . . . to take effect at once, in order that I might have time for study and preparation. I then started into town to buy [scripture]."

Then these stirring words:

> Remarkable as it may seem, and has since appeared to me, a thought of disregarding the call, or of refusing to comply with the requirement, never once entered my mind. The only question I asked—and I asked it a thousand times—was: "How can I accomplish this mission? How can I, who am so shamefully ignorant and untaught in doctrine, do honor to God and justice to the souls of men, and merit the trust reposed in me by the Priesthood?"

With such genuine humility fostering resolution rather than defeating it, Eli Pierce fulfilled a remarkable mission. His journal could appropriately close on a completely renovated life with this one line: "Throughout our entire mission we were greatly blessed." But I add one experience to make the point.

During his missionary service, Brother Pierce was called in to administer to the infant child of a branch president he knew and loved. Unfortunately, the wife of the branch president had become embittered and now seriously objected to any religious activity within the home, including a blessing for this dying child. With the mother refusing to leave the bedside and the child too ill to move, this humble branch president with his missionary friend retired to a small upper room in the house to pray for the baby's life. The mother, suspecting just such an act, sent one of the older children to observe and report back.

There in that secluded chamber the two knelt and prayed fervently until, in Brother Pierce's own words, "We felt that the child would live and knew that our prayers had been heard."

Arising from their knees, they turned slowly only to see the young girl standing in the partially open doorway gazing intently into the room. She seemed, however, quite oblivious to the movements of the two men. She stood entranced for some seconds, her eyes immovable. Then she said, "Papa, who was that . . . man in there?"

Her father said, "That is Brother Pierce. You know him."

"No," she said, matter-of-factly, "I mean the *other* man."

"There was no other, darling, except Brother Pierce and myself. We were praying for baby."

"Oh, there was another man," the child insisted, "for I saw him standing [above] you and Brother Pierce and he was dressed [all] in white."

Now if God in his heavens will do that for a repentant old cigar-smoking, inactive, swearing pool player, don't you think he'll do it for you? He will if your resolve is as deep and permanent as Eli Pierce's. In this church we ask for faith, not infallibility. (See *Biography and Family Record of Lorenzo Snow*, pp. 407–13.)

Immerse yourself in the scriptures. You will find your own experiences described there. You will find spirit and strength there. You will find solutions and counsel. Nephi says, "The words of Christ will tell you all things . . . ye should do" (2 Nephi 32:3).

Pray earnestly and fast with purpose and devotion. Some difficulties, like devils, come not out "but by prayer and fasting."

Serve others. The heavenly paradox is that only in so doing can you save yourself.

Be patient. As Robert Frost said, with many things the only way out is through. Keep moving. Keep trying.

Have faith. "Has the day of miracles ceased?"

> Or have angels ceased to appear unto the children of men? Or has he withheld the power of the Holy Ghost from them? Or will he, so long as time shall last, or the earth shall stand, or there shall be one man upon the face thereof to be saved?
>
> Behold I say unto you, Nay; for it is by faith . . . that angels appear and minister unto men. [Moroni 7:35–37]

Several decades ago an acquaintance of mine left a small southern Utah town to travel to the East. He had never traveled much beyond his little hometown and certainly had never ridden a train. But his older sister and brother-in-law needed him under some special circumstances, and his parents agreed to free him from the farm work in order to go. They drove him to Salt Lake City and put him onto the train—new Levi's, not-so-new boots, very frightened, and eighteen years old.

There was one major problem, and it terrified him. He had to change trains in Chicago. Furthermore, it involved a one-night layover, and that was a fate worse than death. His sister had written, carefully outlining when the incoming train would arrive and how and where and when he was to catch the outgoing line, but he was terrified.

And then his humble, plain, sun-scarred father did something no one in this room should ever forget. He said, "Son, wherever you go in this Church there will always be somebody to stand by you. That's part of what it means to be a Latter-day Saint." And then he stuffed into the pocket of his calico shirt the name of a bishop he had taken the time to identify from sources at Church headquarters. If the boy had troubles, or became discouraged and afraid, he was to call the bishop and ask for help.

Well, the train ride progressed rather uneventfully until the train pulled into Chicago. And even then the young man did pretty well at collecting his luggage and making it to the nearby hotel room that had been prearranged by his brother-in-law. But then the clock began to tick and night began to fall and faith began to fail. Could he find his way back to the station? Could he find the right track and train? What if it was late? What if he was late? What if he lost his ticket? What if his sister had made a mistake and he ended up in New York? What if? What if? What if?

Without those well-worn boots ever hitting the floor, that big, raw-boned boy flew across the room, nearly pulled the telephone out of the wall, and, fighting back tears and troubles, called the bishop. Alas, the bishop was not home, but the bishop's wife was. She spoke long enough to reassure him that absolutely nothing could go wrong that night. He was, after all, safe in the room, and what he needed more than anything else was a night's rest. Then she said, "If tomorrow morning you are still concerned, follow these directions and you can be with our family and other ward members until train time. We will make sure you get safely on your way." She then carefully spelled out the directions, had him repeat them back, and suggested a time for him to come.

With slightly more peace in his heart, he knelt by his bed in prayer (as he had every night of his eighteen years) and then waited for morning to come. Somewhere in the night the hustle and bustle of Chicago in the 1930s subsided into peaceful sleep.

At the appointed hour the next morning he set out. A long walk, then catch a bus. Then transfer to another. Watch for the stop. Walk a block, change sides of the street, and then one last bus. Count the streets carefully. Two more to go. One more to go. I'm here. Let me out of this bus. It worked, just like she said.

Then his world crumbled, crumbled before his very eyes. He stepped out of the bus onto the longest stretch of shrubbery and grass he had ever seen in his life. She had said something about a park, but he thought a park was a dusty acre in southern Utah with a netless tennis court in one corner. Here he stood looking in vain at the vast expanse of Lincoln Park with not a single friendly face in sight.

There was *no* sign of a bishop or a ward or a meetinghouse. And the bus was gone. It struck him that he had no idea where he was or what combination of connections with who knows what number of buses would be necessary to get him back to the station. Suddenly he felt more alone and overwhelmed than he had at any moment in his life. As the tears welled up in his eyes, he despised himself for feeling so afraid—but he was, and the tears would not stop. He stepped off the sidewalk away from the bus stop into the edge of the park. He needed some privacy for his tears, as only an eighteen-year-old from southern Utah could fully appreciate. But as he stepped away from the noise, fighting to control his emotions, he thought he heard something hauntingly familiar in the distance. He moved cautiously in the direction of the sound. First he walked, and then he walked quickly. The sound was stronger and firmer and certainly it was familiar. Then he started to smile, a smile that erupted into an audible laugh, and then he started to run. He wasn't sure that was the most dignified thing for a newcomer to Chicago to do, but this was no time for discretion. He ran, and he ran fast. He ran as fast as those cowboy boots would carry him—over shrubs, through trees, around the edge of a pool.

> Though hard to you this journey may appear,
> Grace shall be as your day.

The sounds were crystal clear, and he was weeping newer, different tears. For there over a little rise huddled around a few picnic tables and bundles of food were the bishop and his wife and their children and most of the families of that little ward. The date: July 24, 1934. The sound: a slightly off-key a cappella rendition of lines that even a boy from southern Utah could recognize.

> Gird up your loins; fresh courage take;
> Our God will never us forsake;
> And soon we'll have this tale to tell—
> All is well! All is well!
> ["Come, Come, Ye Saints, *Hymns,* 1985, no. 30]

It was Pioneer Day. The gathering to which he had been invited was a Twenty-Fourth of July celebration. Knowing that it was about time for the boy to arrive, the ward had thought it a simple matter to sing a verse or two of "Come, Come, Ye Saints" to let him know their location.

Elisha, with a power known only to the prophets, had counseled the king of Israel on how and where and when to defend against the warring Syrians. The king of Syria, of course, wished to rid his armies of this prophetic problem. So—and I quote:

> Therefore sent he thither horses, and chariots, and a great host: and they came by night, and compassed the city about.
>
> . . . an host compassed the city both with horses and chariots. [2 Kings 6:14–15]

If Elisha is looking for a good time to be depressed, this is it. His only ally is the president of the local teachers quorum. It is one prophet and one lad against the world. And the boy is petrified. He sees the enemy everywhere—difficulty and despair and problems and burdens everywhere. The bus is gone and all he can see is Chicago. With faltering faith the boy cries, "Alas, my master! how shall we do?"

And Elisha's reply? "Fear not: for they that be with us are more than they that be with them" (2 Kings 6:15–16).

"They that be with us?" Now just an Israelite minute here. Faith is fine and courage is wonderful, but this is ridiculous, the boy thinks. There *are* no others with them. He can recognize a Syrian army when he sees one, and he knows that one child and an old man are not strong odds against it. But then comes Elisha's promise:

> Fear not: for they that be with us are more than they that be with them.
>
> And Elisha prayed, and said, Lord, I pray thee, open his eyes, that he may see. And the Lord opened the eyes of the young man; and he saw: and, behold, the mountain was full of horses and chariots of fire round about Elisha. [2 Kings 6:16–17]

In the gospel of Jesus Christ you have help from both sides of the veil, and you must never forget that. When disappointment and discouragement strike—and they will—you remember and never forget that if our eyes could be opened we would see horses and chariots of fire as far as the eye can see riding at reckless speed to come to our protection. They will always be there, these armies of heaven, in defense of Abraham's seed.

I close with this promise from heaven:

> Verily, verily, I say unto you, ye are little children, and ye have not as yet understood how great blessings the Father hath in his own hands and prepared for you;
>
> And ye cannot bear all things now; nevertheless, be of good cheer, for I will lead you along. [D&C 78:17–18]

> I will go before your face. I will be on your right hand and on your left, . . . and mine angels [shall be] round about you, to bear you up. [D&C 84:88]

> The kingdom is yours and the blessings thereof are yours, and the riches of eternity are yours. [D&C 78:18]

Oh, yes, "We'll find the place which God for us prepared." And on the way "We'll make the air with music ring, Shout praises to our God and King; Above the rest these words we'll tell—All is well! All is well!" ("Come, Come, Ye Saints," *Hymns,* 1985, no. 30).

I say this in the name of Jesus Christ. Amen.

Jeffrey R. Holland was commissioner of education for the Church Educational System when this devotional address was given in the Marriott Center on 18 March 1980.

An Anchor to the Souls of Men

HOWARD W. HUNTER

It is a wonderful privilege for me to be with all of the students and young adults gathered here in the Marriott Center tonight and in many other locations throughout North America. I am also aware that videotapes of these firesides will be sent to many of our international areas where English, Spanish, and French are spoken. I am thrilled that modern technology allows us to reach out to so many of you marvelous young people at a time when the Church is growing very rapidly.

The General Authorities of the Church have great confidence in you and have a genuine desire to stay in touch with you, to know of your concerns, and to offer some words of encouragement, counsel, and reassurance. My purpose tonight is to give just such encouragement and reassurance. I am delighted to be with you.

Life has a fair number of challenges in it, and that's true of life in the 1990s. Indeed, you may be feeling that you have more than your share of problems. These concerns may be very global difficulties, such as the devastating famine we see in Somalia and other places in the world, or the incessant sounds of war in Yugoslavia, or the Middle East, or India, or Ireland, or so many other locations around the world.

Unfortunately, some of these wars have religious or ethnic overtones, and that makes them even more tragic, if that is possible. These last few years we have seen our fair share of economic difficulties and recession in every nation. Sometimes these economic challenges get translated into very immediate problems for college students and those trying to earn a living, and perhaps start a family, in their early adult years.

Years ago there was a popular music group formed at BYU that went on to considerable local stardom and acclaim, a group named The Three D's. They took the name from their three singers: Duane Hiatt, Richard (Dick) Davis, and Denis Sorenson. My fear is that in the nineties, if we were to form a popular singing group among our young people, it might still be called The Three D's, but that could be for Despair, Doom, and Discouragement.

I am here tonight to tell you that Despair, Doom, and Discouragement are not an acceptable view of life for a Latter-day Saint. However high on the charts they are on the hit parade of contemporary news, we must not walk on our lower lip every time a few difficult moments happen to confront us.

I am just a couple of years older than most of you, and in those few extra months I have seen a bit more of life than you have. I want you to know that there have always been some difficulties in mortal life and there always will be. But knowing what we know, and living as we are supposed to live, there really is no place, no excuse, for pessimism and despair.

In my lifetime I have seen two world wars plus Korea plus Vietnam and all that you are currently witnessing. I have worked my way through the depression and managed to go to law school while starting a young family at the same time. I have seen stock markets and world economics go crazy and have seen a few despots and tyrants go crazy, all of which causes quite a bit of trouble around the world in the process.

So I am frank to say tonight that I hope you won't believe all the world's difficulties have been wedged into your decade, or that things have never been worse than they are for you personally, or that they will never get better. I reassure you that things have been worse and they *will* always get better. They always do—especially when we live and love the gospel of Jesus Christ and give it a chance to flourish in our lives.

Here are some actual comments that have been made and passed on to me in recent months. This comes from a fine returned missionary:

> Why should I date and get serious with a girl? I am not sure I even want to marry and bring a family into this kind of a world. I am not very sure about my own future. How can I take the responsibility for the future of others whom I would love and care about and want to be happy?

Here's another from a high school student:

> I hope I die before all these terrible things happen that people are talking about. I don't want to be on the earth when there is so much trouble.

And this from a recent college graduate:

> I am doing the best I can, but I wonder if there is much reason to even plan for the future, let alone retirement. The world probably won't last that long anyway.

Well, isn't that a fine view of things? Sounds like we all ought to go and eat a big plate of worms.

I want to say to all within the sound of my voice tonight that you have every reason in this world to be happy and to be optimistic and to be confident. Every generation since time began has had some things to overcome and some problems to work out. Furthermore, every individual person has a particular set of challenges that sometimes seem to be earmarked for us individually. We understood that in our premortal existence.

Prophets and apostles of the Church have faced some of those personal difficulties. I acknowledge that I have faced a few, and you will undoubtedly face some of your own now and later in your life. When these experiences humble us and refine us and teach us and bless us, they can be powerful instruments in the hands of God to make us better people, to make us more grateful and more loving, to make us more considerate of other people in their own times of difficulty.

Yes, we all have difficult moments individually and collectively, but even in the most severe of times, anciently or modern, those problems and prophecies were never intended to do anything but bless the righteous and help those who are less righteous move toward repentance. God loves us, and the scriptures tell us he

> gave his only begotten Son, that whosoever believeth in him should not perish, but have everlasting life.
>
> For God sent not his Son into the world to condemn the world; but that the world through him might be saved. [John 3:16–17]

The scriptures also indicate that there will be seasons of time when the whole world will have some difficulty. We know that in our dispensation unrighteousness will, unfortunately, be quite evident, and it will bring its inevitable difficulties and pain and punishment. God will cut short that unrighteousness in his own due time, but our task is to live fully and faithfully and not worry ourselves sick about the woes of the world or when it will end. Our task is to have the gospel in our lives and to be a bright light, a city set upon a hill that reflects the beauty of the gospel of Jesus Christ and the joy and happiness that will always come to every people in every age who keep the commandments.

In this last dispensation there will be great tribulation (Matthew 24:21). We know that from the scriptures. We know there will be wars and rumors of wars and that the whole earth will be in commotion (D&C 45:26). All dispensations have had their perilous times, but our day will include genuine peril (2 Timothy 3:1). Evil men will flourish (2 Timothy 3:13), but then evil men have very often flourished. Calamities will come and iniquity will abound (D&C 45:27).

Inevitably, the natural result of some of these kinds of prophecies is fear, and that is not fear limited to a younger generation. It is fear shared by those of any age who don't understand what we understand.

But I want to stress that these feelings are not necessary for faithful Latter-day Saints, and they do not come from God. To ancient Israel, the great Jehovah said:

> Be strong and of a good courage, fear not, nor be afraid of them: for the Lord thy God, he it is that doth go with thee; he will not fail thee, nor forsake thee. . . .
>
> And the Lord, he it is that doth go before thee; he will be with thee, he will not fail thee, neither forsake thee: fear not, neither be dismayed. [Deuteronomy 31:6, 8]

And to you, our marvelous generation in modern Israel, the Lord has said: "Therefore, fear not, little flock; do good; let earth and hell combine against you, for if ye are built upon my rock, they cannot prevail. . . . Look unto me in every thought; doubt not, fear not" (D&C 6:34, 36).

Such counsel is laced throughout our modern scriptures. Listen to this wonderful reassurance:

> Fear not, little children, for you are mine, and I have overcome the world, and you are of them that my Father hath given me. [D&C 50:41]

> Verily I say unto you my friends, fear not, let your hearts be comforted; yea, rejoice evermore, and in everything give thanks. [D&C 98:1]

In light of such wonderful counsel, I think it is incumbent upon us to rejoice a little more and despair a little less, to give thanks for what we have and for the magnitude of God's blessings to us, and to talk a little less about what we may not have or what anxiety may accompany difficult times in this or any generation.

For Latter-day Saints this is a time of great hope and excitement—one of the greatest eras of the Restoration and therefore one of the greatest eras in any dispensation, inasmuch as ours is the greatest of all dispensations. We need to have faith and hope, two of the greatest fundamental virtues of any discipleship of Christ. We must continue to exercise confidence in God, inasmuch as that is the first principle in our code of belief. We must believe that God has all power, that he loves us, and that his work will not be stopped or frustrated in our individual lives or in the world generally. He will bless us as a people because he always has blessed us as a people. He will bless us as individuals because he always has blessed us as individuals.

Listen to this marvelous counsel given by President Joseph F. Smith nearly ninety years ago. It sounds as if young people in that day might have been a little anxious about their future as well. I quote:

> You do not need to worry in the least, the Lord will take care of you and bless you. He will also take care of His servants, and will bless them and help them to accomplish His purposes; and all the powers of darkness combined in earth and in hell cannot prevent it. . . . He has stretched forth His hand to accomplish His purposes, and the arm of flesh cannot stay it. He will cut His work short in righteousness, and will hasten His purposes in His own time. It is only necessary to try with our might to keep pace with the onward progress of the work of the Lord, then God will preserve and protect us, and will prepare the way before us, that we shall live and multiply and replenish the earth and always do His will. [Joseph F. Smith, *CR,* October 1905, pp. 5–6]

More recently, Elder Marion G. Romney, then of the Quorum of the Twelve, counseled the Church. This was twenty-five years ago, when the world also knew some difficulty. An American president had been assassinated, communism was alive and menacing, and a war was building up in Southeast Asia. My sons were just exactly your age at that time, and they had some of the same anxieties you have about life and marriage and the future. Here's what President Romney said then:

> Naturally, believing Christians, even those who have a mature faith in the gospel, are concerned and disturbed by the lowering clouds on the horizon. But they need not be surprised or frantic about their portent, for, as has already been said, at the very beginning of this last dispensation the Lord made it abundantly clear that through the tribulations and calamity that he foresaw and foretold and that we now see coming upon us, there would be a people who, through acceptance and obedience to the gospel, would be able to recognize and resist the powers of evil, build up the promised Zion, and prepare to meet the Christ and be with him in the blessed millennium. And we know further that it is possible for every one of us, who will, to have a place among those people. It is this assurance and this expectation that gives us understanding of the Lord's admonition, "be not troubled." [Marion G. Romney, *CR,* 1966, pp. 53–54]

Let me offer a third example from yet another moment of difficulty in this century. In the midst of the most devastating international conflagration the modern world has ever seen, Elder John A. Widtsoe of the Council of the Twelve counseled people who were worried. Nazism was on the march, there was war in the Pacific, nation after nation seemed to be drawn into war. Mind you this was 1942, not 1992 or 1993. This is what Brother Widtsoe said:

> Above the roar of cannon and airplane, the maneuvers and plans of men, the Lord always determines the tide of battle. So far and no farther does He permit the evil one to go in his career to create human misery. The Lord is ever victorious; He is the Master to whose will Satan is subject. Though all hell may rage, and men may follow evil, the purposes of the Lord will not fail. [John A. Widtsoe, *CR,* April 1942, p. 34]

I promise you tonight in the name of the Lord whose servant I am that God will always protect and care for his people. We will have our difficulties the way every generation and people have had difficulties. Your life as a young college student or working person in the 1990s is no different than any young person's life has been in any age of time. But with the gospel of Jesus Christ you have every hope and promise and reassurance. The Lord has power over his Saints and will always prepare places of peace, defense, and safety for his people. When we have faith in God we can hope for a better world—for us personally and for all mankind. The prophet Ether taught anciently (and he knew something about troubles):

> Wherefore, whoso believeth in God might with surety hope for a better world, yea, even a place at the right hand of God, which hope cometh of faith, maketh an anchor to the souls of men, which would make them sure and steadfast, always abounding in good works, being led to glorify God. [Ether 12:4]

Disciples of Christ in every generation are invited, indeed commanded, to be filled with a perfect brightness of hope (2 Nephi 31:20).

This faith and hope of which I speak is not a Pollyanna-like approach to significant personal and public problems. I don't believe we can wake up in the morning and simply by drawing a big "happy face" on the chalkboard believe that is going to take care of the world's difficulties. But if our faith and hope is anchored in Christ, and in his teachings, commandments, and promises, then we are able to count on something truly remarkable, genuinely miraculous, that can part the Red Sea and lead modern Israel to a place "where none shall come to hurt or make afraid" ("Come, Come, Ye Saints," *Hymns,* 1985, no. 30). Fear, which can come upon people in difficult days, is a principal weapon in the arsenal that Satan uses to make mankind unhappy. He who fears loses strength for the combat of life in the fight against evil. Therefore, the power of the evil one always tries to generate fear in human hearts. In every age and in every era fear has faced mankind.

As children of God and descendants of Abraham, Isaac, and Jacob, we must seek to dispel fear from among people. A timid, fearing people cannot do their work well, and they cannot do God's work at all. Latter-day Saints have a divinely assigned mission to fulfill that simply must not be dissipated in fear and anxiety.

An apostle of the Lord in an earlier day said this:

> The key to the conquest of fear has been given through the Prophet Joseph Smith. "If ye are prepared ye shall not fear." (D.&C. 38:30) That divine message needs repeating today in every stake and ward. [And, I might add, among every group of college students and young adults in the Church.] [John A. Widtsoe, *CR*, April 1942, p. 33]

Are we prepared to surrender to God's commandments? Are we prepared to achieve victory over our appetites? Are we prepared to obey righteous law? If we can honestly answer yes to those questions, we can bid fear to depart from our lives. Surely the degree of fear in our hearts may well be measured by our preparation to live righteously—living that should characterize every Latter-day Saint in every age and time.

Let me close tonight with one of the greatest statements I have ever read from the Prophet Joseph Smith, who faced such immense difficulties in his life and who of course paid the ultimate price for his victory. But he *was* victorious, and he was a happy, robust, optimistic man. Those who knew him felt his strength and courage, even in the darkest of times. He did not sag in spirits or long remain in any despondency.

He said about our time—yours and mine—that ours is the moment

> upon which prophets, priests and kings [in ages past] have dwelt with peculiar delight; [all these ancient witnesses for God] have looked forward with joyful anticipation to the day in which we live; and fired with heavenly and joyful anticipations they have sung and written and prophesied of this our day; . . . we are the favored people that God has [chosen] to bring about the Latter-day glory. [*HC* 4:609–10]

That is a thrilling statement to me: that the ancients whom we love and read and quote so much—Adam and Abraham, Joshua and Joseph, Isaiah and Ezekiel and Ezra, Nephi and Alma, and Mormon and Moroni—all of these ancient prophets, priests, and kings focused their prophetic vision "with peculiar delight" on our day, on our time. It is this hour to which they have looked forward "with joyful anticipation," and "fired with heavenly and joyful anticipation they have sung and written and prophesied of this our day." They saw us as "the favored people" upon whom God would shower his full and complete latter-day glory, and I testify that is our destiny. What a privilege! What an honor! What a responsibility! And what joy! We have every reason in time and eternity to rejoice and give thanks for the quality of our lives and the promises we have been given. That we may do so, I pray in the name of Jesus Christ. Amen.

Howard W. Hunter was the president of the Council of the Twelve Apostles of The Church of Jesus Christ of Latter-day Saints when this fireside address was delivered in the Marriott Center on 7 February 1993.

The Second Century of Brigham Young University

SPENCER W. KIMBALL

My BELOVED brothers and sisters: It was almost eight years ago that I had the privilege of addressing an audience at the Brigham Young University about "Education for Eternity." Some things were said then that I believe, then and now, about the destiny of this unique university. I shall refer to several of those ideas again, combining them with some fresh thoughts and impressions I have concerning Brigham Young University as it enters its second century.

I am grateful to all who made possible the Centennial Celebration for the Brigham Young University, including those who have developed the history of this university in depth. A centennial observance is appropriate, not only to renew our ties with the past, but also to review and reaffirm our goals for the future. My task is to talk about BYU's second century. Though my comments will focus on Brigham Young University, it is obvious to all of us here that the university is, in many ways, the center of the Church Educational System. President McKay described the university as "the hub of the Church educational wheel." Karl G. Maeser described the Brigham Young Academy as "the parent trunk of the great education banyan tree," and recently it has been designated "the flagship." However it is stated, the centrality of this university to the entire system is a very real fact of life. What I say to you, therefore, must take note of things beyond the borders of this campus, but not beyond its influence. We must ever keep firmly in mind the needs of those ever-increasing numbers of LDS youth in other places in North America and in other lands who cannot attend this university, whose needs are real, and who represent, in fact, the majority of LDS college and university students.

In a speech I gave to many of the devoted alumni of this university in the Arizona area, I employed a phrase to describe the Brigham Young University as becoming an "educational Everest." There are many ways in which BYU can tower above other universities—not simply because of the size of its student body or its beautiful campus—but because of the unique light BYU can send forth into the educational world. Your light must have a special glow, for while you will do many things in the programs of this university that are done elsewhere, these same things can and must be done better here than others do them. You will also do some special things here that are left undone by other institutions.

First among these unique features is the fact that education on this campus deliberately and persistently concerns itself with "education for eternity," not just for time. The faculty has a double heritage that they must pass along: the secular knowledge that history has washed to the feet of mankind along with the new knowledge brought by scholarly research, and also the vital and revealed truths that have been sent to us from heaven.

This university shares with other universities the hope and the labor involved in rolling back the frontiers of knowledge even further, but we also know that through the process of revelation there are yet "many great and important things" to be given to mankind that will have an intellectual and spiritual impact far beyond what mere men can imagine. Thus, at this university among faculty, students, and administration there is and must be an excitement and an expectation about the very nature and future of knowledge that underwrites the uniqueness of BYU.

Your double heritage and dual concerns with the secular and the spiritual require you to be "bilingual." As scholars you must speak with authority and excellence to your professional colleagues in the language of scholarship, and you must also be literate in the language of spiritual things. We must be more bilingual, in that sense, to fulfill our promise in the second century of BYU.

BYU is being made even more unique, not because what we are doing is changing, but because of the general abandonment by other universities of their efforts to lift the daily behavior and morality of their students.

From the administration of BYU in 1967 came this thought:

> Brigham Young University has been established by the prophets of God and can be operated only on the highest standards of Christian morality. . . . Students who instigate or participate in riots or open rebellion against the policies of the University cannot expect to remain at the university.
>
> The standards of the Church are understood by students who have been taught these standards in the home and at Church throughout their lives.
>
> First and foremost, we expect BYU students to maintain a single standard of Christian morality. . . .
>
> . . . attendance at BYU is a privilege and not a right, and . . . students who attend must expect to live its standards or forfeit the privilege. [Ernest L. Wilkinson, President of BYU, July 1967]

We have no choice at BYU except to "hold the line" regarding gospel standards and values and to draw men and women from other campuses also—all we can—into this same posture, for people entangled in sin are not free. At this university (that may to some of our critics seem unfree) there will be real individual freedom. Freedom from worldly ideologies and concepts unshackles man far more than he knows. It is the truth that sets men free. BYU, in its second century, must become the last remaining bastion of resistance to the invading ideologies that seek control of curriculum as well as classroom. We do not resist such ideas because we fear them, but because they are false. BYU, in its second century, must continue to resist false fashions in education, staying with those basic principles that have proved right and have guided good men and women and good universities over the centuries. This concept is not new, but in the second hundred years we must do it even better.

When the pressures mount for us to follow the false ways of the world, we hope in the years yet future that those who are part of this university and the Church Educational System will not attempt to counsel the board of trustees to follow false ways. We want, through your administration, to receive all your suggestions for making BYU even better. I hope none will presume on the prerogatives of the prophets of God to set the basic direction for this university. No man comes to the demanding position of the Presidency of the Church except his heart and mind are constantly open to the impressions, insights, and revelations of God. No one is more anxious than the Brethren who stand at the head of this Church to receive such guidance as the Lord would give them for the benefit of mankind and for the people of the Church. Thus, it is important to remember what we have in the revelations of the Lord: "And thou shalt not command him who is at thy head, and at the head of the church" (D&C 28:6). If the governing board has as much loyalty from faculty and students, from administration and staff as we have had in the past, I do not fear for the future!

The Church Board of Education and the Brigham Young University Board of Trustees involve individuals who are committed to truth as well as to the order of the kingdom. I observed while I was here in 1967 that this institution and its leaders should be like the Twelve as they were left in a very difficult world by the Savior:

> The world hath hated them, because they are not of the world, even as I am not of the world.
>
> I pray not that thou shouldest take them out of the world, but that thou shouldest keep them from the evil.
>
> They are not of the world, even as I am not of the world. [John 17:14–16]

This university is not of the world any more than the Church is of the world, and it must not be made over in the image of the world.

We hope that our friends, and even our critics, will understand why we must resist anything that would rob BYU of its basic uniqueness in its second century. As the Church's commissioner of education said on the occasion of the inaugural of President Oaks:

> Brigham Young University seeks to improve and to "sanctify" itself for the sake of others—not for the praise of the world, but to serve the world better.

That task will be persisted in. Members of the Church are willing to doubly tax themselves to support the Church Educational System, including this university, and we must not merely "ape the world." We must do special things that would justify the special financial outpouring that supports this university.

As the late President Stephen L Richards once said, "Brigham Young University will never surrender its spiritual character to sole concern for scholarship." BYU will be true to its charter and to such addenda to that charter as are made by living prophets.

I am both hopeful and expectant that out of this university and the Church Educational System there will rise brilliant stars in drama, literature, music, sculpture, painting, science, and in all the scholarly graces. This university can be the refining host for many such individuals who will touch men and women the world over long after they have left this campus.

We must be patient, however, in this effort, because just as the City of Enoch took decades to reach its pinnacle of performance in what the Lord described as occurring "in process of time" (Moses 7:21), so the quest for excellence at BYU must also occur "in process of time."

> Ideals are like stars; you will not succeed in touching them with your hands. But like the seafaring man on the desert of waters, you choose them as your guides, and following them you will reach your destiny. [Carl Schurz, 18 April 1975, address in Faneuil Hall, Boston]

I see even more than was the case nearly a decade ago a widening gap between this university and other universities both in terms of purposes and in terms of directions. Much has happened in the intervening eight years to make that statement justifiable. More and more is being done, as I hoped it would, to have here "the greatest collection of artifacts, records, writings . . . in the world." BYU is moving toward preeminence in many fields, thanks to the generous support of the tithe payers of the Church and the excellent efforts of its faculty and students under the direction of a wise administration.

These changes do not happen free of pain, challenge, and adjustment. Again, harking back, I expressed the hope that the BYU vessel would be kept seaworthy by taking "out all old planks as they decay and put[ting] in new and stronger timber in their place," because the *Flagship BYU* must sail on and on and on. The creative changes in your academic calendar, your willingness to manage your curriculum more wisely, your efforts to improve general education, your interaction of disciplines across traditional departmental lines, and the creation of new research institutes here on this campus—all are evidences that the captain and crew are doing much to keep the BYU vessel seaworthy and sailing. I refer to the centers of research that have been established on this campus, ranging from family and language research on through to research on food, agriculture, and ancient studies. Much more needs to be done, but you must "not run faster or labor more than you have strength and means provided" (D&C 10:4). While the discovery of new knowledge must increase, there must always be a heavy and primary emphasis on transmitting knowledge—on the quality of teaching at BYU. Quality teaching is a tradition never to be abandoned. It includes a quality relationship between faculty and students. Carry these over into BYU's second century!

Brigham Young undoubtedly meant both teaching and learning when he said:

> Learn everything that the children of men know, and be prepared for the most refined society upon the face of the earth, then improve on this until we are prepared and permitted to enter the

> society of the blessed—the holy angels that dwell in the presence of God. [*JD* 16:77]

We must be certain that the lessons are not only taught but are also absorbed and learned. We remember the directive that President John Taylor made to Karl G. Maeser "that no infidels will go forth from this school."

> Whatever you do, be choice in your selection of teachers. We do not want infidels to mould the minds of our children. They are a precious charge bestowed upon us by the Lord, and we cannot be too careful in rearing and training them. I would rather have my children taught the simple rudiments of a common education by men of God, and have them under their influence, than have them taught in the most abstruce sciences by men who have not the fear of God in their hearts. . . . We need to pay more attention to educational matters, and do all we can to procure the services of competent teachers. Some people say, we cannot afford to pay them. You cannot afford not to pay them; you cannot afford not to employ them. We want our children to grow up intelligent, and to walk abreast with the peoples of any nation. God expects us to do it; and therefore I call attention to this matter. I have heard intelligent practical men say, it is quite as cheap to keep a good horse as a poor one, or to raise good stock as inferior animals. And is it not quite as cheap to raise good intelligent children as to rear children in ignorance. [*JD* 24:168–69]

Thus, we can continue to do as the Prophet Joseph Smith implied that we should when he said: "Man was created to dress the earth, to cultivate his mind, and to glorify God."

We cannot do these things except we continue, in the second century, to be concerned about the spiritual qualities and abilities of those who teach here. In the book of Mosiah we read, "Trust no one to be your teacher nor your minister, except he be a man of God, walking in his ways and keeping his commandments" (Mosiah 23:14). William R. Inge said, "I have no fear that the candle lighted in Palestine years ago will ever be put out."

We must be concerned with the spiritual worthiness, as well as the academic and professional competency, of all those who come here to teach. William Lyon Phelps said:

> I thoroughly believe in a university education for both men and women; but I believe a knowledge of the Bible without a college course is more valuable than a college course without the Bible.

Students in the second century must continue to come here to learn. We do not apologize for the importance of students' searching for eternal companions at the same time that they search the scriptures and search the shelves of libraries for knowledge. President McKay observed on one occasion that "the university is not a dictionary, a dispensary, nor is it a department store. It is more than a storehouse of knowledge and more than a community of scholars. The university life is essentially an exercise in thinking, preparing, and living." We do not want BYU ever to become an educational factory. It must concern itself with not only the dispensing of facts but with the preparation of its students to take their place in society as thinking, thoughtful, and sensitive individuals who, in paraphrasing the motto of your Centennial, come here dedicated to love of God, pursuit of truth, and service to mankind.

There are yet other reasons why we must not lose either our moorings or our sense of direction in the second century. We still have before us the remarkable prophecy of John Taylor when he observed:

> You will see the day that Zion will be as far ahead of the outside world in everything pertaining to learning of every kind as we are today in regard to religious matters. You mark my words, and write them down, and see if they do not come to pass. [*JD* 21:100]

Surely we cannot refuse that rendezvous with history because so much of what is desperately needed by mankind is bound up in our being willing to contribute to the fulfillment of that prophecy.

Others, at times, also seem to have a sensing of what might happen. Charles H. Malik, former president of the United Nations General Assembly, voiced a fervent hope when he said that

> one day a great university will arise somewhere . . . I hope in America . . . to which Christ will return in His full glory and power, a university which will, in the promotion of scientific, intellectual, and artistic excellence, surpass by far even the best secular universities of the present, but which will at the same time enable Christ to bless it and act and feel perfectly at home in it. ["Education and Upheaval: The Christian's Responsibility," *Creative Help for Daily Living,* 21 September 1970]

Surely BYU can help to respond to that call!

By dealing with basic issues and basic problems, we can be effective educationally. Otherwise, we will simply join the multitude who have so often lost their way in dark, sunless forests even while working hard. It was Thoreau who said, "There are a thousand hacking at the branches of evil to one who is striking at the root" (*Walden* [1854], I, "Economy"). We should deal statistically and spiritually with root problems, root issues, and root causes in BYU's second century. We seek to do so, not in arrogance or pride, but in the spirit of service. We must do so with a sense of trembling and urgency because what Edmund Burke said is true: "The only thing necessary for the triumph of evil is for good men to do nothing" (letter to William Smith, 9 January 1795).

Learning that includes familiarization with facts must not occur in isolation from concern over our fellowmen. It must occur in the context of a commitment to serve them and to reach out to them.

In many ways the dreams that were once generalized as American dreams have diminished and faded. Some of these dreams have now passed so far as institutional thrust is concerned to The Church of Jesus Christ of Latter-day Saints and its people for their fulfillment. It was Lord Acton who said on one occasion:

> It was from America that the plain ideas that men ought to mind their business, and that the nation is responsible to Heaven for the acts of the State—ideas long locked in the breast of solitary

> thinkers, and hidden among Latin folios—burst forth like a conqueror upon the world they were destined to transform, under the title of the Rights of Man . . . and the principle gained ground, that a nation can never abandon its fate to an authority it cannot control. [*The History of Freedom and Other Essays,* 1907]

Too many universities have given themselves over to such massive federal funding that they should not wonder why they have submitted to an authority they can no longer control. Far too many no longer assume that nations are responsible to heaven for the acts of the state. Far too many now see the Rights of Man as merely access rights to the property and money of others, and not as the rights traditionally thought of as being crucial to our freedom.

It will take just as much sacrifice and dedication to preserve these principles in the second century of BYU,—even more than that required to begin this institution in the first place, when it was once but a grade school, and then an academy supported by a stake of the Church. If we were to abandon our ideals, would there be any left to take up the torch of some of the principles I have attempted to describe?

I am grateful, therefore, that, as President Oaks observed, "There is no anarchy of values at Brigham Young University." There never has been. There never will be. But we also know, as President Joseph Fielding Smith observed in speaking on this campus, that "knowledge comes both by reason and by revelation." We expect the natural unfolding of knowledge to occur as a result of scholarship, but there will always be that added dimension that the Lord can provide when we are qualified to receive and he chooses to speak:

> A time to come in the which nothing shall be withheld, whether there be one God or many gods, they shall be manifest.

And further,

> All thrones and dominions, principalities and powers, shall be revealed and set forth upon all who have endured valiantly for the gospel of Jesus Christ. [D&C 121:28–29]

As the pursuit of excellence continues on this campus and elsewhere in the Church Educational System, we must remember the great lesson taught to Oliver Cowdery, who desired a special outcome—just as we desire a remarkable blessing and outcome for BYU in the second century. Oliver Cowdery wished to be able to translate with ease and without real effort. He was reminded that he erred, in that he "took no thought save it was to ask" (D&C 9:7). We must do more than ask the Lord for excellence. Perspiration must precede inspiration; there must be effort before there is excellence. We must do more than pray for these outcomes at BYU, though we must surely pray. We must take thought. We must make effort. We must be patient. We must be professional. We must be spiritual. Then, in the process of time, this will become the fully anointed university of the Lord about which so much has been spoken in the past.

We can sometimes make concord with others, including scholars who have parallel purposes. By reaching out to the world of scholars, to thoughtful men and women everywhere who share our concerns and at least some of the items on our agenda of action, we can multiply our influence and give hope to others who may assume that they are alone.

In other instances, we must be willing to break with the educational establishment (not foolishly or cavalierly, but thoughtfully and for good reason) in order to find gospel ways to help mankind. Gospel methodology, concepts, and insights can help us to do what the world cannot do in its own frame of reference.

In some ways the Church Educational System, in order to be unique in the years that lie ahead, may have to break with certain patterns of the educational establishment. When the world has lost its way on matters of principle, we have an obligation to point the way. We can, as Brigham Young hoped we would, "be a people of profound learning pertaining to the things of this world," but without being tainted by what he regarded as the "pernicious, atheistic influences" that flood in unless we are watchful. Our scholars, therefore, must be sentries as well as teachers!

We surely cannot give up our concerns with character and conduct without also giving up on mankind. Much misery results from flaws in character, not from failures in technology. We cannot give in to the ways of the world with regard to the realm of art. President Romney brought to our attention not long ago a quotation in which Brigham Young said there is "no music in hell." Our art must be the kind that edifies man, which takes into account his immortal nature, and which prepares us for heaven, not hell.

One peak of educational excellence that is highly relevant to the needs of the Church is the realm of language. BYU should become the acknowledged language capital of the world in terms of our academic competency and through the marvelous "laboratory" that sends young men and women forth to service in the mission field. I refer, of course, to the Language Training Mission. There is no reason why this university could not become the place where, perhaps more than anywhere else, the concern for literacy and the teaching of English as a second language is firmly headquartered in terms of unarguable competency as well as deep concern.

I have mentioned only a few areas. There are many others of special concern, with special challenges and opportunities for accomplishment and service in the second century.

We can do much in excellence and, at the same time, emphasize the large-scale participation of our students, whether it be in athletics or in academic events. We can bless many and give many experience, while, at the same time, we are developing the few select souls who can take us to new heights of attainment.

It ought to be obvious to you, as it is to me, that some of the things the Lord would have occur in the second century of BYU are hidden from our immediate view. Until we have climbed the hill just before us, we are not apt to be given a glimpse of what lies beyond. The hills ahead are higher than we think. This means that accomplishments and further direction must occur in proper order, after we have done our part. We will not be transported from point A to point Z without having to pass through the developmental and demanding experiences of all the points of achievement and all the milestone markers that lie between!

This university will go forward. Its students are idealists who have integrity, who love to work in good causes. These students will not only have a secular training but will have come to understand what Jesus meant when he said that the key of knowledge, which had been lost by society centuries before, was "the fulness of the scriptures." We understand, as few people do, that education is a part of being about our Father's business and that the scriptures contain the master concepts for mankind.

We know there are those of unrighteous purposes who boast that time is on their side. So it may seem to those of very limited vision. But of those engaged in the Lord's work, it can be truly said, "Eternity is on our side! Those who fight that bright future fight in vain!"

I hasten to add that as the Church grows global and becomes more and more multicultural, a smaller and smaller percentage of all our LDS college-age students will attend BYU or the Hawaii Campus, or Ricks College, or the LDS Business College. It is a privileged group who are able to come here. We do not intend to neglect the needs of the other Church members wherever they are, but those who do come here have an even greater follow-through responsibility to make certain that the Church's investment in them provides dividends through service and dedication to others as they labor in the Church and in the world elsewhere.

> To go to BYU is something special. There were Brethren who had dreams regarding the growth and maturity of Brigham Young University, even to the construction of a temple on the hill they had long called Temple Hill, yet "dreams and prophetic utterances are not self-executing. They are fulfilled usually by righteous and devoted people making the prophecies come true." [Ernest L. Wilkinson, *Brigham Young University: The First One Hundred Years*]

So much of our counsel given to you here today as you begin your second century is the same counsel we give to others in the

Church concerning other vital programs—you need to lengthen your stride, quicken your step, and (to use President Tanner's phrase) continue your journey. You are headed in the right direction! Such academic adjustments as need to be made will be made out of the individual and collective wisdom we find when a dedicated faculty interacts with a wise administration, an inspired governing board, and an appreciative body of students.

I am grateful that the Church can draw upon the expertise that exists here. The pockets of competency that are here will be used by the Church increasingly and in various ways.

We want you to keep free as a university—free of government control, not only for the sake of the university and the Church, but also for the sake of our government. Our government, state and federal, and our people are best served by free colleges and universities, not by institutions that are compliant out of fears over funding.

We look forward to developments in your computer-assisted translation projects and from the Ezra Taft Benson Agriculture and Food Institute. We look forward to more being done in the field of education, in the fine arts, in the J. Reuben Clark Law School, in the Graduate School of Management, and in the realm of human behavior.

We appreciate the effectiveness of the programs here, such as our Indian program with its high rate of completion for Indian students. But we must do better in order to be better, and we must be better for the sake of the world!

As previous First Presidencies have said, and we say again to you, we expect (we do not simply hope) that Brigham Young University will "become a leader among the great universities of the world." To that expectation I would add, "Become a unique university in all of the world!"

May I thank now all those who have made this Centennial Celebration possible and express appreciation to the alumni, students, and friends of the university for the Centennial Carillon Tower that is being given to the university on its 100th birthday. Through these lovely bells will sound the great melodies that have motivated the people of the Lord's church in the past and will lift our hearts and inspire us in the second century—with joy and even greater determination. This I pray in the name of Jesus Christ. Amen.

Spencer W. Kimball was president of The Church of Jesus Christ of Latter-day Saints when this Founders Day address was given in the Marriott Center on 10 October 1975.

Meeting the Challenges of Today

NEAL A. MAXWELL

THANK YOU very much, President Oaks. And thank you, sisters, for that lovely music. This is always a great experience for any of us to have.

Often, when speaking to student leaders in higher education, I have used the analogy that—in a university—the faculty, staff, and administration are like the natives, and the students are like the tourists. In many ways, a recurring devotional speaker is more like one of the natives. Even so, I thank President Oaks for once again extending this precious privilege to me. You may conclude today, however, that I am becoming more like a tourist, since I shall try to cover two topics in order to make the most of these fleeting moments.

Discipleship includes good citizenship; and in this connection, if you are careful students of the statements of the modern prophets, you will have noticed that with rare exceptions—especially when the First Presidency has spoken out—the concerns expressed have been over moral issues, not issues between political parties. The declarations are about principles, not people, and causes, not candidates. On occasions, at other levels in the Church, a few have not been so discreet, so wise, or so inspired.

But make no mistake about it, brothers and sisters: In the months and years ahead, events will require of each member that he or she decide whether or not he or she will follow the First Presidency. Members will find it more difficult to halt longer between two opinions (see 1 Kings 18:21).

President Marion G. Romney said, many years ago, that he had "never hesitated to follow the counsel of the Authorities of the Church even though it crossed my social, professional, or political life" (*CR,* April 1941, p. 123). This is a hard doctrine, but it is a particularly vital doctrine in a society that is becoming more wicked. In short, brothers and sisters, not being ashamed of the gospel of Jesus Christ includes not being ashamed of the prophets of Jesus Christ.

We are now entering a period of incredible ironies. Let us cite but one of these ironies that is yet in its subtle stages: We shall see in our time a maximum of indirect effort made to establish irreligion as the state religion. It is actually a new form of paganism that uses the carefully preserved and cultivated freedoms of Western civilization to shrink freedom even as it rejects the value essence of our rich Judeo-Christian heritage.

M. J. Sobran wrote recently:

> The Framers of the Constitution . . . forbade the Congress to make any law "respecting" the establishment of religion, thus leaving the states free to do so (as several of them did); and they explicitly forbade the Congress to abridge "the free exercise" of religion, thus giving actual religious observance a rhetorical emphasis that fully accords with the special concern we know they had for religion. It takes a special ingenuity to wring out of this a governmental indifference to religion, let alone an aggressive secularism. Yet there are those who insist that the First Amendment actually proscribes governmental partiality not only to any single religion, but to religion as such; so that tax exemption for churches is now thought to be unconstitutional. It is startling to consider that a clause clearly protecting religion can be construed as requiring that it be denied a status routinely granted to educational

> and charitable enterprises, which have no overt constitutional protection. Far from *equalizing* unbelief, secularism has succeeded in virtually *establishing* it. . . .
>
> . . . What the secularists are increasingly demanding, in their disingenuous way, is that religious people, when they act politically, act only on secularist grounds. They are trying to equate *acting* on religion with *establishing* religion. And—I repeat—the consequence of such logic is really to establish secularism. It is, in fact, to force the religious to internalize the major premise of secularism: that religion has no proper bearing on public affairs. ["The Established Irreligion," *Human Life Review* 4 (Summer 1978), pp. 51–52, 60–61]

Brothers and sisters, irreligion as the state religion would be the worst of all combinations. Its orthodoxy would be insistent and its inquisitors inevitable. Its paid ministry would be numerous beyond belief. Its Caesars would be insufferably condescending. Its majorities—when faced with clear alternatives—would make the Barabbas choice, as did a mob centuries ago when Pilate confronted them with the need to decide.

Your discipleship may see the time come when religious convictions are heavily discounted. M. J. Sobran also observed, "A religious conviction is now a second-class conviction, expected to step deferentially to the back of the secular bus, and not to get uppity about it" (ibid., p. 58). This new irreligious imperialism seeks to disallow certain of people's opinions simply because those opinions grow out of religious convictions. Resistance to abortion will soon be seen as primitive. Concern over the institution of the family will be viewed as untrendy and unenlightened.

In its mildest form, irreligion will merely be condescending toward those who hold to traditional Judeo-Christian values. In its more harsh forms, as is always the case with those whose dogmatism is blinding, the secular church will do what it can to reduce the influence of those who still worry over standards such as those in the Ten Commandments. It is always such an easy step from dogmatism to unfair play—especially so when the dogmatists believe themselves to be dealing with primitive people who do not know what is best for them. It is the secular bureaucrat's burden, you see.

Am I saying that the voting rights of the people of religion are in danger? Of course not! Am I saying, "It's back to the catacombs"? No! But there is occurring a discounting of religiously based opinions. There may even be a covert and subtle disqualification of some for certain offices in some situations, in an ironic "irreligious test" for office.

However, if people are not permitted to advocate, to assert, and to bring to bear, in every legitimate way, the opinions and views they hold that grow out of their religious convictions, what manner of men and women would they be, anyway? Our founding fathers did not wish to have a state church established nor to have a particular religion favored by government. They wanted religion to be free to make its own way. But neither did they intend to have irreligion made into a favored state church. Notice the terrible irony if this trend were to continue. When the secular church goes after its heretics, where are the sanctuaries? To what landfalls and Plymouth Rocks can future pilgrims go?

If we let come into being a secular church shorn of traditional and divine values, where shall we go for inspiration in the crises of tomorrow? Can we appeal to the rightness of a specific regulation to sustain us in our hours of need? Will we be able to seek shelter under a First Amendment which by then may have been twisted to favor irreligion? Will we be able to rely for counterforce on value education in school systems that are increasingly secularized? And if our governments and schools were to fail us, would we be able to fall back upon the institution of the family, when so many secular movements seek to shred it?

It may well be, as our time comes to "suffer shame for his name" (Acts 5:41), that some of this special stress will grow out of that portion of discipleship which involves citizenship. Remember that, as Nephi and Jacob said, we must learn to endure "the crosses of the world" (2 Nephi 9:18) and yet to despise "the shame of [it]" (Jacob 1:8). To go on clinging to the iron rod in spite of the mockery and scorn that flow at us from the multitudes in that great and spacious building seen by Father Lehi, which is the "pride of the world," is to disregard the shame of the world (1 Nephi 8:26–27, 33; 11:35–36). Parenthetically, why—really, why—do the disbelievers who line that spacious building watch so intently what the believers are doing? Surely there must be other things for the scorners to do—unless, deep within their seeming disinterest, there is interest.

If the challenge of the secular church becomes very real, let us, as in all other human relationships, be principled but pleasant. Let us be perceptive without being pompous. Let us have integrity and not write checks with our tongues that our conduct cannot cash.

Before the ultimate victory of the forces of righteousness, some skirmishes will be lost. Even these, however, must leave a record so that the choices before the people are clear, and let others do as they will in the face of prophetic counsel. There will also be times, happily, when a minor defeat seems probable, that others will step forward, having been rallied to rightness by what we do. We will know the joy, on occasion, of having awakened a slumbering majority of the decent people of all races and creeds—a majority which was, till then, unconscious of itself.

Jesus said that when the fig trees put forth their leaves "summer is nigh" (Matthew 24:32). Thus warned that summer is upon us, let us not then complain of the heat.

Have I come today only to add one more to the already long list of special challenges faced by you and me? Not really. I have also come to say to you that God, who foresaw all challenges, has given to us a precious doctrine that can encourage us in meeting this and all other challenges.

The combined doctrine of God's foreknowledge and of foreordination is one of the doctrinal roads least traveled by, yet these clearly underline how very long and how perfectly God has loved us and known us with our individual needs and capacities. Isolated from other doctrines or mishandled, though, these truths can stoke the fires of fatalism, impact adversely upon our agency, cause us to focus on status rather than service, and carry us over into predestination. President Joseph Fielding Smith once warned:

> It is very evident from a thorough study of the gospel and the plan of salvation that a conclusion that those who accepted the Savior were predestined to be saved no matter what the nature of their lives must be an error. . . . Surely Paul never intended to convey such a thought. [*Improvement Era,* May 1963, pp. 350–51]

Paul, you will recall, brothers and sisters, stressed running the life's race the full distance; he did *not* intend a casual Christianity in which some had won the race even before the race had started.

Yet, though foreordination is a difficult doctrine, it has been given to us by the living God, through living prophets, for a purpose. It can actually increase our understanding of how crucial this mortal estate is, and it can encourage us in further good works. This precious doctrine can also help us to go the second mile because we are doubly called.

In some ways, our second estate, in relationship to our first estate, is like agreeing in advance to surgery. Then the anesthetic of forgetfulness settles in upon us. Just as doctors do not de-anesthetize a patient in the midst of authorized surgery to ask him again if the surgery should be continued, so, after divine tutoring, we agreed once to come here and to submit ourselves to certain experiences and have no occasion to revoke that decision.

Of course, when we mortals try to comprehend, rather than merely accept, foreordination, the result is one in which finite minds futilely try to comprehend omniscience. A full understanding is impossible; we simply have to trust in what the Lord has told us, knowing enough, however, to realize that we are not dealing with *guarantees* from God but extra *opportunities*—and heavier responsibilities. If those responsibilities are in some ways linked to past performance or to past capabilities, it should not surprise us.

The Lord has said,

> There is a law, irrevocably decreed in heaven before the foundations of this world, upon which all blessings are predicated—
>
> And when we obtain any blessing from God, it is by obedience to that law upon which it is predicated. [D&C 130:20–21]

This is an eternal law, brothers and sisters—it prevailed in the first estate as well as in the second. It should not disconcert us, therefore, that the Lord has indicated that he chose some individuals before they came here to carry out certain assignments and, hence, these individuals have been foreordained to those assignments. Joseph Smith said, "Every man who has a calling to minister to the inhabitants of the world was ordained to that very purpose in the Grand Council of heaven before this world was. I suppose I was ordained to this very office in that Grand Council" (*Teachings*, p. 365).

Foreordination is like any other blessing—it is a conditional bestowal subject to our faithfulness. Prophecies foreshadow events without determining the outcomes, because of a divine foreseeing of outcomes. So foreordination is a conditional bestowal of a role, a responsibility, or a blessing which, likewise, foresees but does not fix the outcome.

There have been those who have failed or who have been treasonous to their trust such as David, Solomon, Judas. God foresaw the fall of David, but was not the cause of it. It was David who saw Bathsheba from the balcony and sent for her. But neither was God surprised by such a sad development. God foresaw, but did not cause, Martin Harris' loss of certain pages of the translated Book of Mormon; God made plans to cope with that failure over fifteen hundred years before it was to occur (see D&C 10 and Words of Mormon).

Thus foreordination is clearly no excuse for fatalism or arrogance or the abuse of agency. It is not, however, a doctrine that can simply be ignored because it is difficult. Indeed, deep inside the hardest doctrines are some of the pearls of greatest price. The doctrine pertains not only to the foreordination of the prophets, but to each of us. God—in his precise assessment, beforehand, as to those who will respond to the words of the Savior and the prophets—is a part of that plan. From the Savior's own lips came these words: "I am the good shepherd, and know my sheep, and am known of mine" (John 10:14). Similarly the Savior said, "My sheep hear my voice, and I know them, and they follow me"

(John 10:27). And further in this dispensation, he declared, "And ye are called to bring to pass the gathering of mine elect; for mine elect hear my voice and harden not their hearts" (D&C 29:7).

This responsiveness could not have been gauged without divine foreknowledge concerning all of us mortals and our response, one way or another, to the gospel. God's foreknowledge is so perfect it leaves the realm of prediction and enters the realm of prophecy.

The foreseeing of those who would accept the gospel in mortality, gladly and with alacrity, is based upon their parallel responsiveness in the premortal world. No wonder the Lord could say as he did to Jeremiah, "Before I formed thee in the belly I knew thee; . . . and I ordained thee a prophet unto the nations" (Jeremiah 1:5). Paul, when writing to the Saints in Rome, said, "God hath not cast away his people which he foreknew" (Romans 11:2). Paul also said of God that "he hath chosen us in him before the foundation of the world" (Ephesians 1:4).

The Lord, who was able to say to his disciples, "Cast the net on the right side of the ship," knew beforehand there was a multitude of fishes there (John 21:6). If he knew beforehand the movements and whereabouts of fishes in the little Sea of Tiberias, should it offend us that he knows beforehand which mortals will come into the gospel net?

It does no violence even to our frail human logic to observe that there cannot be a grand plan of salvation for all mankind, unless there is also a plan for each individual. The salvational sum will reflect all its parts. Once the believer acknowledges that the past, present, and future are before God simultaneously—even though we do not understand how—then the doctrine of foreordination may be seen somewhat more clearly. For instance, it was necessary for God to know how the economic difficulties and crop failures of the Joseph Smith, Senior, family in New England would move this special family to Cumorah country where the Book of Mormon plates were buried. God's plans could scarcely have so unfolded if—willy-nilly—the Smiths had been born Manchurians and if, meanwhile, the plates had been buried in Belgium!

The Lord would need to have perfect comprehension of all the military and political developments, including those now underway in the Middle East—which, when they unfold, will combine to bring to pass a latter-day condition in which "all nations" will be gathered against Jerusalem to battle (Zechariah 14:2–4). It should not surprise us that the Lord who notices the fall of each sparrow and the hair from every head would know centuries before how much money Judas would receive—thirty pieces of silver—at the time he betrayed the Savior (Matthew 26:15; 27:3; Zechariah 11:12).

Quite understandably, the manner in which things unfold seems to us mortals to be so natural. Our not knowing what is to come (in the perfect way that God knows) thus preserves our free agency completely. When, through a process we call inspiration and revelation, we are permitted at times to tap that divine data bank, we are accessing, for the narrow purposes at hand, the knowledge of God. No wonder that experience is so unforgettable!

There are clearly special cases of individuals in mortality who have special limitations in life, which conditions we mortals cannot now fully fathom. For all we now know, the seeming limitations may have been an agreed-upon spur to achievement—a "thorn in the flesh." Like him who was blind from birth, some come to bring glory to God (John 9:1–3). We must be exceedingly careful about imputing either wrong causes or wrong rewards to all in such circumstances. They are in the Lord's hands, and he loves them perfectly. Indeed, some of those who have required much waiting upon in this life may be waited upon again by the rest of us in the next world—but for the highest of reasons.

Thus, when we are elected to certain mortal chores, we are elected "according to the foreknowledge of God the Father" (1 Peter 1:2). When Abraham was advised that he was chosen before he was born and that he was among the "noble and great ones" (Abraham 3:22–23), we received a marvelous insight. Through the revelation given to us by the prophet Joseph F. Smith we read that "The Prophet Joseph Smith, . . . Hyrum Smith, Brigham Young, John Taylor, Wilford Woodruff, and other choice spirits" were also reserved by God "to come forth in the fulness of times to take part in laying the foundations of the great latter-day work" (D&C 138:53). These individuals are among the rulers whom Abraham had had described to him centuries earlier by God. They were chosen to be "rulers in the Church of God" (D&C 138:55), not necessarily rulers in secular kingdoms. Thus those seen by Abraham were the Pauls, not the Caesars; the Spencer W. Kimballs, not the Churchills. Wise secular leaders do much lasting and commendable good; but as Paul observed to the Saints in Corinth, as the world measured greatness and wisdom "not many wise men after the flesh, not many mighty, not many noble, are called" (1 Corinthians 1:26).

President Joseph Fielding Smith wrote: "In regard to the holding of the priesthood in pre-existence, I will say that there was an organization there just as well as an organization here, and men there held authority. Men chosen to positions of trust in the spirit world held priesthood" (*Doctrines of Salvation* 3:81). Alma speaks about foreordination with great effectiveness and links it to the foreknowledge of God and, perhaps, even to our previous performance (Alma 13:3–5). The omniscience of God made it possible, therefore, for him to determine the boundaries and times of nations (Acts 17:26; Deuteronomy 32:8).

Elder Orson Hyde said of our life in the premortal world, "We understood things better there than we do in this lower world." Elder Hyde also surmised as to the agreements we made there as follows: "It is not impossible that we signed the articles thereof with our own hands,—which articles may be retained in the archives above, to be presented to us when we rise from the dead, and be judged out of our own mouths, according to that which is written in the books." Just because we have forgotten, said Elder Hyde, "our forgetfulness cannot alter the facts" (*JD* 7:314–15). Brothers and sisters, the degree of detail involved in the covenants and promises we participated in at that time may be a much more highly customized thing than many of us surmise. Yet, on occasion, even with our forgetting, there may be inklings. President Joseph F. Smith wrote:

> But in coming here, we forgot all, that our agency might be free indeed, to choose good or evil, that we might merit the reward of our own choice and conduct. But by the power of the Spirit, in the redemption of Christ, *through obedience, we often catch a spark from the awakened memories of the immortal soul,* which lights up our whole being as with the glory of our former home. [*GD,* pp. 13–14; emphasis added]

As indicated earlier, this powerful teaching of foreordination is bound to be a puzzlement in some respects, especially if we do not have faith and trust in the Lord. Yet if we think about it, even within our finite framework of experience, it should not startle us. Mortal parents are reasonably good at predicting the behavior of their children in certain circumstances. Of this Elder James E. Talmage wrote:

> Our Heavenly Father has a full knowledge of the nature and disposition of each of His children, a knowledge gained by long observation and experience in the past eternity of our primeval childhood; a knowledge compared with which that gained by earthly parents through mortal experience with their children is infinitesimally small. By reason of that surpassing knowledge, God reads the future of child and children, of men individually and of men collectively as communities and nations; He knows what each will do under given conditions, and sees the end from the beginning. His foreknowledge is based on intelligence and reason. He foresees the future as a state which naturally and surely will be; not as one which must be because He has arbitrarily willed that it shall be.—From the author's *Great Apostasy,* p. 20. [*Jesus the Christ,* 3rd ed. (Salt Lake City: The Church of Jesus Christ of Latter-day Saints, 1916), p. 29]

Another helpful analogy for students is the reality that universities, including this one, can and do predict with a high degree of accuracy the grades entering students will receive in their college careers based upon certain tests, past performances, and so forth. If mortals can do this with reasonable accuracy (and even with a short span of familiarity and finite data), God, the Father, who knows us perfectly, surely can foresee how we will respond to various challenges. While we often do not rise to our opportunities, God is neither pleased nor surprised. But we cannot say to him later on that we could have achieved if we had just been given the chance! This is all part of the justice of God.

One of the most helpful—indeed, very necessary—parallel truths to be pondered when studying this powerful doctrine of foreordination is given in the revelation of the Lord to Moses in which the Lord says, "And all things are present with me, for I know them all" (Moses 1:6). God does not live in the dimension of time as do we. Moreover, since "all things are present with" God, his is not simply a predicting based solely upon the past. In ways that are not clear to us, he actually *sees,* rather than *foresees,* the future—because all things are, at once, present before him.

In a revelation given to the Prophet Joseph Smith, the Lord described himself as "The same which knoweth all things, for all things are present before mine eyes" (D&C 38:2). From the prophet Nephi we receive the same basic insight in which we, likewise, must trust: "But the Lord knoweth all things from the beginning; wherefore, he prepareth a way to accomplish all his works among the children of men" (1 Nephi 9:6). It was by divine design that Mary became the mother of Jesus. Further, Lucy Mack Smith, who played such a crucial role in the rearing of Joseph Smith, did not come to that assignment by chance.

One of the dimensions of worshipping a living God is to know that he is alive and living in the sense of seeing and acting. He is not a retired God whose best years are past, to whom we should pay a retroactive obeisance, worshipping him for what he has already done. He is the living God who is, at once, in all the dimensions of time—the past and present and future—while we labor constrained by the limitations of time itself.

It is imperative, brothers and sisters, that we always keep in mind the caveats noted earlier, so that we do not indulge ourselves, or our whims, simply because of the presence of this powerful doctrine of foreordination, for with special opportunities come special responsibilities and much greater risks. But the doctrine of foreordination properly understood and humbly pursued can help us immensely in coping with the vicissitudes of life. Otherwise, time can tug at us and play so many tricks upon us. We should always understand that while God is never surprised, we often are.

Life episodes can take on a new meaning. For instance, Simon, the Cyrenian, wandered into Jerusalem that very day and was pressed into service by Roman soldiers to help carry the cross of Christ (see Mark 15:21). Simon's son, Rufus, joined the Church, and was so well thought of by the apostle Paul that the latter mentioned Rufus in his epistle to the Romans, describing him as "chosen in the Lord" (Romans 16:13). Was it, therefore, a mere accident that Simon, "who passed by, coming out of the country" (Mark 15:21), was asked to bear the cross of Jesus?

Properly humbled and instructed concerning the great privileges that are ours, we can cope with what seem to be very dark days and difficult developments, because we will have a true perspective about "things as they really are," and we can see in them a great chance to contribute. Churchill, in trying to rally his countrymen in an address at Harrow School (29 October 1941), said to them:

> Do not let us speak of darker days; let us speak rather of sterner days. These are not dark days: these are great days—the greatest days our country has ever lived; and we must all thank God that we have been allowed, each of us according to our stations, to play a part in making these days memorable in the history of our race.

Brothers and sisters, so we should regard the dispensation of the fulness of times—even when we face stern challenges and circumstances, "these are great days"! Our hearts need not fail us. We can be equal to our challenges, including the aforementioned challenge of the secular church.

The truth about foreordination also helps us to taste the deep wisdom of Alma, when he said we ought to be content with things that God hath allotted to each of us (Alma 29:3, 4). If, indeed, the things allotted to each of us have been divinely customized according to our ability and capacity, then for us to seek to wrench ourselves free of our schooling circumstances could be to tear ourselves away from carefully matched opportunities. To rant and to rail could be to go against divine wisdom, wisdom in which we may have once concurred before we came here. God knew beforehand each of our coefficients for coping and contributing and has so ordered our lives.

The late President Henry D. Moyle said,

> I believe that we, as fellow workers in the priesthood, might well take to heart the admonition of Alma and be content with that which God hath allotted us. We might well be assured that we had something to do with our "allotment" in our preexistent state. This would be an additional reason for us to accept our present condition and make the best of it. It is what we agreed to do. [*CR,* October 1952, p. 71]

By the way, brothers and sisters, I hasten to add that among the things "allotted" are not included things like a bad temper. The deficiencies of a developmental variety are those we are expected to overcome.

Now, as I prepare to conclude, may I point out what a vastly different view of life the doctrine of foreordination gives to us. Shorn of this perspective, others are puzzled or bitter about life. Without gospel perspective, life would be a punishment, not a joy—like trying to play a game of billiards on a table with a rumpled cloth, with a crooked cue, and an elliptical billiard ball (from Sir William S. Gilbert's libretto of *The Mikado*). (Perhaps the moral of that analogy is that we should stay out of pool halls.) In any event, pessimism does not really reckon with life and the universe as these things "really are." The disciple will be puzzled at times, too. But he persists. Later he rejoices over how wonderfully things fit together, realizing only then that, with God, things never were apart.

Jacob said that the Spirit teaches us the truth "of things as they really are, and of things as they really will be" (Jacob 4:13). Centuries later Paul said that "the Spirit searcheth . . . the deep things of God" (1 Corinthians 2:10). Of some of these deep things we have spoken today, and of how things really are. Brothers and sisters, in some of those precious and personal moments of deep discovery, there will be a sudden surge of recognition of an immortal insight, a doctrinal déjà vu. We will sometimes experience a flash from the mirror of memory that beckons us forward toward a far horizon.

When in situations of stress we wonder if there is any more in us to give, we can be comforted to know that God, who knows our capacity perfectly, placed us here to succeed. No one was foreordained to fail or to be wicked. When we have been weighed and found wanting, let us remember that we were measured before, and we were found equal to our tasks; and, therefore, let us continue, but with a more determined discipleship. When we feel overwhelmed, let us recall the assurance that God will not overprogram us; he will not press upon us more than we can bear (D&C 50:40).

The doctrine of foreordination, therefore, is not a doctrine of repose; it is a doctrine for the second-milers; it can draw out of us the last full measure of devotion. It is a doctrine of perspiration, not aspiration. Moreover, it discourages aspiring, lest we covet, like two early disciples, that which has already been given to another (Matthew 20:20–23). Foreordination is a doctrine for the deep believer and will only bring scorn from the skeptic.

When, as Joseph F. Smith said, we "catch a spark from the awakened memories of the immortal soul," let us be quietly grateful. And when of great truths we can come to say, "I know," that powerful spiritual witness may also carry with it the sense of our having known before. With rediscovery, what we are really saying is, "I know—again!" No wonder that, so often, real teaching is mere reminding.

God bless you and keep you, my special friends, to the end that you will each carry out all of the assignments given to you so very long ago. You have been measured and found adequate for the challenges that will face you as citizens of the kingdom of God; of that you should have a deep inner assurance. Be true to that trust, as all of us must, I pray in the name of Jesus Christ. Amen.

Neal A. Maxwell was a president of the First Quorum of the Seventy of The Church of Jesus Christ of Latter-day Saints when this devotional address was given in the Marriott Center on 10 October 1978.

The Seven Deadly Heresies

BRUCE R. MCCONKIE

I HAVE SOUGHT and do now seek that guidance and enlightenment that come from the Holy Spirit of God. I desire to speak by the power of the Holy Ghost so that my words will be true and wise and proper. When any of us speaks by the power of the Spirit, we say what the Lord wants said, or, better, what he would say if he were here in person.

I shall depart from my normal and usual pattern and read portions of my presentation because I want to state temperately and accurately the doctrinal principles involved and to say them in a way that will not leave room for doubt or question. I shall speak on some matters that some may consider to be controversial, though they ought not to be. They are things on which we ought to be united, and to the extent we are all guided and enlightened from on high we will be. If we are so united—and there will be no disagreement among those who believe and understand the revealed word—we will progress and advance and grow in the things of the Spirit; we will prepare ourselves for a life of peace and happiness and joy here and now, and for an eventual eternal reward in the kingdom of our Father.

There is a song or a saying or a proverb or a legend or a tradition or something that speaks of seven deadly sins. I know nothing whatever about these and hope you do not. My subject is one about which some few of you, unfortunately, do know a little. It is "The Seven Deadly Heresies"—not the great heresies of a lost and fallen Christendom, but some that have crept in among us.

Now I take a text. These words were written by Paul to certain ancient Saints. In principle they apply to us:

> I hear that there be divisions among you; and I partly believe it.
>
> For there must be also heresies among you, that they which are approved may be made manifest among you. [1 Corinthians 11:18–19]

Now let me list some axioms (I guess in academic circles we call these caveats):

—There is no salvation in believing a false doctrine.

—Truth, diamond truth, truth unmixed with error, truth alone leads to salvation.

—What we believe determines what we do.

—No man can be saved in ignorance of God and his laws.

—Man is saved no faster than he gains knowledge of Jesus Christ and the saving truths of his everlasting gospel.

—Gospel doctrines belong to the Lord, not to men. They are his. He ordained them, he reveals them, and he expects us to believe them.

—The doctrines of salvation are not discovered in a laboratory or on a geological field trip or by accompanying Darwin around the world. They come by revelation and in no other way.

—Our sole concern in seeking truth should be to learn and believe what the Lord knows and believes. Providentially he has set forth some of his views in the holy scriptures.

—Our goal as mortals is to gain the mind of Christ, to believe what he believes, to think what he thinks, to say what he says, to do what he does, and to be as he is.

—We are called upon to reject all heresies and cleave unto all truth. Only then can we progress according to the divine plan.

As the Lord has said,

> Whatever principle of intelligence we attain unto in this life, it will rise with us in the resurrection.
>
> And if a person gains more knowledge and intelligence in this life through his diligence and obedience than another, he will have so much the advantage in the world to come. [D&C 130:18–19]

Please note that knowledge is gained by obedience. It comes by obedience to the laws and ordinances of the gospel. In the ultimate and full sense it comes only by revelation from the Holy Ghost. There are some things a sinful man does not and cannot know. The Lord's people are promised: "By the power of the Holy Ghost ye may know the truth of all things" (Moroni 10:5). But if they do not seek the Spirit, if they do not accept the revelations God has given, if they cannot distinguish between the revealed word and the theories of men, they have no promise of gaining a fullness of truth by the power of the Holy Ghost.

Now may I suggest the list of heresies.

Heresy one: There are those who say that God is progressing in knowledge and is learning new truths.

This is false—utterly, totally, and completely. There is not one sliver of truth in it. It grows out of a wholly twisted and incorrect view of the King Follett sermon and of what is meant by eternal progression.

God progresses in the sense that his kingdoms increase and his dominions multiply—not in the sense that he learns new truths and discovers new laws. God is not a student. He is not a laboratory technician. He is not postulating new theories on the basis of past experiences. He has indeed graduated to that state of exaltation that consists of knowing all things and having all power.

The life that God lives is named *eternal life*. His name, one of them, is "Eternal," using that word as a noun and not as an adjective, and he uses that name to identify the type of life that he lives. God's life is eternal life, and eternal life is God's life. They are one and the same. Eternal life is the reward we shall obtain if we believe and obey and walk uprightly before him. And eternal life consists of two things. It consists of life in the family unit, and, also, of inheriting, receiving, and possessing the fullness of the glory of the Father. Anyone who has each of these things is an inheritor and possessor of the greatest of all gifts of God, which is eternal life.

Eternal progression consists of living the kind of life God lives and of increasing in kingdoms and dominions everlastingly. Why anyone should suppose that an infinite and eternal being who has presided in our universe for almost 2,555,000,000 years, who made the sidereal heavens, whose creations are more numerous than the particles of the earth, and who is aware of the fall of every sparrow—why anyone would suppose that such a being has more to learn and new truths to discover in the laboratories of eternity is totally beyond my comprehension.

Will he one day learn something that will destroy the plan of salvation and turn man and the universe into an uncreated nothingness? Will he discover a better plan of salvation than the one he has already given to men in worlds without number?

The saving truth, as revealed to and taught, formally and officially, by the Prophet Joseph Smith in the *Lectures on Faith* is that God is omnipotent, omniscient, and omnipresent. He knows all things, he has all power, and he is everywhere present by the power of his Spirit. And unless we know and believe this doctrine we cannot gain faith unto life and salvation.

Joseph Smith also taught in the *Lectures on Faith* "that three things are necessary in order that any rational and intelligent being may exercise faith in God unto life and salvation." These he named as

1. the idea that he actually exists;

2. a *correct* idea of his character, perfections, and attributes; and

3. an actual knowledge that the course of life which he is pursuing is according to the divine will.

The attributes of God are given as knowledge, faith or power, justice, judgment, mercy, and truth. The perfections of God are named as "the perfections which belong to all of the attributes of his nature," which is to say that God possesses and has all knowledge, all faith or power, all justice, all judgment, all mercy, and all truth. He is indeed the very embodiment and personification and source of all these attributes. Does anyone suppose that God can be more honest than he already is? Neither need any suppose there are truths he does not know or knowledge he does not possess.

Thus Joseph Smith taught, and these are his words:

> Without the knowledge of all things, God would not be able to save any portion of his creatures; for it is by reason of the knowledge which he has of all things, from the beginning to the end, that enables him to give that understanding to his creatures by which they are made partakers of eternal life; and if it were not for the idea existing in the minds of men that God had all knowledge it would be impossible for them to exercise faith in him. [N. B. Lundwall, comp., *Lectures on Faith* (Salt Lake City: N. B. Lundwall, n.d.), p. 43]

If God is just dabbling with a few truths he has already chanced to learn or experimenting with a few facts he has already discovered, we have no idea as to the real end and purpose of creation.

Heresy two concerns itself with the relationship between organic evolution and revealed religion and asks the question whether they can be harmonized.

There are those who believe that the theory of organic evolution runs counter to the plain and explicit principles set forth in the holy scriptures as these have been interpreted and taught by Joseph Smith and his associates. There are others who think that evolution is the system used by the Lord to form plant and animal life and to place man on earth.

May I say that all truth is in agreement, that true religion and true science bear the same witness, and that in the true and full sense, true science is part of true religion. But may I also raise some questions of a serious nature. Is there any way to harmonize the false religions of the Dark Ages with the truths of science as they have now been discovered? Is there any way to harmonize the revealed religion that has come to us with the theoretical postulates of Darwinism and the diverse speculations descending therefrom?

Should we accept the famous document of the First Presidency issued in the days of President Joseph F. Smith and entitled "The Origin of Man" as meaning exactly what it says? Is it the doctrine of the gospel that Adam stood next to Christ in power and might and intelligence before the foundations of the world were laid; that Adam was placed on this earth as an immortal being; that there was no death in the world for him or for any form of life until after the Fall; that the fall of Adam brought temporal and spiritual death into the world; that this temporal death passed upon all forms of life, upon man and animal and fish and fowl and plant life; that Christ came to ransom man and all forms of life from the effects of the temporal death brought into the world through the Fall, and in the case of man from a spiritual death also; and that this ransom includes a resurrection for man and for all forms of life? Can you harmonize these things with the evolutionary postulate that death has always existed and that the various forms of life have evolved from preceding forms over astronomically long periods of time?

Can you harmonize the theories of men with the inspired words that say:

> And now, behold, if Adam had not transgressed he would not have fallen, but he would have remained in the garden of Eden. And all things which were created must have remained in the same state in which they were after they were created; and they must have remained forever, and had no end.
>
> And they [meaning Adam and Eve] would have had no children; wherefore they would have remained in a state of innocence, having no joy, for they knew no misery; doing no good, for they knew no sin.
>
> But behold, all things have been done in the wisdom of him who knoweth all things.
>
> Adam fell that men might be; and men are, that they might have joy.
>
> And the Messiah cometh in the fulness of time, that he may redeem the children of men from the fall. [2 Nephi 2:22–26]

These are questions to which all of us should find answers. Every person must choose for himself what he will believe. I recommend that all of you study and ponder and pray and seek light and knowledge in these and in all fields.

I believe that the atonement of Christ is the great and eternal foundation upon which revealed religion rests. I believe that no man can be saved unless he believes that our Lord's atoning sacrifice brings immortality to all and eternal life to those who believe and obey, and no man can believe in the Atonement unless he accepts both the divine sonship of Christ and the fall of Adam.

My reasoning causes me to conclude that if death has always prevailed in the world, then there was no fall of Adam that brought death to all forms of life; that if Adam did not fall, there is no need for an atonement; that if there was no atonement, there is no salvation, no resurrection, and no eternal life; and that if there was no atonement, there is nothing in all of the glorious promises that the Lord has given us. I believe that the Fall affects man, all forms of life, and the earth itself, and that the Atonement affects man, all forms of life, and the earth itself.

Heresy three: There are those who say that temple marriage assures us of an eventual exaltation. Some have supposed that couples married in the temple who commit all manner of sin, and who then pay the penalty, will gain their exaltation eventually.

This notion is contrary to the whole system and plan that the Lord has ordained, a system under which we are privileged to work out our salvation with fear and trembling before him. If we believe and obey, if we enter the waters of baptism and make solemn covenants with the Lord to keep his commandments, we thereby get on a strait and narrow path that leads from the gate of repentance and baptism to a reward that is called eternal life. And if we traverse the length of the path going upward and forward and onward, keeping the commandments, loving the Lord, and doing all that we ought to do, eventually we will be inheritors of that reward.

And in exactly and precisely the same sense, celestial marriage is a gate that puts us on a path leading to exaltation in the highest heaven of the celestial world. It is in that highest realm of glory and dignity and honor hereafter that the family unit continues. Those who inherit a place in the highest heaven receive the reward that is named eternal life. Baptism is a gate; celestial marriage is a gate. When we get on the paths of which I speak, we are then obligated to keep the commandments. My suggestion in this field is that you go to the temple and listen to a ceremony of celestial marriage, paying particular and especial attention to the words, and learn what the promises are that are given. And you will learn that all of the promises given are conditioned upon subsequent compliance with all of the terms and conditions of that order of matrimony.

Heresy four: There are those who believe that the doctrine of salvation for the dead offers men a second chance for salvation.

I knew a man, now deceased, not a member of the Church, who was a degenerate old reprobate who found pleasure, as he supposed, in living after the manner of the world. A cigarette dangled from his lips, alcohol stenched his breath, and profane and bawdy stories defiled his lips. His moral status left much to be desired.

His wife was a member of the Church, as faithful as she could be under the circumstances. One day she said to him, "You know the Church is true; why won't you be baptized?" He replied, "Of course I know the Church is true, but I have no intention of changing my habits in order to join it. I prefer to live the way I do. But that doesn't worry me in the slightest. I know that as soon as I die, you will have someone go to the temple and do the work for me and everything will come out all right in the end anyway."

He died and she had the work done in the temple. We do not sit in judgment and deny vicarious ordinances to people. But what will it profit him?

There is no such thing as a second chance to gain salvation. This life is the time and the day of our probation. After this day of life, which is given us to prepare for eternity, then cometh the night of darkness wherein there can be no labor performed.

For those who do not have an opportunity to believe and obey the holy word in this life, the first chance to gain salvation will come in the spirit world. If those who hear the word for the first time in the realms ahead are the kind of people who would have accepted the gospel here, had the opportunity been afforded them, they will accept it there. Salvation for the dead is for those whose first chance to gain salvation is in the spirit world.

In the revelation recently added to our canon of holy writ, these words are found:

> Thus came the voice of the Lord unto me, saying: All who have died without a knowledge of this gospel, who would have received it if they had been permitted to tarry, shall be heirs of the celestial kingdom of God;
>
> Also all that shall die henceforth without a knowledge of it, who would have received it with all their hearts, shall be heirs of that kingdom;
>
> For I, the Lord, will judge all men according to their works, according to the desire of their hearts. [D&C 137:7–9]

There is no other promise of salvation than the one recited in that revelation. Those who reject the gospel in this life and then receive it in the spirit world go not to the celestial, but to the terrestrial kingdom.

Heresy five: There are those who say that there is progression from one kingdom to another in the eternal worlds or that lower kingdoms eventually progress to where higher kingdoms once were.

This belief lulls men into a state of carnal security. It causes them to say, "God is so merciful; surely he will save us all eventually; if we do not gain the celestial kingdom now, eventually we will; so why worry?" It lets people live a life of sin here and now with the hope that they will be saved eventually.

The true doctrine is that all men will be resurrected, but they will come forth in the Resurrection with different kinds of bodies—some celestial, others terrestrial, others telestial, and some with bodies incapable of standing any degree of glory. The body we receive in the Resurrection determines the glory we receive in the kingdoms that are prepared.

Of those in the telestial world it is written: "And they shall be servants of the Most High; but where God and Christ dwell they cannot come, worlds without end" (D&C 76:122).

Of those who had the opportunity to enter into the new and everlasting covenant of marriage in this life and who did not do it, the revelation says:

> Therefore, when they are out of the world they neither marry nor are given in marriage; but are appointed angels in heaven; which angels are ministering servants, to minister for those who are worthy of a far more, and an exceeding, and an eternal weight of glory.
>
> For these angels did not abide my law; therefore, they cannot be enlarged, but remain separately and singly, without exaltation, in their saved condition, to all eternity; and from henceforth are not gods, but are angels of God forever and ever. [D&C 132:16–17]

They neither progress from one kingdom to another, nor does a lower kingdom ever get where a higher kingdom once was. Whatever eternal progression there is, it is within a sphere.

Heresy six: There are those who believe or say they believe that Adam is our father and our god, that he is the father of our spirits and our bodies, and that he is the one we worship.

The devil keeps this heresy alive as a means of obtaining converts to cultism. It is contrary to the whole plan of salvation set forth in the scriptures, and anyone who has read the book of Moses, and anyone who has received the temple endowment, has no excuse whatever for being led astray by it. Those who are so ensnared reject the living prophet and close their ears to the apostles of their day. "We will follow those who went before," they say. And having so determined, they soon are ready to enter polygamous relationships that destroy their souls.

We worship the Father, in the name of the Son, by the power of the Holy Ghost; and Adam is their foremost servant, by whom the peopling of our planet was commenced.

Heresy seven: There are those who believe we must be perfect to gain salvation.

This is not really a great heresy, only a doctrinal misunderstanding that I mention here in order to help round out our discussion and to turn our attention from negative to positive things. If we keep two principles in mind we will thereby know that good and faithful members of the Church will be saved, even though they are far from perfect in this life.

These two principles are (1) that this life is the appointed time for men to prepare to meet God—this life is the day of our probation; and (2) that the same spirit which possesses our bodies at the time we go out of this mortal life shall have power to possess our bodies in that eternal world.

What we are doing as members of the Church is charting a course leading to eternal life. There was only one perfect being, the Lord Jesus. If men had to be perfect and live all of the law strictly, wholly, and completely, there would be only one saved person in eternity. The Prophet taught that there are many things to be done, even beyond the grave, in working out our salvation.

And so what we do in this life is chart a course leading to eternal life. That course begins here and now and continues in the realms ahead. We must determine in our hearts and in our souls, with all the power and ability we have, that from this time forward we will press on in righteousness; by so doing we can go where God and Christ are. If we make that firm determination, and are in the course of our duty when this life is over, we will continue in that course in eternity. That same spirit that possesses our bodies at the time we depart from this mortal life will have power to possess our bodies in the eternal world. If we go out of this life loving the Lord, desiring righteousness, and seeking to acquire the attributes of godliness, we will have that same spirit in the eternal world, and we will then continue to advance and progress until an ultimate, destined day when we will possess, receive, and inherit all things.

Now I do not say these are the only great heresies that prevail among us. There are others that might be mentioned. My suggestion, relative to all doctrines and all principles, is that we become students of holy writ, and that we conform our thinking and our beliefs to what is found in the standard works. We need to be less concerned about the views and opinions that others have expressed and drink directly from the fountain the Lord has given us. Then we shall come to a true understanding of the points of his doctrine. And if we pursue such a course, we will soon find that it proceeds in a different direction than the one that the world pursues. We will not be troubled with the intellectual views and expressions of uninspired people. We will soon obtain for ourselves the witness of the Spirit that we are pursuing a course that is pleasing to the Lord, and this knowledge will have a cleansing and sanctifying and edifying influence upon us.

Now, in order to have things in perspective, let me identify the three greatest heresies in all Christendom. They do not prevail among us, fortunately, but they are part of the gross and universal darkness that covers the earth and blots out from the minds of men those truths upon which salvation rests.

The greatest truth known to man is that there is a God in heaven who is infinite and eternal; that he is the creator, upholder, and preserver of all things; that he created us and the sidereal heavens and ordained and established a plan of salvation whereby we might advance and progress and become like him. The truth pertaining to him is that he is our Father in Heaven, that he has a body of flesh and bones as tangible as man's, that he is a literal person, and that if we believe and obey his laws we can gain the exaltation that he possesses. Now that is the greatest truth and the most glorious concept known to the human mind, and the reverse of it is the greatest heresy in all Christendom.

The Christian heresy, where God is concerned, is that deity is a spirit essence that fills the immensity of space; that he is three beings in one; that he is uncreated, incorporeal, and incomprehensible; that he is without body, parts, or passions; that he is a spirit nothingness that is everywhere and nowhere in particular present. These are concepts written in the creeds had in the churches of the world.

The second greatest truth in all eternity pertains to the divine sonship of the Lord, Jesus Christ. It includes the eternal verity that he was foreordained in the councils of eternity to come to earth and be the redeemer of men, to come and ransom men from the temporal and spiritual death brought upon them by the fall of Adam. This second greatest truth is that Christ worked out the infinite and eternal atoning sacrifice because of which all men are raised in immortality and those who believe and obey are raised also unto eternal life.

Now the second greatest heresy in all Christendom is designed to destroy the glories and wonders of the infinite and eternal atonement. It is that men are saved by some kind of lip service, by the grace of God, without work and without effort on their part.

The third greatest truth known to mankind is that the Holy Spirit of God is a revelator and a sanctifier, that he is a personage of spirit, that his assigned ministry and work in the eternal Godhead is to bear record of the Father and of the Son, to reveal them and their truths to men. His work is to cleanse and perfect human souls, to burn dross and evil out of human souls as though by fire. We call that the baptism of fire.

Now the opposite of that is the third greatest heresy in all Christendom. It is that revelation has ceased, that God's mouth is closed, that the Holy Ghost no longer inspires men, that the gifts of the Spirit were done away with after the death of the ancient apostles, and that we no longer need to follow the course they charted.

I simply name these things; I think you will want to weigh and evaluate what is involved. I think you will want to ponder and wonder and search the scriptures. After Jesus had been teaching the Nephites as a resurrected person, giving them as much truth as in his wisdom he felt they could absorb at one time, he counseled them to go to their homes, and to ponder in their hearts the things he had said, and to pray to the Father in his name to find out if they were true, and then to come again on the morrow and he would teach them more.

Now that gives us the pattern by which we should operate in the Church. We come together in congregations, seeking the guidance of the Holy Spirit, studying the revelations, reading the scriptures, and hearing expressions of doctrine and counsel given by those who are appointed. These teachings ought to be delivered by the power of the Holy Spirit. They ought to be received by the same power. And if they are, then the speaker and the hearer will be mutually edified, and we will have true and proper worship.

Then when the meeting is over, the "amen" should not end it. We should go to our homes and to our families and to our circles, and we should search out the revelations and find out what the Lord has said on the subjects involved. We should seek to get in tune with the Holy Spirit and to gain a witness, not solely of the truth and divinity of the work in which we are engaged but also of the doctrines that are taught by those who preach to us. We come into these congregations, and sometimes a speaker brings a jug of living water that has in it many gallons. And when he pours it out on the congregation, all the members have brought is a single cup and so that's all they take away. Or maybe they have their hands over the cups, and they don't get anything to speak of.

On other occasions we have meetings where the speaker comes and all he brings is a little cup of eternal truth, and the members of the congregation come with a large jug, and all they get in their jugs is the little dribble that came from a man who should have known better and who should have prepared himself and talked from the revelations and spoken by the power of the Holy Spirit. We are obligated in the Church to speak by the power of the Spirit. We are commanded to treasure up the words of light and truth and then give forth the portion that is appropriate and needful on every occasion.

I do not think that the heresies I have named are common in the Church. I think that the great majority of the members of the

Church believe and understand true doctrines and seek to apply true principles in their lives. Unfortunately, there are a few people who agitate and stir these matters up, who have some personal ax to grind, and who desire to spread philosophies of their own, philosophies that, as near as the judges in Israel can discern, are not in harmony with the mind and will and purpose of the Lord. It is incumbent upon us to believe the truth, and then we have the obligation to walk in the light and to apply the truths that we have learned to ourselves and to influence others to do likewise.

Now the glorious and wondrous thing about this whole system of revealed religion that the Lord, our God, has given us is the fact that it is true. There isn't a grander, a more glorious, a more wondrous concept than the simple one that the work in which we are engaged is true. And because it is true it will triumph and prevail, and the knowledge of God and his truths will roll forth until it covers the whole earth as the waters cover the sea. We do not expect to have a perfect society among us until the millennial day dawns. But that is not far distant. And when that day comes, we will all, as the scriptures say, see eye to eye and speak with one voice, and the Lord himself will dwell among us. He could not dwell among us now because we are divided and we are not living in that perfect harmony and unity and with that devotion that prevailed among the Saints in the city of Enoch.

God grant that we may be wise in what we do, that we may seek truth, that we may live in harmony with the truth, that we may bear testimony of the truth, and that we may, as a consequence, have a joy and peace and happiness here and now and be inheritors, in due course, of eternal reward in our Father's kingdom. This is my prayer for myself and for all of you, and for all of the members of the Church, and for honest truthseekers everywhere, and I offer it in the name of the Lord Jesus Christ. Amen.

Bruce R. McConkie was a member of the Council of the Twelve of The Church of Jesus Christ of Latter-day Saints when this fireside address was given in the Marriott Center on 1 June 1980.

Leaders and Managers

HUGH NIBLEY

TWENTY-THREE YEARS AGO on this same occasion, I gave the opening prayer, in which I said: "We have met here today clothed in the black robes of a false priesthood." Many have asked me since whether I really said such a shocking thing, but nobody has ever asked what I meant by it. Why not? Well, some knew the answer already, and as for the rest, we do not question things at the BYU. But for my own relief, I welcome this opportunity to explain: a "false priesthood"?

Why a PRIESTHOOD? Because these robes originally denoted those who had taken clerical orders, and a college was a "mystery" with all the rites, secrets, oaths, degrees, tests, feasts, and solemnities that go with initiation into higher knowledge.

But why FALSE? Because it is borrowed finery, coming down to us through a long line of unauthorized imitators. It was not until 1893 that "an intercollegiate commission was formed to draft a uniform code for caps, gowns, and hoods" in the United States. Before that there were no rules—you designed your own; and that liberty goes as far back as these fixings can be traced. The late Roman emperors, as we learn from the infallible Du Cange, marked each step in the decline of their power and glory by the addition of some new ornament to the resplendent vestments that proclaimed their sacred office and dominion. Branching off from them, the kings of the tribes who inherited the lands and the claims of the Empire vied with each other in imitating the Roman masters, determined to surpass even them in the theatrical variety and richness of caps and gowns.

One of the four crowns worn by the emperor was the mortarboard. The French kings got it from Charlemagne, the model and founder of their royal lines. To quote Du Cange:

> When the French kings quitted the palace at Paris to erect a Temple of Justice, at the same time they conferred their royal adornments on those who would preside therein, so that the judgments that came from their mouths would have more weight and authority with the people, as if they were coming from the mouth of the prince himself [the idea of the Robe of the Prophet, conferring his glory on his successor]. It is to these concessions that the mortar-boards and the scarlet and ermine robes of the chancellors of France and the presidents of Parlement are to be traced. Their gowns or *epitogia* [the loose robe thrown over the rest of the clothing, to produce the well-known greenhouse effect], are still made in the ancient fashion. . . . The name "mortar-board" is given to the diadem because it is shaped like a mortar-board which serves for mixing plaster, and is bigger on top than on the bottom. [Charles Du Fresne, Sieur Du Cange, *Glossarium ad Scriptores Mediae et Infimae Graecitatis* (Graz, Austria: Akademische Druck u. Verlagsanstalt, 1958; Unveränderter Abdruck der 1688 bei Anisson, Joan. Posuel u. Claud. Rigaud in Lyon erschiehenen Ausgabe)]

But where did the Roman emperors get it? For one thing, the mortarboard was called a *Justinianeion,* because of its use by the Emperor Justinian, who introduced it from the East. He got his court trappings and protocol from the monarchs of Asia, in particular the Grand Shah, from whom it can be traced to the khans of the steppes and the Mongol emperors, who wore the golden button of all wisdom on the top of the cap even as I do now; the shamans of the north also had it, and among the Laplanders it is still called "the Cap of the Four Winds." The four-square headpiece topped by the golden tassel—"the emergent Flame of Full Enlightenment"—also figures in some Buddhist and Lamaist representations. But you get the idea—this Prospero suit is pretty strong medicine—"rough magic" indeed! (See Shakespeare, *The Tempest,* act 5, scene 1, line 51.)

There is another type of robe and headdress described in Exodus and Leviticus and the third book of Josephus' *Antiquities,* i.e., the white robe and linen cap of the Hebrew priesthood, which have close resemblance to some Egyptian vestments. They were given up entirely, however, with the passing of the temple, and were never even imitated again by the Jews. Both their basic white and their peculiar design, especially as shown in the latest studies from Israel, are much like our own temple garments. This is not the time or the place to pursue a subject in which Brother Packer wisely recommends a judicious restraint; I bring it up only to ask myself, "What if I appeared for an endowment session in the temple dressed in this outfit?" There would be something incongruous about it, of course, even comical. But why should that be so? The original idea behind both garments is the same—to provide a clothing more fitting to another ambience, action, and frame of mind than that of the warehouse, office, or farm. Section 109 of the Doctrine and Covenants describes the function and purpose of the temple as much the same as those of a university: a house where all seek learning by study and faith, by discriminating search among the best books (no official list is given), and by constant discussion—diligently teaching "*one another* words of wisdom"; everybody seeking greater light and knowledge as all things come to be "gathered in one"—hence *uni*versity.

Both the black and the white robes proclaim a primary concern for things of the mind and the spirit, sobriety of life, and concentration of purpose removed from the largely mindless, mechanical routines of your everyday world. Cap and gown announced that the wearer had accepted certain rules of living and been tested in special kinds of knowledge.

What is wrong, then, with the flowing robes? For one thing, they are somewhat theatrical and too easily incline the wearer, beguiled by their splendor, to masquerade and affectation. In the time of Socrates the Sophists were making a big thing of their special manner of dress and delivery. It was all for show, of course, but it was "dressing for success" with a vengeance, for the whole purpose of the rhetorical brand of education which they inaugurated and sold at top prices to the ambitious youth was to make the student successful as a paid advocate in the law courts, a commanding figure in public assemblies, or a successful promoter of daring business enterprises by mastering those irresistible techniques of persuasion and salesmanship which the Sophists had to offer.

That was the classical education which Christianity embraced at the urging of the great St. Augustine. He had learned by hard experience that you can't trust revelation because you can't control it—the Spirit bloweth where *it* listeth, and what the Church needed was something more available and reliable than that, something, he says, *commodior et multitudini tutior*—"handier and more reliable for the public"—than revelation or even reason, and that is exactly what the rhetorical education had to offer.

At the beginning of this century scholars were strenuously debating the momentous transition from *Geist* to *Amt,* from Spirit to office, from inspiration to ceremony in the leadership of the Early Church, when the inspired leader was replaced by the typical city bishop, an appointed and elected official—ambitious, jealous, calculating, power-seeking, authoritarian; an able politician and a master of public relations—St. Augustine's trained rhetorician. At the same time the charismatic gifts, the spiritual gifts, not to be trusted, were replaced by rites and ceremonies that could be timed and controlled, all following the Roman imperial model, as Alfoeldi has shown, including the caps and gowns.

And down through the centuries the robes have never failed to keep the public at a respectful distance, inspire a decent awe for the professions, and impart an air of solemnity and mystery that has been as good as money in the bank. The four faculties of

Theology, Philosophy, Medicine, and Law have been the perennial seedbeds not only of professional wisdom, but of the quackery and venality so generously exposed to public view by Plato, Rabelais, Molière, Swift, Gibbon, A. E. Housman, H. L. Mencken, and others.

What took place in the Greco-Roman as in the Christian world was that fatal shift from *leadership* to *management* that marks the decline and fall of civilizations.

At the present time, Captain Grace Hopper, that grand old lady of the Navy, is calling our attention to the contrasting and conflicting natures of management and leadership. No one, she says, ever managed men into battle. She wants more emphasis in teaching leadership. But leadership can no more be taught than creativity or how to be a genius. The *Generalstab* tried desperately for a hundred years to train up a generation of leaders for the German army, but it never worked, because the men who delighted their superiors, i.e., the managers, got the high commands, while the men who delighted the lower ranks, i.e., the leaders, got reprimands. Leaders are movers and shakers, original, inventive, unpredictable, imaginative, full of surprises that discomfit the enemy in war and the main office in peace. For managers are safe, conservative, predictable, conforming organization men and team players, dedicated to the establishment.

The leader, for example, has a passion for *equality.* We think of great generals from David and Alexander on down, sharing their beans or *maza* with their men, calling them by their first names, marching along with them in the heat, sleeping on the ground, and first over the wall. A famous ode by a long-suffering Greek soldier, Archilochus, reminds us that the men in the ranks are not fooled for an instant by the executive type who thinks he is a leader.

For the manager, on the other hand, the idea of equality is repugnant and indeed counterproductive. Where promotion, perks, privilege, and power are the name of the game, awe and reverence for *rank* is everything, the inspiration and motivation of all good men. Where would management be without the inflexible paper processing, dress standards, attention to proper social, political, and religious affiliation, vigilant watch over habits and attitudes, and so forth, that gratify the stockholders and satisfy security?

"If you love me," said the Greatest of all leaders, "you will keep my commandments." "If you know what is good for me," says the manager, "you will keep *my* commandments, and not make waves." That is why the rise of management always marks the decline of culture. If the management does not go for Bach, very well, there will be no Bach in the meeting; if management favors vile, sentimental doggerel verse extolling the qualities that make for success, young people everywhere will be spouting long trade-journal jingles from the stand; if the management's taste in art is what will sell—trite, insipid, folksy kitsch—that is what we will get; if management finds maudlin, saccharine commercials appealing, that is what the public will get; if management must reflect the corporate image in tasteless, trendy new buildings, down come the fine old pioneer monuments.

To Parkinson's Law, which shows how management gobbles up everything else, he added what he calls the "Law of Injelitance": Managers do not promote individuals whose competence might threaten their own position; and so as the power of management spreads ever wider, the quality deteriorates, if that is possible. In short, while management shuns *equality,* it feeds on *mediocrity.*

On the other hand, leadership is an escape from mediocrity. All the great deposits of art, science, and literature from the past on which all civilization is nourished come to us from a mere handful of leaders. For the qualities of leadership are the same in all fields, the leader being simply the one who sets the highest example; and to do that and open the way to greater light and knowledge, the leader must break the mold. "A ship in port is safe," says Captain Hopper, speaking of management; "but that is not what ships were built for," she adds, calling for leadership. True leaders are inspiring because they are inspired, caught up in a higher purpose, devoid of personal ambition, idealistic, and incorruptible.

There is necessarily some of the manager in every leader (what better example than Brigham Young?), as there should be some of the leader in every manager. Speaking in the temple to the temple management, the scribes and Pharisees all in their official robes, the Lord chided them for one-sidedness: They kept careful accounts of the most trivial sums brought into the temple, but in their dealings they neglected fair play, compassion, and good faith, which happen to be the prime qualities of leadership. The Lord insisted that *both* states of mind are necessary, and that is important: "This ye must do [speaking of the bookkeeping] but not neglect the other." But it is "the blind leading the blind," he continues, who reverse priorities, who "choke on a gnat and gulp down a camel" (see Matthew 23:23ff). So vast is the discrepancy between management and leadership that only a blind man would get them backwards. Yet that is what we do. In that same chapter of Matthew, the Lord tells the same men that they do not really take the temple seriously while the business contracts registered in the temple they take very seriously indeed (see Matthew 23:16–18). I am told of a meeting of very big businessmen in a distant place, who happened also to be the heads of stakes, where they addressed the problem of "how to stay awake in the temple." For them what is done in the house of the Lord is mere quota-filling until they can get back to the real work of the world.

History abounds in dramatic confrontations between the two types, but none is more stirring than the epic story of the collision between Moroni and Amalickiah—the one the most charismatic *leader,* the other the most skillful *manager* in the Book of Mormon. We are often reminded that Moroni "did not delight in the shedding of blood" and would do anything to avoid it, repeatedly urging his people to make covenants of peace and preserve them by faith and prayer. He refused to talk about "the enemy"—for him they were always "our brethren," misled by the traditions of their fathers; he fought them only with heavy reluctance, and he *never* invaded their lands, even when they threatened intimate invasion of his own; for he never felt threatened, since he trusted absolutely in the Lord. At the slightest sign of weakening by an enemy in battle, Moroni would instantly propose a discussion to put an end to the fighting. The idea of total victory was alien to him—no revenge, no punishment, no reprisals, no reparations, even for an aggressor who had ravaged his country. He would send the beaten enemy home after battle, accepting their word for good behavior or inviting them to settle on Nephite lands, even when he knew he was taking a risk. Even his countrymen who fought against him lost their lives only while opposing him on the field of battle—there were no firing squads, and former conspirators and traitors had only to agree to support his popular army to be reinstated. And, like Helaman, he insisted that conscientious objectors keep their oaths and not go to war even when he desperately needed their help. Always concerned with doing the decent thing, he would never take what he called unfair advantage of an enemy. Devoid of personal ambition, the moment the war was over he "yielded up the command of his armies . . . and he retired to his own house . . . in peace" (Alma 62:43), though as a national hero he could have had any office or honor. For his motto was, "I seek not for power," and as to rank, he thought of himself only as one of the despised and outcast of Israel. If all this sounds a bit too idealistic, may I remind you that there really have been such men in history, hard as that is to imagine today.

Above all, Moroni was the charismatic leader, personally going about to rally the people, who came running together spontaneously to his "title of liberty," the banner of the poor and downtrodden of Israel (Alma 46:12–13, 19–21). He had little patience with management and let himself get carried away and wrote tactless and angry letters to the big men sitting on their thrones "in a state of thoughtless stupor" back in the capital. And when it was necessary, he bypassed the whole system; he "altered the *management* of affairs among the Nephites," to counter Amalickiah's managerial skill (Alma 49:11; emphasis added). Yet he could apologize handsomely when he learned that he had been wrong, led by his generous impulses to an exaggerated contempt for management, and he gladly shared with Pahoran the glory of the final victory—the one thing that ambitious generals jealously reserve for themselves.

But if Moroni hated war so much, why was he such a dedicated general? He leaves us in no doubt on that head—he took up the sword only as a last resort: "I seek not for power, but to pull it down" (Alma 60:36). He was determined "to pull down their pride and their nobility"—the pride and nobility of those groups who were trying to take things over (Alma 51:17). The "Lamanite brethren" he fought were the reluctant auxiliaries of Zoramites and Amalickiahites, his own countrymen. They "grew proud . . . , because of their exceedingly great riches," and sought to seize power for themselves (Alma 45:23ff). Enlisting the aid of "those who were in favor of kings . . . those of high birth . . . supported by those who sought power and authority over the people" (Alma 51:8), they were further joined by important judges who had many friends and kindreds (the right connections are everything) plus almost all the lawyers and the high priests, to which were added "the lower judges of the land, and they were seeking for power" (Alma 46:4). All these Amalickiah welded together with immense managerial skill to form a single ultraconservative coalition who agreed to "support him and establish him to be their king," expecting that "he would make them rulers over the people" (Alma 46:5). Many in the church were won over by Amalickiah's skillful oratory, for he was a charming (*flattering* is the Book of Mormon word) and persuasive communicator. He made war the cornerstone of his policy and power, using a systematic and carefully planned communication system of towers and trained speakers to stir up the people to fight for their rights, meaning Amalickiah's career. For while Moroni had kind feelings for the enemy, Amalickiah "did care not for the blood of his people" (Alma 49:10). His object in life was to become king of both the Nephites and Lamanites, using the one to subdue the other (see Alma 46:5). He was a master of dirty tricks, to which he owed some of his most brilliant achievements as he maintained his upward mobility by clever murders, high-powered public relations, and great executive ability. His competitive spirit was such that he swore to drink the blood of Alma, who stood in his way. In short, he was "one very wicked man" (Alma 46:9), who stood for everything that Moroni loathed.

It is at this time in Book of Mormon history that the word *management* makes its only appearances (three of them) in all the scriptures. First there was that time when Moroni on his own "altered the management of affairs among the Nephites" (Alma 49:11) during a crisis. Then there was Korihor, the ideological spokesman for the Zoramites and Amalickiahites, who preached that "every man fared in this life according to the *management* of the creature; therefore every man prospered according to his genius [ability, talent, brains, and so forth], and . . . conquered according to his strength; and whatsoever a man did was no crime" (Alma 30:17; emphasis added). He raged against the government for taking people's property, that "they durst not make use of that which is their own" (Alma 30:28). Finally, as soon as Moroni disappeared from the scene, the old coalition "did obtain the sole *management* of the government," and immediately did "turn their backs upon the poor" (Helaman 6:39; emphasis added), while they appointed judges to the bench who displayed the spirit of cooperation by "letting the guilty and the wicked go unpunished because of their money" (Helaman 7:5). (All this took place in Central America.)

Such was the management that Moroni opposed. By all means, brethren, let us take "Captain Moroni" for our model, and never forget what he fought for—the poor, outcast, and despised; and what he fought against—pride, power, wealth, and ambition; or *how* he fought, as the generous, considerate, and magnanimous foe—a leader in every sense.

(Even at the risk of running overtime I must pause and remind you that this story of which I have given just a few small excerpts is supposed to have been cooked up back in the 1820s somewhere in the backwoods by some abysmally ignorant, disgustingly lazy, and shockingly unprincipled hayseed. Aside from a light mitigation of those epithets, that is the only alternative to believing that the story is *true;* nobody made it up, for the situation is equally fantastic no matter what kind of author you choose to invent.)

That Joseph Smith is beyond compare the greatest leader of modern times is a proposition that needs no comment. Brigham Young recalled that many of the brethren considered themselves better managers than Joseph and were often upset by his economic naiveté. Brigham was certainly a better manager than the Prophet (or anybody else, for that matter), and he knew it, yet he always deferred to and unfailingly followed Brother Joseph all the way while urging others to do the same, because he knew only too well how small is the wisdom of men compared with the wisdom of God.

Moroni scolded the management for their "love of glory and the vain things of the world" (Alma 60:32), and *we* have been warned against the things of this world as recently as the last general conference. But exactly what are the things of the world? An easy and infallible test has been given us in the well-known maxim "You can have anything in this world for money." If a thing is of this world, you can have it for money; if you cannot have it for money, it does not belong to this world. That is what makes the whole thing *manageable*—money is pure number; by converting all values to numbers, everything can be fed into the computer and handled with ease and efficiency. "How much?" becomes the only question we need to ask. The manager "knows the price of everything, and the value of nothing" (Oscar Wilde, *Lady Windermere's Fan,* act 3), because for him the value *is* the price.

Look around you here. Do you see anything that cannot be had for money? Is there anything here you couldn't have if you were rich enough? Well, for one thing you may think you detect intelligence, integrity, sobriety, zeal, character, and other such noble qualities—don't the caps and gowns prove that? But hold on! I have always been taught that those are the very things that managers are looking for—they bring top prices in the marketplace. Does their value in *this* world mean, then, that they have no value in the *other* world? It means exactly that: such things have no price and command no salary in Zion; you cannot bargain with them because they are as common as the once-pure air around us; they are not negotiable in the kingdom because there everybody possesses all of them in full measure, and it would make as much sense to demand pay for having bones or skin as it would to collect a bonus for honesty or sobriety. It is only in our world that they are valued for their scarcity. "Thy money perish with thee," said Peter to a gowned quack (Simon Magus), who sought to include "the gift of God" in a business transaction (see Acts 8:9–24).

The group leader of my high priests quorum is a solid and stalwart Latter-day Saint who was recently visited by a young returned missionary who came to sell him some insurance. Cashing in on his training in the mission field, the fellow assured the brother that he knew that he had the right policy for him just as he knew the gospel was true. Whereupon my friend, without further ado, ordered him out of the house. For one with a testimony should hold it sacred and not sell it for money. The early Christians called *Christemporoi* those who made merchandise of spiritual gifts or Church connections. The things of the world and the things of eternity cannot be thus conveniently conjoined, and it is because many people are finding this out today that I am constrained at this time to speak on this unpopular theme.

For the past year I have been assailed by a steady stream of visitors, phone calls, and letters from people agonizing over what might be called a change of major. Heretofore the trouble has been the repugnance the student (usually a graduate) has felt at entering one line of work when he or she would greatly prefer another. But what can they do? "If you leave my employ," says the manager, "what will become of you?" But today it is not boredom or disillusionment, but conscience that raises the problem: To "seek ye first financial independence and all other things shall be added," is recognized as a rank *per*version of the scriptures and an immoral *in*version of values.

To question that sovereign maxim, one need only consider what strenuous efforts of wit, will, and imagination have been required to defend it. I have never heard, for example, of artists, astronomers, naturalists, poets, athletes, musicians, scholars, or even politicians coming together in high-priced institutes, therapy groups, lecture series, outreach programs, or clinics to get themselves psyched up by GO! GO! GO! slogans, moralizing clichés, or the spiritual exercises of a careful dialectic, to give themselves what is called a "wealth mind-set" with the assurance that (in the words of Korihor) "whatsoever a man [does is] no crime" (Alma 30:17). Nor do those ancient disciplines lean upon lawyers, those managers of managers, to prove to the world that they are not cheating. Those who have something to give to humanity revel in their work and do not have to rationalize, advertise, or evangelize to make themselves feel good about what they are doing.

In my latest class a graduating honors student in business management wrote this—the assignment was to compare oneself with some character in the Pearl of Great Price, and he quite seriously chose Cain:

> Many times I wonder if many of my desires are too self-centered. Cain was after personal gain. He knew the impact of his decision to kill Abel. Now, I do not ignore God and make murderous pacts with Satan; however, I desire to get gain. Unfortunately, my desire to succeed in business is not necessarily to help the Lord's kingdom grow [a refreshing bit of honesty]. Maybe I am pessimistic, but I feel that few businessmen have actually dedicated themselves to the furthering of the church without first desiring personal gratification. As a business major, I wonder about the ethics of business—"charge as much as possible for a product which was made by someone else who was paid as little as possible. You live on the difference." As a businessman will I be living on someone's industry and not my own? Will I be contributing to society, or will I receive something for nothing, as did Cain? While being honest, these are difficult questions for me.

They have been made difficult by the rhetoric of our times. The Church was full of men in Paul's day "supposing that gain is godliness" (1 Timothy 6:5) and making others believe it. Today the black robe puts the official stamp of approval on that very proposition. But don't blame the College of Commerce! The Sophists, those shrewd businessmen and showmen, started that game 2,500 years ago, and you can't blame others for wanting to get in on something so profitable. The learned doctors and masters have always known which side their bread was buttered on and have taken their place in the line. Business and "Independent Studies," the latest of the latecomers, have filled the last gaps, and today, no matter what your bag, you can put in for a cap and gown.

And be not alarmed that management is running the show—they always have.

Most of you are here today only because you believe that this charade will help you get ahead in the world. But in the last few years things have got out of hand; "the economy," once the most important thing in our materialistic lives, has become the *only* thing. We have been swept up in a total dedication to "the economy," which like the massive mud slides of our Wasatch Front, is rapidly engulfing and suffocating everything. If President Kimball is "frightened and appalled" by what he sees, I can do no better than to conclude with his words: "We must leave off the worship of modern-day idols and a reliance on the 'arm of flesh,' for the Lord has said to all the world in our day, 'I will not spare any that remain in Babylon'" ("The False Gods We Worship," *Ensign,* July 1976, p. 6). And Babylon is where we are.

In a forgotten time, before the Spirit was exchanged for the office and inspired leadership for ambitious management, these robes were designed to represent withdrawal from the things of this world—as the temple robes *still* do. That we may become more fully aware of the real significance of both is my prayer in the name of Jesus Christ. Amen.

Hugh Nibley was a professor emeritus of the Department of Ancient Scripture when this commencement address was given in the Marriott Center on 19 August 1983.

Revelation

DALLIN H. OAKS

I AM GOING to speak this morning about revelation. Revelation is communication from God to man. It can occur in many different ways. Some prophets, like Moses and Joseph Smith, have talked with God face to face. Some persons have had personal communication with angels. Other revelations have come, as Elder James E. Talmage described it, "through the dreams of sleep or in waking visions of the mind" (*The Articles of Faith,* 12th ed. [Salt Lake City: The Church of Jesus Christ of Latter-day Saints, 1924], p. 229). In its more familiar forms, revelation or inspiration comes by means of words or thoughts communicated to the mind (D&C 8:2–3; Enos 1:10), by sudden enlightenment (D&C 6:14–15), by positive or negative feelings about proposed courses of action, or even by inspiring performances, as in the performing arts, the beautiful music we heard at the beginning of this devotional assembly being a notable example. As Elder Boyd K. Packer has stated, "Inspiration comes more as a feeling than as a sound" ("Prayers and Answers," *Ensign,* November 1979, p. 20).

Assuming you are familiar with these different forms of revelation or inspiration, I have chosen to discuss this subject in terms of a different classification—the purpose of the communication. I can identify eight different purposes served by communication from

God: (1) to testify; (2) to prophesy; (3) to comfort; (4) to uplift; (5) to inform; (6) to restrain; (7) to confirm; and (8) to impel. I will describe each of these in that order, giving examples.

My purpose in suggesting this classification and in giving these examples is to persuade each of you to search your own experience and to conclude that you have already received revelations and that you can receive more revelations because communication from God to men and women is a reality. President Lorenzo Snow declared that it is "the grand privilege of every Latter-day Saint . . . to have the manifestations of the spirit every day of our lives" (*CR,* April 1899, p. 52). President Harold B. Lee taught:

> Every man has the privilege to exercise these gifts and these privileges in the conduct of his own affairs; in bringing up his children in the way they should go; in the management of his business, or whatever he does. It is his right to enjoy the spirit of revelation and of inspiration to do the right thing, to be wise and prudent, just and good, in everything that he does. [*Stand Ye in Holy Places* (Salt Lake City: Deseret Book, 1974), p. 141–42]

As I review the following eight purposes of revelation, I hope you will recognize the extent to which you have already received revelation or inspiration and resolve to cultivate this spiritual gift for more frequent use in the future.

1. The *testimony* or witness of the Holy Ghost that Jesus is the Christ and that the gospel is true is a revelation from God. When the apostle Peter affirmed that Jesus Christ was the Son of the living God, the Savior called him blessed, "for flesh and blood hath not revealed it unto thee, but my Father which is in heaven" (Matthew 16:17). This precious revelation can be part of the personal experience of every seeker after truth and, once received, becomes a pole star to guide in all the activities of life.

2. *Prophecy* is another purpose or function of revelation. Speaking under the influence of the Holy Ghost and within the limits of his or her stewardship, a person may be inspired to predict what will come to pass in the future. This is the office of the Prophet, Seer, and Revelator, who prophesies for the Church, as Joseph

Smith prophesied the Civil War (D&C 87) and foretold that the Saints would become a mighty people in the Rocky Mountains. Prophecy is part of the calling of a patriarch. Each of us is privileged to receive prophetic revelation illuminating future events in our lives, like a Church calling we are to receive. To cite another example, after our fifth child was born, my wife and I did not have any more children. After more than ten years, we concluded that our family would not be any larger, which grieved us. Then one day, while my wife was in the temple, the Spirit whispered to her that she would have another child. That prophetic revelation was fulfilled a year and a half later with the birth of our sixth child, for whom we had waited thirteen years.

3. A third purpose of revelation is to give *comfort.* Such a revelation came to the Prophet Joseph Smith in Liberty Jail. After many months in deplorable conditions, he cried out in agony and loneliness, pleading with the Lord to remember the persecuted Saints. The comforting answer came:

> My son, peace be unto thy soul; thine adversity and thine afflictions shall be but a small moment;
>
> And then, if thou endure it well, God shall exalt thee on high; thou shalt triumph over all thy foes. [D&C 121:7–8]

In that same revelation the Lord declared that, no matter what tragedies or injustices should befall the Prophet, "Know thou, my son, that all these things shall give thee experience, and shall be for thy good" (D&C 122:7).

Each of us knows of other examples of revelations of comfort. Some have been comforted by visions of departed loved ones or by feeling their presence. The widow of a good friend told me how she had felt the presence of her departed husband, giving her assurance of his love and concern for her. Others have been comforted in adjusting to the loss of a job or a business advantage or even a marriage. A revelation of comfort can also come in connection with a blessing of the priesthood, either from the words spoken or from the feeling communicated in connection with the blessing.

Another type of comforting revelation is the assurance received that a sin has been forgiven. After praying fervently for an entire day and night, a Book of Mormon prophet recorded that he heard a voice, which said, "Thy sins are forgiven thee, and thou shalt be blessed."

"Wherefore," Enos wrote, "my guilt was swept away" (Enos 1:5–6; also see D&C 61:2). This assurance, which comes when a person has completed all the steps of repentance, gives assurance that the price has been paid, that God has heard the repentant sinner, and that his or her sins are forgiven. Alma described that moment as a time when he was no longer "harrowed up by the memory" of his sins. "And oh, what joy, and what marvelous light I did behold; yea, my soul was filled with joy. . . . There can be nothing so exquisite and sweet as was my joy" (Alma 36:19–21).

4. Closely related to the feeling of comfort is the fourth purpose or function of revelation, to *uplift.* At some time in our lives, each of us needs to be lifted up from a depression, from a sense of foreboding or inadequacy, or just from a plateau of spiritual mediocrity. Because it raises our spirits and helps us resist evil and seek good, I believe that the feeling of uplift that is communicated by reading the scriptures or by enjoying wholesome music, art, or literature is a distinct purpose of revelation.

5. The fifth purpose of revelation is to *inform.* This may consist of inspiration giving a person the words to speak on a particular occasion, such as in the blessings pronounced by a patriarch or in sermons or other words spoken under the influence of the Holy Ghost. The Lord commanded Joseph Smith and Sidney Rigdon to lift up their voices and speak the thoughts that he would put in their hearts,

> For it shall be given you in the very hour, yea, in the very moment, what ye shall say. [D&C 100:5–6; see also D&C 84:85 and 124:97]

On some sacred occasions, information has been given by face-to-face conversations with heavenly personages, such as in the visions related in ancient and modern scriptures. In other circumstances, needed information is communicated by the quiet whisperings of the Spirit. A child loses a treasured possession, prays for help, and is inspired to find it; an adult has a problem at work, at home, or in genealogical research, prays, and is led to the information necessary to resolve it; a Church leader prays to know whom the Lord would have him call to fill a position, and the Spirit whispers a name. In all of these examples—familiar to each of us—the Holy Ghost acts in his office as a teacher and revelator, communicating information and truths for the edification and guidance of the recipient.

Revelation from God serves all five of these purposes: testimony, prophecy, comfort, uplift, and information. I have spoken of them only briefly, giving examples principally from the scriptures. I will speak at greater length about the remaining three purposes of revelation, giving examples from my personal experience.

6. The sixth type or purpose of revelation is to *restrain* us from doing something. Thus, in the midst of a great sermon explaining the power of the Holy Ghost, Nephi suddenly declared,

> And now I . . . cannot say more; the Spirit stoppeth mine utterance. [2 Nephi 32:7]

The revelation that restrains is one of the most common forms of revelation. It often comes by surprise, when we have not asked for revelation or guidance on a particular subject. But if we are keeping the commandments of God and living in tune with his Spirit, a restraining force will steer us away from things we should not do.

One of my first experiences in being restrained by the Spirit came soon after I was called as a counselor in a stake presidency in Chicago. In one of our first presidency meetings, our stake president made a proposal that our new stake center be built in a particular location. I immediately saw four or five good reasons why that was the wrong location. When asked for my counsel, I opposed the proposal, giving each of those reasons. The stake president wisely proposed that each of us consider the matter prayerfully for another week and discuss it further in our next meeting. Almost perfunctorily I prayed about the subject and immediately received a strong impression that I was wrong, that I was standing in the way of the Lord's will, and that I should remove myself from opposition to it. Needless to say, I was restrained and promptly gave my approval to the proposed construction. Incidentally, the wisdom of constructing the stake center in that location was soon evident, even to me. My reasons to the contrary turned out to be shortsighted, and I was soon grateful to have been restrained from relying on them.

Several years ago I picked up the desk pen in my office at BYU to sign a paper that had been prepared for my signature, something I did at least a dozen times each day. That document committed the university to a particular course of action we had decided to follow. All the staff work had been done, and all appeared to be in order. But as I went to sign the document, I was filled with such negative thoughts and forebodings that I put it to one side and asked for the entire matter to be reviewed again. It was, and within a few days additional facts came to light that showed that the proposed course of action would have caused the university serious problems in the future.

On another occasion, the Spirit came to my assistance as I was editing a casebook on a legal subject. A casebook consists of several hundred court opinions, together with explanatory material and text written by the editor. My assistant and I had finished all of the work on the book, including the necessary research to assure that these court opinions had not been reversed or overruled. Just before sending it to the publisher, I was leafing through the manuscript, and a particular court opinion caught my attention. As I looked at it, I had a profoundly uneasy feeling. I asked my assistant to check that opinion again to see if everything was in order. He did and reported that it was. In a subsequent check of the completed manuscript, I was again stopped at that case, again with a great feeling of uneasiness. This time I went to the law library myself. There, in some newly received publications, I discovered that this case had just been reversed on appeal. If that opinion had been published in my casebook, it would have been a serious professional embarrassment. I was saved by the restraining power of revelation.

7. A common way to seek revelation is to propose a particular course of action and then pray for inspiration to *confirm* it. The Lord explained the confirming type of revelation when Oliver Cowdery failed in his efforts to translate the Book of Mormon:

> Behold, you have not understood; you have supposed that I would give it unto you, when you took no thought save it was to ask me.
>
> But, behold, I say unto you, that you must study it out in your mind; then you must ask me if it be right, and if it is right I will cause that your bosom shall burn within you; therefore, you shall feel that it is right. [D&C 9:7–8]

Similarly, the prophet Alma likens the word of God to a seed and tells persons studying the gospel that if they will give place for the seed to be planted in their hearts, the seed will enlarge their souls and enlighten their understanding and begin to be delicious to them (Alma 32). That feeling is the Holy Ghost's confirming revelation of the truth of the word.

When he spoke on the BYU campus some years ago on the subject "Agency or Inspiration," Elder Bruce R. McConkie stressed our responsibility to do all that we can before we seek a revelation. He gave a very personal example. When he set out to choose a companion for eternity, he did not go to the Lord and ask whom he ought to marry. "I went out and found the girl I wanted," he said. "She suited me; . . . it just seemed . . . as though this ought to be. . . . [Then] all I did was pray to the Lord and ask for some guidance and direction in connection with the decision that I'd reached" (*Speeches of the Year,* 1972–73 [Provo, Utah: Brigham Young University Press, 1973], p. 111).

Elder McConkie summarized his counsel on the balance between agency and inspiration in these sentences:

> We're expected to use the gifts and talents and abilities, the sense and judgment and agency with which we are endowed. [p. 108]

> . . . Implicit in asking in faith is the precedent requirement that we do everything in our power to accomplish the goal that we seek. [p. 110]
>
> . . . We're expected to do everything in our power that we can, and then to seek an answer from the Lord, a confirming seal that we've reached the right conclusion. [p. 113]

As a regional representative, I was privileged to work with four different members of the Council of the Twelve and with other General Authorities as they sought revelation in connection with the calling of stake presidents. All proceeded in the same manner. They interviewed persons residing in the stake—counselors in the stake presidency, members of the high council, bishops, and others who had gained special experience in Church administration—asking them questions and hearing their counsel. As these interviews were conducted, the servants of the Lord gave prayerful consideration to each person interviewed and mentioned. Finally, they reached a tentative decision on the new stake president. This proposal was then prayerfully submitted to the Lord. If it was confirmed, the call was issued. If it was not confirmed, or if they were restrained, that proposal was tabled, and the process continued until a new proposal was formed and the confirming revelation was received.

Sometimes confirming and restraining revelations are combined. For example, during my service at BYU, I was invited to give a speech before a national association of attorneys. Because it would require many days to prepare, this was the kind of speaking invitation I had routinely declined. But as I began to dictate a letter declining this particular invitation, I felt restrained. I paused and reconsidered my action. I then considered how I might accept the invitation, and as I came to consider it in that light, I felt the confirming assurance of the Spirit and knew that this was what I must do. The speech that resulted, "A Private University Looks at Government Regulation," opened the door to a host of important opportunities. I was invited to repeat that same speech before several other nationally prominent groups. It was published in *Vital Speeches,* in a professional journal, and in several other periodicals and books, from which it was used as a leading statement of the private university's interest in freedom from government regulation. This speech led to BYU's being consulted by various church groups on the proper relationship between government and a church-related college. These consultations in turn contributed to the formation of a national organization of church-related colleges and universities that has provided a significant coalition to oppose unlawful or unwise government regulation. I have no doubt, as I look back on the event, that this speaking invitation I almost declined was one of those occasions when a seemingly insignificant act made a great deal of difference. Those are the times when it is vital for us to receive the guidance of the Lord, and those are the times when revelation will come to aid us if we hear and heed it.

8. The eighth purpose or type of revelation consists of those instances when the Spirit *impels* a person to action. This is not a case where a person proposes to take a particular action and the Spirit either restrains or confirms. This is a case where revelation comes when it is not being sought and impels some action not proposed. This type of revelation is obviously less common than other types, but its rarity makes it all the more significant.

A scriptural example is recorded in the first book of Nephi. When Nephi was in Jerusalem to obtain the precious records from the treasury, the Spirit of the Lord directed him to kill Laban as he lay drunk in the street. This act was so far from Nephi's heart that he recoiled and wrestled with the Spirit, but he was again directed to slay Laban, and he finally followed that revelation (1 Nephi 4).

Students of Church history will recall Wilford Woodruff's account of an impression that came to him in the night telling him to move his carriage and mules away from a large tree. He did so, and his family and livestock were saved when the tree crashed to the ground in a tornado that struck 30 minutes later (see Matthias F. Cowley, *Wilford Woodruff: History of His Life and Labors* [Salt Lake City: Bookcraft, 1964], pp. 331–32).

As a young girl, my grandmother, Chasty Olsen Harris, had a similar experience. She was tending some children who were playing in a dry riverbed near their home in Castle Dale, Utah. Suddenly she heard a voice that called her by name and directed her to get the children out of the riverbed and up on the bank. It was a clear day, and there was no sign of rain. She saw no reason to heed the voice and continued to play. The voice spoke to her again, urgently. This time she heeded the warning. Quickly gathering the children, she made a run for the bank. Just as they reached it, an enormous wall of water, originating with a cloudburst in the mountains many miles away, swept down the canyon and roared across where the children had played. Except for this impelling revelation, she and the children would have been lost.

For nine years Professor Marvin Hill and I had worked on the book *Carthage Conspiracy*, which concerns the 1845 court trial of the murderers of Joseph Smith. We had several different sources of minutes on the trial, some bearing their authors' names and others unsigned. The fullest set of minutes was unsigned, but because we had located them in the Church Historian's Office, we were sure they were the minutes kept by George Watt, the Church's official scribe who was sent to record the proceedings of the trial. We so stated in seven drafts of our manuscript, and we analyzed all our sources on that assumption.

Finally, the book was completed, and within a few weeks the final manuscript would be sent to the publisher. As I sat in my office at BYU one Saturday afternoon, I felt impelled to go through a pile of unexamined books and pamphlets accumulated on the table behind my desk. At the very bottom of the pile of 50 or 60 publications, I found a printed catalog of the contents of the Wilford C. Wood Museum, which Professor LaMar Berrett, the author, had sent to me a year and a half earlier. As I quickly flipped through the pages of this catalog of Church history manuscripts, my eyes fell on a page describing the manuscript of the trial minutes we had attributed to George Watt. This catalog page told how Wilford Wood had purchased the original of that set of minutes in Illinois and had given the Church a typewritten version, the same version we had obtained from the Church Historian. We immediately visited the Wilford Wood Museum in Woods Cross, Utah, and obtained additional information that enabled us to determine that the minutes we had thought were the official Church source had been prepared by one of the lawyers for the defense. With this knowledge, we returned to the Church Historian's Office and were able to locate for the first time George Watt's official and highly authentic set of minutes on the trial. This discovery saved us from a grievous error in the identification of one of our major sources and also permitted us to enrich the contents of our book significantly. The impression I received that day in my office was a cherished example of the way the Lord will help us in our righteous professional pursuits when we qualify for the impressions of his Spirit.

I had another choice experience with impelling revelation a few months after I began my service at BYU. As a new and inexperienced president, I had many problems to analyze and many decisions to reach. I was very dependent on the Lord. One day in October, I drove up Provo Canyon to ponder a particular problem. Although alone and without any interruption, I found myself unable to think of the problem at hand. Another pending issue I was not yet ready to consider kept thrusting itself into my mind: Should we modify BYU's academic calendar to complete the fall semester before Christmas? After ten or fifteen minutes of unsuccessful efforts to exclude thoughts of this subject, I finally realized what was happening. The issue of the calendar did not seem timely to me, and I was certainly not seeking any guidance on it, but the Spirit was trying to communicate with me on that subject. I immediately turned my full attention to that question and began to record my thoughts on a piece of paper. Within a few minutes, I had recorded the details of a three-semester calendar, with all of its powerful advantages. Hurrying back to the campus, I reviewed it with my colleagues and found them enthusiastic. A few days later the board of trustees approved our proposed new calendar, and we published its dates, barely in time to make them effective in the fall of 1972. Since that time, I have reread these words of the Prophet Joseph Smith and realized that I had the experience he described:

> A person may profit by noticing the first intimation of the spirit of revelation; for instance, when you feel pure intelligence flowing into you, it may give you sudden strokes of ideas . . . ; and thus by learning the Spirit of God and understanding it, you may grow into the principle of revelation. [*Teachings,* p. 151]

I have now described eight different purposes or types of revelation: (1) testifying, (2) prophesying, (3) comforting, (4) uplifting, (5) informing, (6) restraining, (7) confirming, and (8) impelling. Each of these refers to revelations that are received. Before concluding I will suggest a few ideas about revelations that are *not* received.

First, we should understand what can be called the principle of "stewardship in revelation." Our Heavenly Father's house is a house of order, where his servants are commanded to "act in the office in which [they are] appointed" (D&C 107:99). This principle applies to revelation. Only the president of the Church receives revelation to guide the entire Church. Only the stake president receives revelation for the special guidance of the stake. The person who receives revelation for the ward is the bishop. For a family, it is the priesthood leadership of the family. Leaders receive revelation for their own stewardships. Individuals can receive revelation to guide their own lives. But when one person purports to receive revelation for another person outside his or her own stewardship—such as a Church member who claims to have revelation to guide the entire Church or a person who claims to have a revelation to guide another person over whom he or she has no presiding authority according to the order of the Church—you can be sure that such revelations are not from the Lord. "There are counterfeit signals" (Boyd K. Packer, "Prayers and Answers," *Ensign,* November 1979, p. 20). Satan is a great deceiver, and he is the source of some of these spurious revelations. Others are simply imagined.

If a revelation is outside the limits of stewardship, you know it is not from the Lord, and you are not bound by it. I have heard of cases where a young man told a young woman she should marry him because he had received a revelation that she was to be his eternal companion. If this is a true revelation, it will be confirmed directly to the woman if she seeks to know. In the meantime, she is under no obligation to heed it. She should seek her own guidance and make up her own mind. The man can receive revelation to guide his own actions, but he cannot properly receive revelation to direct hers. She is outside his stewardship.

What about those times when we seek revelation and do not receive it? We do not always receive inspiration or revelation when we request it. Sometimes we are delayed in the receipt of revelation, and sometimes we are left to our own judgment. We cannot force spiritual things. It must be so. Our life's purpose to obtain experience and to develop faith would be frustrated if our Heavenly Father directed us in every act, even in every important act. We must make decisions and experience the consequences in order to develop self-reliance and faith.

Even in decisions we think very important, we sometimes receive no answers to our prayers. This does not mean that our prayers have not been heard. It only means that we have prayed about a decision that, for one reason or another, we should make without guidance by revelation. Perhaps we have asked for guidance in choosing between alternatives that are equally acceptable or equally unacceptable. I suggest that there is *not* a right and wrong to *every* question. To many questions, there are only two wrong answers or two right answers. Thus, a person who seeks guidance on which of two different ways he should pursue to get even with a person who has wronged him is not likely to receive a revelation. Neither is a person who seeks guidance on a choice he will never have to make because some future event will intervene, such as a third alternative that is clearly preferable. On one occasion, my wife and I prayed earnestly for guidance on a decision that seemed very important. No answer came. We were left to proceed on our own best judgment. We could not imagine why the Lord had not aided us with a confirming or restraining impression. But it was not long before we learned that we did not have to make a decision on that question because something else happened that made a decision unnecessary. The Lord would not guide us in a selection that made no difference.

No answer is likely to come to a person who seeks guidance in choosing between two alternatives that are equally acceptable to the Lord. Thus, there are times when we can serve productively in two different fields of labor. Either answer is right. Similarly, the Spirit of the Lord is not likely to give us revelations on matters that are trivial. I once heard a young woman in a testimony meeting praise the spirituality of her husband, indicating that he submitted every question to the Lord. She told how he accompanied her shopping and would not even choose between different brands of canned vegetables without making his selection a matter of prayer. That strikes me as improper. I believe the Lord expects us to use the intelligence and experience he has given us to make these kinds of choices. When a member asked the Prophet Joseph Smith for advice on a particular matter, the Prophet stated:

> It is a great thing to inquire at the hands of God, or to come into His presence; and we feel fearful to approach Him on subjects that are of little or no consequence. [*Teachings,* p. 22]

Of course we are not always able to judge what is trivial. If a matter appears of little or no consequence, we can proceed on the basis of our own judgment. If the choice is important for reasons unknown to us, such as the speaking invitation I mentioned earlier or even a choice between two cans of vegetables when one contains a hidden poison, the Lord will intervene and give us guidance. When a choice will make a real difference in our lives—obvious or not—and when we are living in tune with the Spirit and seeking his guidance, we can be sure we will receive the guidance we need to attain our goal. The Lord will not leave us unassisted when a choice is important to our eternal welfare.

I know that God lives and that revelation to his children is a reality. I pray that we will be worthy and willing, and that he will bless us to grow in this principle of revelation. I bear you my testimony of the truthfulness of the gospel, in the name of Jesus Christ. Amen.

Dallin H. Oaks was a justice of the Utah Supreme Court when this devotional address was given in the Marriott Center on 29 September 1981.

The Arts and the Spirit of the Lord

BOYD K. PACKER

I AM PARTICULARLY appreciative of the music we've just heard, and quote from section 25 of the Doctrine and Covenants:

> For my soul delighteth in the song of the heart; yea, the song of the righteous is a prayer unto me, and it shall be answered with a blessing upon their heads. [D&C 25:12]

I very anxiously lay claim to those blessings from these righteous young men and women who have sung so beautifully this sacred hymn of Zion. My gratitude to them will, I'm sure, be more obvious when I move into the message that I have chosen to speak upon tonight.

I want to respond to a question that I face with some frequency. It has many variations, but the theme is this: Why do we not have more inspired and inspiring music in the Church? Or why do we have so few great paintings or sculptures depicting the Restoration? Why is it when we need a new painting for a bureau of information, or perhaps for a temple, frequently nonmember painters receive the commission? The same questions have an application to poetry, to drama, to dance, to creative writing, to all the fine arts.

Now, I'm sure there are those who will say, "Why does he presume to talk about that? He is uninformed. He is just out of his province." It may comfort them to know that I know that. My credentials to speak do not come from being a musician, for I'm not. I am not a composer, nor a conductor, and certainly I am not a vocalist. I cannot, for example, play the piano. I would be very unwilling to do so. However, should I be pressed to it, I could, without much difficulty, prove my point. I am not adequate as an artist, nor as a sculptor, a poet, or a writer.

But then I do not intend to train you in any of those fields. My credentials, if I have any (some of them should be obvious), relate to spiritual things.

I hope for sufficient inspiration to comment on how the Spirit of the Lord influences or is influenced by the art forms that I have mentioned. Since I have been interested in these matters, I have, over the years, listened very carefully when they have been discussed by the Brethren. I have studied expressions of my Brethren and of those who have led us in times past, in order to determine how those questions should be answered.

The reason we have not yet produced a greater heritage in art and literature and music and drama is not, I am very certain, because we have not had talented people. For over the years we have had not only good ones but great ones. Some have reached great heights in their chosen fields. But few have captured the spirit of the gospel of Jesus Christ and the restoration of it in music, in art, in literature. They have not, therefore, even though they were gifted, made a lasting contribution to the onrolling of the Church and kingdom of God in the dispensation of the fulness of times. They have therefore missed doing what they might have done, and they have missed being what they might have become. I am reminded of the statement "There are many who struggle and climb and finally reach the top of the ladder, only to find that it is leaning against the wrong wall."

If you are willing to listen, I would like to express some concerns I have had over these matters and describe to you some disappointments I have heard expressed among the leaders of the Church.

Because I intend to be quite direct in my comments, I am a bit concerned. For I know when we touch this subject we talk of people who are very gifted. And people who are very gifted, it would seem, tend to be temperamental.

We were discussing some time ago the music and musicians of the Church, when one of the Twelve pointed out that it may be difficult to get instruction across because some of our musicians, among others, have a tendency to be temperamental. "Yes," observed one of the senior members of our Quorum, "More temper than mental." That, I suppose, describes all of us at one time or another.

Before I continue, I want it clearly understood that we have in the Church tens of thousands of gifted people who not only have talent, but who are generous with it. Our gifted people are greatly needed in the Church.

The work of the Lord has been moved by the members in the wards and stakes and branches who have been blessed with special gifts and who use them unselfishly. Because of what they do, we are able to feel and learn very quickly through music, through art, through poetry some spiritual things that we would otherwise learn very slowly. All of us are indebted to them for their generous service. I am humbly grateful to those who render such service in the Church. But then it is only right that they should contribute.

You who have such talents might well ask, "Whence comes this gift?" And gift it is. You may have cultivated it and developed it, but it was given to you. Most of us do not have it. You were not more deserving than we, but you are a good deal more responsible. If you use your gift properly, opportunities for service are opened that will be beneficial eternally for you and for others.

Has it ever occurred to you that you may leave this life without it? If the gift is yours because of the shape of your vocal cords, or the strength of your lungs, or because of the coordination of your hands, or because your eye registers form and color, you may leave the gift behind. You may have to be content with what you have become, because you possessed it while you were here. It has not been revealed just how this would be. I rather suspect that those gifts which we use properly will stay with us beyond the veil. And, I repeat, you who are gifted may not be more deserving, but you are much more responsible than the rest of us.

Elder Orson F. Whitney said:

> We will yet have Miltons and Shakespeares of our own. God's ammunition is not exhausted. His brightest spirits are held in reserve for the latter times. In God's name and by His help we will build up a literature whose top shall touch heaven, though its foundations may now be low in earth. [Lecture delivered at YMMIA conference, 3 June 1888, in Brian H. Stuy, comp. and ed., *Collected Discourses,* vol. 1 (Burbank, California: B.H.S. Publishing, 1987), p. 154]

Since that statement was made in 1888, those foundations have been raised up very slowly. The greatest poems are not yet written, nor the paintings finished. The greatest hymns and anthems of the Restoration are yet to be composed. The sublimest renditions of them are yet to be conducted. We move forward much slower than need be, and I would like to underline some things that stand in our way.

You will quickly notice that I refer frequently to music. There is a reason for that. We use it more often. But the point that I shall make about the musician applies to all the arts: painting, poetry, drama, dance, and others.

For some reason it takes a constant vigilance on the part of priesthood leaders—both general and local—to ensure that music presented in our worship and devotional services is music that is appropriate for worship and devotional services. I have heard presidents of the Church declare after a general conference, or after a temple dedication, words to this effect (and I am quoting verbatim from one such experience):

> I suppose we did not give enough attention to the music. It seems that our musicians must take such liberties. Something spiritual

> was lost from our meetings because the music was not what it should have been. Next time we must remember to give them more careful instructions.

Why is it that the president of the Church, or the president of the stake, or the bishop of the ward must be so attentive in arranging music for worship services and conference meetings? Why should the anxiety persist that, if the musicians are left to do what they want to do, the result will not invite the Spirit of the Lord?

I have in the past made not altogether successful attempts to set a mood of devotion on a very sacred subject, having been invited to the pulpit immediately after a choir or choral number that was well performed but did nothing to inspire the spirit of devotion; or after a brass ensemble has rendered music that has nothing to do with spiritual inspiration.

The selections, which for other purposes might have been admirable, even impressive, failed in their inspiration simply because they were not appropriate. For some other gathering, some other time, some other place, yes—but they did not do what the hymns of the Restoration could have done. How sad when a gifted person has no real sense of propriety!

Let me illustrate this matter of propriety. Suppose you sponsor a pep rally in the stadium with the purpose of exciting the student body to a high point of enthusiasm. Suppose you invite someone to present a musical number with the expectation that the music would contribute to your purpose. Imagine him playing a sonata on an organ in subdued tones that lulls everyone into a contemplative and reflective mood. However well composed the music, or however well performed, it would not be appropriate for the occasion.

This example, of course, is obvious. It makes me wonder, therefore, why we must be constantly alert to have appropriate music in our sacrament meetings, conference sessions, and other worship services. Music and art and dance and literature can be very appropriate in one place and in one setting and for one purpose and be very wrong in another. That can be true of instruments as well.

We have, in our instruction to the musicians of the Church, this suggestion:

> Organs and pianos are the standard musical instruments used in sacrament meetings. Other instruments, such as orchestral strings, may be used when appropriate, but the music presented must be in keeping with the reverence and spirituality of the meeting. Brass and percussion instruments generally are not appropriate. [*General Handbook of Instructions,* 1976, p. 23]

We are under resistance from some highly trained musicians who insist that they can get as much inspiration from brass instruments or a guitar solo as from a choir. I believe that an organ perhaps could be played at a pep rally in a way to incite great enthusiasm. And I think a brass section could play a hymn in such a way as to be reverent and fitting in a worship service. But if it should happen, it would have to be an exception. We cannot convey a sacred message in an art form that is not appropriate and have anything spiritual happen. But there is a constant attempt to do it.

Several years ago one of the organizations of the Church produced a filmstrip. The subject matter was very serious and the script was well written. The producer provided a story board. A story board is a series of loose, almost scribbled sketches, sometimes with a little color brushed across them, to roughly illustrate each frame of the filmstrip. Very little work is invested in a story board. It is merely to give an idea and is always subject to revision.

Some members of the committee were amused by the story board itself. It had a loose, comical air about it. They decided to photograph the illustrations on the story board and use them in the filmstrip. They thought they would be quite amusing and entertaining.

When the filmstrip was reviewed by four members of the Council of the Twelve, it was rejected. It had to be made over again. Why? Because the art form used simply was not appropriate to the message. You just don't teach sacred, serious subjects with careless, scribbled illustrations.

Now, again to music. There have been a number of efforts to take sacred gospel themes and tie them to modern music in the hope of attracting our young people to the message. Few events in all of human history surpass the spiritual majesty of the First Vision. We would be ill-advised to describe that event, the visit of Elohim and Jehovah, in company with rock music, even soft rock music, or to take equally sacred themes and set them to a modern beat. I do not know how that can be done and result in increased spirituality. I think it cannot be done.

When highly trained artists insist, as they occasionally do, that they receive spiritual experience in tying a sacred gospel theme to an inappropriate art form, I must conclude that they do not know, not really, the difference between when the Spirit of the Lord is present and when it is not.

Very frequently when our musicians, particularly the more highly trained among them, are left to do what they want to do, they perform in such a way as to call attention to themselves and their ability. They do this rather than give prayerful attention to what will inspire. I do not mean "inspire" as the music or art of the world can inspire. I mean *inspire!*

They are not content to use the hymns and anthems of the Restoration, for such a presentation, they feel, will not demonstrate their full capacities. When pressed to do so, they may grudgingly put a hymn on the program. But it is obvious that their heart isn't in it, for the numbers they select themselves seem to say, "Now let us show you what we really can do."

We instruct stake presidents that "preference should be given to the singing of well-known hymns" at stake conferences (1976 Stake Conference Program Schedules).

I know there are those who think that our Church music is limited. Some with professional abilities evidently soon get very tired of it. They want to stray from it and reach out into the world. They present the argument that many of the hymns in our hymnbook were not written for the Church or by members of the Church. I know that already. And some of them are not really as compelling as they might be. Their messages are not as specific as we could have if we produced our own. But by association they have taken on a meaning that reminds members of the Church, whenever they hear them, of the restoration of the gospel, of the Lord, and of his ministry.

Sometimes, to ensure that music will be appropriate, one of the hymns or anthems of the Restoration is specifically requested. "Oh, but they sang that last conference," our conductors will say. Indeed we did, and we preached the same gospel last conference also. The preaching of it over and over again gives it a familiar and a warm feeling. We build it into our lives.

As speakers we are not trying to impress the world with how talented we are as preachers. We are simply trying to get across, by repetition, if that's the only way, the sacred message that has been entrusted to us.

Those of us who lead the Church are not constantly seeking new doctrine to introduce. We simply teach over and over again that which was in the beginning. It is with great difficulty that we try to pass on to the next generation, in some form of purity, that which was given to us. We will lose it if we are not wise.

The musician may say, "Do you really want us to take those few familiar hymns and present them over and over again with no introduction of anything new?" No, that is not what I would want, but it is close.

What I would desire would be to have the hymns of the Restoration *characteristic* of our worship services, with others added if they are appropriate. There are a great many things from elsewhere that are very appropriate. Many numbers can be used in our worship services with complete propriety.

Our hymns speak the truth as far as they go. They could speak more of it if we had more of them, specifically teaching the principles of the restored gospel of Jesus Christ.

If I had my way there would be many new hymns with lyrics near scriptural in their power, bonded to music that would inspire people to worship. Think how much we could be helped by another inspired anthem or hymn of the Restoration. Think how we could be helped by an inspired painting on a scriptural theme or depicting our heritage. How much we could be aided by a graceful and modest dance, by a persuasive narrative, or poem, or drama. We could have the Spirit of the Lord more frequently and in almost unlimited intensity if we would.

For the most part, we do without because the conductor wants to win the acclaim of the world. He does not play to the Lord, but to other musicians. The composer and the arranger want to please the world. The painter wants to be in style. And so our resources of art and music grow ever so gradually. And we find that there have marched through this grand parade of mortality men and women who were sublimely gifted, but who spent all, or most, in the world and for the world. And I repeat that they may well one day come to learn that "many men struggle to reach the top of the ladder, only to find that it is leaning against the wrong wall."

It is a mistake to assume that one can follow the ways of the world and then somehow, in a moment of intruded inspiration, compose a great anthem of the Restoration, or in a moment of singular inspiration paint the great painting. When it is done, it will be done by one who has yearned and tried and longed fervently to do it, not by one who has condescended to do it. It will take quite as much preparation and work as any masterpiece, and a different kind of inspiration.

There is a test you might apply if you are among the gifted. Ask yourself this question: When I am free to do what I really want to do, what will it be?

If you find that you are ashamed of our humble heritage in the arts, that ought to be something of a signal to you. Often artists are not free to create what they most desire because the market demands other things of them. But what about when you are free? Do you have a desire to produce what the Church needs? Or do you desire to convince the Church that it needs to change style so the world will feel comfortable with it? Although our artistic heritage as yet is relatively small, we are losing some of what we have—through neglect!

At the recent rededication of the St. George Temple each session was closed, as is traditional in a temple dedication, with the presentation of the "Hosanna Anthem." The audience, on the signal from the conductor, joins with the choir on that part of the anthem known widely through the Church as "The Spirit of God Like a Fire Is Burning." I sat through those sessions and carefully observed, with great sorrow, that fully 80 percent of those in the audience did not know the words.

We can lose our heritage. We have lost part of it. Let me cite an example in the field of poetry.

William Ernest Henley wrote "Invictus," a proud, almost defiant expression that concludes:

> I am the master of my fate:
> I am the captain of my soul.
> [*Echoes,* 1888, No. 4, In Memoriam R. T. Hamilton Bruce ("Invictus"), stanza 4]

Some years ago an answer to "Invictus" was given. Let me quote it to you:

> Art thou in truth? Then what of him
> Who bought thee with his blood?
> Who plunged into devouring seas
> And snatched thee from the flood?
>
> Who bore for all our fallen race
> What none but him could bear.—
> The God who died that man might live,
> And endless glory share?
>
> Of what avail thy vaunted strength,
> Apart from his vast might?
> Pray that his Light may pierce the gloom,
> That thou mayest see aright.

Men are as bubbles on the wave,
  As leaves upon the tree.
Thou, captain of thy soul, forsooth!
  Who gave that place to thee?

Free will is thine—free agency,
  To wield for right or wrong;
But thou must answer unto him
  To whom all souls belong.

Bend to the dust that head "unbowed,"
  Small part of Life's great whole!
And see in him, and him alone,
  The Captain of thy soul.
["The Soul's Captain," *Improvement Era,* May 1926, opposite inside front cover]

And who wrote that? Orson F. Whitney of the Council of the Twelve Apostles, a gifted and inspired poet whose work is virtually unknown in the Church. Let me quote another of his poems:

There's a mountain named Stern Justice,
  Tall and towering, gloomy, grand,
Frowning o'er a vale called Mercy,
  Loveliest in all the land.

Great and mighty is the mountain,
  But its snowy crags are cold,
And in vain the sunlight lingers
  On the summit proud and bold.

There is warmth within the valley,
  And I love to wander there,
'Mid the fountains and the flowers,
  Breathing fragrance on the air.

Much I love the solemn mountain,
  It doth meet my somber mood,
When, amid the muttering thunders,
  O'er my soul the storm-clouds brood.

But when tears, like rain, have fallen
From the fountain of my woe,
And my soul has lost its fierceness,
Straight unto the vale I go;

Where the landscape, gently smiling,
O'er my heart pours healing balm,
And, as oil on troubled waters,
Brings from out its storm a calm.

Yes, I love both vale and mountain,
Ne'er from either would I part;
Each unto my life is needful,
Both are dear unto my heart.

For the smiling vale doth soften
All the rugged steep makes sad,
And from icy rocks meander
Rills that make the valley glad.

[Orson F. Whitney, "The Mountain and the Vale," *The Poetical Writings of Orson F. Whitney* (Salt Lake City: Juvenile Instructor Office, 1889), p. 183]

Both of these poems are new to most of you. Why would that be? I think it more than a pity that work such as this remains unknown to most students and faculty—even to some of the faculty in the field of literature. It is sad when members of the faculty here would discard them in favor of assigning their students to read degenerate compositions that issue from the minds of perverted and wicked men.

There is the temptation for college teachers, in the Church and outside of it, to exercise their authority to give assignments and thereby introduce their students to degradation under the argument that it is part of our culture. Teachers in the field of literature are particularly vulnerable.

I use the word *warning.* Such will not go unnoticed in the eternal scheme of things. Those who convey a degraded heritage to the next generation will reap disappointment by and by.

Teachers would do well to learn the difference between studying some things, as compared to studying *about* them. There is a great difference.

There is much to be said for a great effort to rediscover the humble and inspired contributions of gifted Saints of the past and thereby inspire the gifted in our day to produce works that will inspire those who come after us.

It is sad but true that, almost as a rule, our most gifted members are drawn to the world. They who are most capable to preserve our cultural heritage and to extend it, because of the enticements of the world, seek rather to replace it. That is so easy to do because for the most part they do not have that intent. They think that what they do is to improve it. Unfortunately many of them will live to learn that indeed, "Many men struggle to climb to reach the top of the ladder, only to find that it is leaning against the wrong wall."

I mentioned earlier that the greatest hymns and anthems have not been composed, nor have the greatest illustrations been set down, nor the poems written, nor the paintings finished. When they are produced, who will produce them? Will it be the most talented and the most highly trained among us? I rather think it will not. They will be produced by those who are the most inspired among us. Inspiration can come to those whose talents are barely adequate, and their contribution will be felt for generations; and the Church and kingdom of God will move forward just a little more easily because they have been here.

Some of our most gifted people struggle to produce a work of art, hoping that it will be described by the world as masterpiece! monumental! epic! when in truth the simple, compelling theme of "I Am a Child of God" has moved and will move more souls to salvation than would such a work were they to succeed.

Some years ago I was chairman of a committee of seminary men responsible to produce a filmstrip on Church history. One of the group, Trevor Christensen, remembered that down in Sanpete County was a large canvas roll of paintings. They had been painted by one of his progenitors, C. C. A. Christensen, who traveled through the settlements giving a lecture on Church history as each painting was unrolled and displayed by lamplight. The roll of paintings had been stored away for generations. We sent a truck for them, and I shall not forget the day we unrolled it.

Brother Christensen was not masterful in his painting, but our heritage was there. Some said it was not great art, but what it lacked in technique was more than compensated in feeling. His work has been shown more widely and published more broadly and received more attention than that of a thousand and one others who missed that point.

I do not think Brother Christensen was a great painter, some would say not even a good one. I think his paintings are masterful. Why? Because the simple, reverent feeling he had for his spiritual heritage is captured in them. I do not think it strange that the world would honor a man who could not paint very well.

The ideal, of course, is for one with a gift to train and develop it to the highest possibility, including a sense of spiritual propriety. No artist in the Church who desires unselfishly to extend our heritage need sacrifice his career or an avocation, nor need he neglect his gift as only a hobby. He can meet the world and "best" it, and not be the loser. In the end, what appears to be such sacrifice will have been but a test.

Abraham did not have to kill Isaac, you know. He had to be willing to. Once that was known, that he would sacrifice his only begotten, he was known to be godlike and the blessings poured out upon him.

A few years ago Sister Packer and I were in Washington, D.C., to represent the Church at an awards banquet held in the reception hall of the Department of State. The elegant and stately surroundings, with a priceless collection of antiques and memorabilia, were impressive. Here, for instance, hangs the painting of George Washington by Gilbert Stuart and other priceless works of art. Both the occasion and the setting were ideal to make reference to the spiritual heritage of our country. And what was the program? A large brass section from one of the service bands played at great length, and with deafening volume, music from *Jesus Christ, Superstar.*

I sat next to a lovely, dignified woman, the wife of an officer of the government. When the crescendo weakened for a moment I was able to ask, by raising my voice a bit, if she was able to hear them all right. Her obvious amusement at the question soon changed to serious disappointment, as she asked in return, "What would Jesus think?"

That is well worth keeping in our minds if we have the talent to compose music or poetry, to illustrate or paint, or sculpt or act, or sing or play or conduct.

What do I think he would think? I think he would rejoice at the playing of militant martial music as men marched to defend a righteous cause. I think that he would think there are times when illustrations should be vigorous, with bold and exciting colors. I think he would chuckle with approval when at times of recreation the music is comical or melodramatic or exciting. Or at times when a carnival air is in order that decorations be bright and flashy, even garish.

I think at times of entertainment he would think it quite in order for poetry that would make one laugh or cry—perhaps both at once. I think that he would think it would be in righteous order on many occasions to perform with great dignity symphonies and operas and ballets. I think that he would think that soloists should develop an extensive repertoire, each number to be performed at a time and in a place that is appropriate.

I would think that he would think there is a place for artwork of every kind—from the scribbled cartoon to the masterpiece in the hand-carved, gold-leaf frame.

But I am sure he would be offended at immodesty and irreverence in music, in art, in poetry, in writing, in sculpture, in dance, or in drama. I know what he would think about music or art or literature or poetry that is purely secular being introduced into our worship services. And how do I know that? Because he has told his servants that. In what ways has he told them? He has told them by either withholding or, on occasions, withdrawing his Spirit when it is done.

I mentioned earlier that I have sometimes struggled without much success to teach sacred things when preceded by music that is secular or uninspired. Let me mention the other side of it.

I have been in places where I felt insecure and unprepared. I have yearned inwardly in great agony for some power to pave the way or loosen my tongue, that an opportunity would not be lost because of my weakness and inadequacy. On more than a few occasions my prayers have been answered by the power of inspired music. I have been lifted above myself and beyond myself when the Spirit of the Lord has poured in upon the meeting, drawn there by beautiful, appropriate music. I stand indebted to the gifted among us who have that unusual sense of spiritual propriety.

Go to, then, you who are gifted; cultivate your gift. Develop it in any of the arts and in every worthy example of them. If you have the ability and the desire, seek a career or employ your talent as an avocation or cultivate it as a hobby. But in all ways bless others with it. Set a standard of excellence. Employ it in the secular sense to every worthy advantage, but never use it profanely. Never express your gift unworthily. Increase our spiritual heritage in music, in art, in literature, in dance, in drama.

When we have done it, our activities will be a standard to the world. And our worship and devotion will remain as unique from the world as the Church is different from the world. Let the use of your gift be an expression of your devotion to him who has given it to you. We who do not share in it will set a high standard of expectation: "For of him unto whom much is given much is required" (D&C 82:3).

Now, in conclusion, may I remind you what I said at the beginning. My credential to speak does not come from personal mastery of the arts. I repeat my confession. I am not gifted as a musician or as a poet, nor adequate as an artist, nor accomplished in the field of dance, or writing, or drama. I speak on this subject because I have a calling, one that not only permits, but even requires, that we stay close to him and to his Spirit.

If we know nothing of the arts, we know something of the Spirit. We know that it can be drawn upon meagerly or almost to the consuming of an individual.

In 1832 the Prophet Joseph Smith received a revelation that now stands as section 88 of the Doctrine and Covenants and was designated by the Prophet as "The Olive Leaf." I quote a few verses:

> Draw near unto me and I will draw near unto you; seek me diligently and ye shall find me; ask, and ye shall receive; knock, and it shall be opened unto you.
>
> Whatsoever ye ask the Father in my name it shall be given unto you, that is expedient for you;
>
> And if ye ask anything that is not expedient for you, it shall turn unto your condemnation.
>
> Behold, that which you hear is as the voice of one crying in the wilderness—in the wilderness, because you cannot see him—my voice, because my voice is Spirit; my Spirit is truth; truth abideth and hath no end; and if it be in you it shall abound.
>
> And if your eye be single to my glory, your whole bodies shall be filled with light, and there shall be no darkness in you; and that body which is filled with light comprehendeth all things.
>
> Therefore, sanctify yourselves that your minds become single to God, and the days will come that you shall see him; for he will unveil his face unto you, and it shall be in his own time, and in his own way, and according to his own will. [D&C 88:63–68]

The Spirit of the Lord can be present on his terms only. God grant that we may learn, each of us, particularly those who are gifted, how to extend that invitation.

He lives. Of him I bear witness. Jesus is the Christ, the Son of God, the Only Begotten of the Father. Spencer W. Kimball is a prophet of God. We have on our shoulders in this generation the Church and kingdom of God to bear away. God grant that those among us who are the most gifted will devote themselves in order that our task may be easier, I pray, in the name of Jesus Christ. Amen.

Boyd K. Packer was a member of the Council of the Twelve of The Church of Jesus Christ of Latter-day Saints when this fireside address was given in the Marriott Center on 1 February 1976.

Necessities of Living

HUGH W. PINNOCK

PRESIDENT OAKS AND brethren and sisters, I am delighted to be here with you this beautiful morning to share the gospel of Jesus Christ with some of the most important people in the kingdom—you.

I would like to discuss five concepts with you today, and my prayer is that these concepts might awaken in you latent thoughts that, once utilized, will make your time on earth more rewarding and exciting. They are these: one, there are thoughts that need thinking; two, there are ideas that need sharing; three, there are words that must be said; four, there are characteristics that need to be developed; and five, there are acts that should be performed.

First, what are these thoughts that need thinking? There are three of them. The first is this: What you are to be, you are now becoming. In Hamlet, Shakespeare's Ophelia said, "We know what we are, but know not what we may be" (act 4, scene 5, lines 42–43). Of course, the gospel had not been restored in the seventeenth century, so even Shakespeare did not really know what man could become; but we do, and this knowledge adds a dimension to our lives that cannot be realized by those who do not have the gospel of Jesus Christ.

Spencer W. Kimball became a prophet not on December 27, 1973, but when he was your age or perhaps even younger, because he was preparing himself for the great things that were to happen. We are becoming exalted today by the acts we perform, by the thoughts we think, and by the words we speak.

At the University of Utah—and I shall not speak those words any more often than I have to—there was a young sorority president, a wonderful musician, who was taught by her parents that her eternal position was being determined by her daily actions. Kathy McKay was an exciting date and a great example to everyone that knew her. One athlete from out of state became interested in the gospel of Jesus Christ just by watching her and recognizing her purity. She knew that the person she was to become she was then becoming.

There are many examples, but let me continue.

The second thought that needs thinking is this: Today might be one of your key days. Vince Lombardi, one of the greatest football coaches who has ever lived and taught, trained his players to give all they had in every play. He explained it this way: "In every football game there are only five or six key plays that determine the final outcome of the game; however, no one knows when those key plays will materialize, and so we must give all we have every play in order to stop the opposition from scoring or to score ourselves."

That is how life is, brothers and sisters. There are only five or six or perhaps a few more key days in our lives—the day that we decide to give all we are and all we have to the Lord Jesus Christ; the day we find that special person with whom we can hold hands throughout eternity; the day we say, "Yes, bishop, I will serve wherever I am sent." There are not many of those days; but we must live the very best we can every day, so when those key days come along we will respond properly and end up with the eternal reward that awaits all of us who are worthy.

The third thought that needs thinking is this: If you do not respond properly to a challenge, maybe no one will. My mind flashes back to Granite High School and a young lady there who had a number of problems. Economically speaking, she was very poor. She could not dress like the other students, and she was insecure and frightened. But there was a young man who knew her and who would say, "Hi, how ya doin'?" One day they were to take a test in history, and he said to her, "Let's sit down and study together." They did, and she could tell that she had value—not romantic value, but value as a fellow human being.

The weeks came and went, and then one day she confessed to that young man that he had saved her life. "What do you mean, I've saved your life?" he asked.

"Do you remember the day we had that history test?"

"Yes."

"I was going to take my life that day. I knew no one cared, that no one loved me. People made fun of the way I dressed and the things I said and the way I looked. But you cared, and because of that I'm still alive."

Incidentally, I saw that woman several years ago. She is a nurse now in Salt Lake City and is doing well, ministering to the needs of others. She is alive because someone who sat in class with her cared. Brothers and sisters, there are people who need you.

Next, there are ideas that need sharing. The first is this: The only effective decision-making apparatus in this life is the gospel of Jesus Christ. In theory, all of the great resources found within a nation can be used for that country's well-being; yet this magnificent nation in which we live is not making the type of decisions that are helpful or lasting, that are providing the stability we need. The philosophies of men are confusing, conflicting, cumbersome, and often contrary to the time frames within which we must live.

Our great educational institutions, with the exception of BYU, do much to facilitate our specializations and career preparations and little else. I say that kindly, but believe it with all of my heart. Our educational institutions worldwide do not provide the type of decision-making capacities that we need to live at peace and in love with others; neither do the great corporations with their millions and often billions of dollars. But the more we utilize this incredible tool of the gospel of Jesus Christ, the happier we will be today, tomorrow (when our todays become yesterdays), and forever. It behooves all of us in this incredible environment of Brigham Young University to study, along with physics and behavioral theory and English and physical development, the gospel of Jesus Christ, that our decisions might be eternally helpful.

The second idea that I would like to share—and it is not unlike the first—is this: We function best in an environment of freedom. We are free when we are independent, and we are totally independent only when we are completely dependent upon the Savior. The Master said, "I can of mine own self do nothing: as I hear, I judge: and my judgment is just; because I seek not mine own will, but the will of the Father which hath sent me" (John 5:30). He did all that he saw his Father do; may we emulate him as he emulated his Father.

Referring to freedom and our relationship with him, the Savior also said, "I, the Lord God, make you free, therefore ye are free indeed" (D&C 98:8). Freedom, like inspired decisions, cannot come from any source other than the Savior. If we were totally dependent on the Savior, we could even find ourselves in prison and still be free.

The next and third part of my discussion is this: There are words that need saying. The first words that need saying are the most beautiful words of all: "I love you," and "I appreciate you." I talked on love at a missionary zone conference in Philadelphia one day, and during interviews a young man from Utah County, a former football player at American Fork High School, came up and said, "President, I've never told my dad that I love him."

I said, "Elder, we're not leaving this office until you do."

"I can't," he protested. "My father works for Geneva, and we can't reach him during the day; but I promise, President, that I'll call him tonight and tell him I love him."

I replied, "Elder, after you do, call me and let me know how it went."

After driving home from Philadelphia, I went through a tall pile of mail and did some dictation. Sister Pinnock went to bed, but I sat up for a while and wrote in my journal—still no telephone call. As I was finally going to bed, much later than I should have been going to bed, the telephone rang.

"President, I did it," he announced.

I said, "Tell me about it."

"Well, I was so frightened that I waited too long, and when I finally called, they had gone to bed. Mother answered the telephone, and because I had called late in the night on other occasions in my life, she thought I was in trouble; so I said, 'No, Mom, everything's okay, but I must talk to Dad.'"

She handed the telephone to her sleepy husband, who said, "Yes, Son, what is it?"

The missionary son said, "Dad, I love you. I want you to know how much I love you."

His father began to sob and handed the telephone back to his wife, who demanded, "What did you tell your father?"

He said, "Mom, I told Dad how much I love him, and I want you to know how much I love you." Then there was crying on both ends of the line.

Brothers and sisters, if you love and appreciate someone, it is a matter of integrity to communicate that fact, because it is not said often enough. I was speaking at a single adults conference in California a few weeks ago about this very topic when an individual jumped up and ran out of the meeting. I am fairly used to having that happen when I speak, so I was not alarmed; but he came back, and that was surprising. Afterwards we talked for a few minutes, and I asked, "Why did you leave?"

He explained: "It has been several years since I told my father I love him, and I couldn't wait until the end of the talk." He had run out and said, "Dad, I love you."

Whom have you thanked today? One of the things we tried to do in the mission field was to say "thank you" to someone each day, to express appreciation to someone deserving. What other words need to be said and said more often? These: "I know that the gospel of Jesus Christ is true and that Joseph Smith is a prophet of God." When seventeen years of age, I took a date to the Garden Park Ward in Salt Lake City to a sacrament meeting followed by a fireside. Elder Richard L. Evans was the speaker. I cannot remember his topic nor any of his words, except that he said, "Young friends, the gospel of Jesus Christ is true." Those words pierced me like a sword; they were exactly the right words at the right time for a young man who was searching and stumbling. Someone needs to hear you say those words and to observe you living the way that you know you should live. Bear your testimony often; bear it to those nearby, because sometimes it is those nearby who need you the most.

I am reminded of the story that Elder L. Tom Perry shared with us just a few weeks ago at general conference time. It took place in the mid-seventies shortly after he had lost his first wife. Before one of the sessions of general conference he looked over where the wives usually sit, and of course his wife's chair was vacant; she was not there. He stood up, ran outside the Tabernacle, and said, "I want to bring someone inside who would not have an opportunity to attend conference today." Accordingly, he went right to the end of the line, found a lovely young lady, and introduced himself. After she had introduced herself as a student from Ricks College, he brought her inside and gave her the privilege of sitting in the seat that his wife would have occupied were she alive. During the session, he glanced over to look at her and observed tears streaming down her face. Afterward he went over and said, "I noticed that you were crying."

"I had lost my testimony," she explained. "I thought, 'One last chance—I'm going to come to Salt Lake to attend general conference, and perhaps then I'll know the gospel is true'; and then you came out and singled me from the crowd, brought me in, and sat me here. Even though I appreciate the great words that were spoken this day, it was your kindly act that let me know the gospel of Jesus Christ is true." Each conference time, she writes a letter to Elder Perry, thanking him for his kindness.

Fourth, there are characteristics that need to be developed. What are they? The first is this: courage. I would suspect that a number of you know Jim Moss; he teaches here. I would like to share with you two instances of courage from his life in order that you will know by his example what I mean .

The first occurred at that educational institution north of here by some forty-five miles—Brigham Young established that school also, I hasten to add. Jim was student body president there; and, because there are so many there that do not believe or do not understand, he searched for a way to teach the gospel of Jesus Christ. The idea came to Jim to honor President David O. McKay as one of their great graduates. He shared that with other student leaders, many of whom were not members of the Church, and they too became enthusiastic. So for one week, the life of David O. McKay, the things that he had taught, and the things that he knew to be true were written in the student newspaper, the *Daily Chronicle.* In a mass teaching effort, thousands learned something about the gospel of Jesus Christ because of the courage of Jim Moss, whose imaginative mind wanted to teach the gospel to others.

I will tell you another story about Jim. After a marvelous mission, he finished an outstanding career as an undergraduate. From there he went to Stanford, graduated in law, and received many fine offers to labor in top law firms. But Jim wanted to teach young people, and so from law school he became a seminary teacher. Now, of course, he is blessing us by his time here.

Another example of courage happened just a few days ago. While I was in one of our great Eastern cities, a young woman came to me and said, "This will be the most difficult half-hour I have ever spent; but I want to go on a mission, and I have not lived a worthy life. I must tell you what I have done; I must confess."

As we sat there, the tears fell from her eyes as she told of a life that had been very difficult. Her relations with her father were almost unbelievable. She had experienced difficulty all through junior high school, high school, and college. But she wanted to live the way she knew she could, the way the Savior wanted her to live; she wanted to tell others about this great gospel of Jesus Christ. Therefore, with all the courage she had and in a very awkward way, she confessed in order that she might serve and live free.

Another example: A missionary in Pennsylvania came to me and said, "President, there is something I have not confessed—when I was a young man, I often stole."

"How much did you steal, Elder?"

"Oh, five or six hundred dollars worth of merchandise and sometimes money."

"Can you remember when you stole and from whom you stole?"

"Yes, I can."

I said, "Then pay it back." The Spirit whispered to both of us that that is what he needed to do. "That means, Elder, that you can't serve as a leader since you can't have an automobile, because every time you have another three or four or five dollars, you're to send it home."

He replied, "I understand, President." Because of his family and other personal considerations, he said, "I can't go to the people I stole from until I return. Would you mail the money back to them?" I said yes; and so I sent envelopes to my friends living in Chicago, New York, Pittsburgh, St. Louis, and other cities, who would then forward the money in plain envelopes postmarked in cities far distant from where this elder was laboring.

About a year ago, I had the opportunity of sealing that young man in the temple; and one of the things he said was that the day his life really changed was when he had made full restitution. The Lord blessed him; he needed him to serve as a leader, but not for many months, because he needed to pay back that which he had taken.

Another characteristic that we must develop is that of personal authenticity. A number of years ago, at Universal International Studios, I watched the filming of television programs and movies. It was delightful, with one exception. Everything that I saw was false—the sheriff's office, the jail, even the running rivers and sagebrush were made from plastic. As I was observing this artificiality, a beautiful young television star came up and asked, "How do you like what you see here?"

"I love it," I answered, "and I'm enjoying myself; but I'm sort of disappointed because everything is false."

She looked up and said, "But that's why we must be so real. The audience must focus on us."

And then I thought, "Oh, how true that is with life!" Almost everything we see outside in the world, brothers and sisters, is false; it is misdirected. That is why we must be so real, why we must be so honest, why integrity must be tattooed upon the spirits of us all.

In conclusion, brothers and sisters, there are acts that need doing. You are the most adequately trained college people the world has ever known. You have not only the finest training available, but also the gospel of Jesus Christ; these form a combination that cannot be found anywhere else. Therefore, the acts that you do today, tomorrow, and forever will affect countless others. What are these acts? The first is this: Being worthy. Staying worthy is a daily task. One of the saddest situations that I have observed lately is that of a marvelous man—top in his field, a wonderful Church leader—who, within twenty minutes during a period of discouragement, injured himself, hurt all of us that know him and love him, injured those in his profession, and impeded the direction of the kingdom. He did not work to remain worthy every day. He slipped just once.

I am sure a number of you are familiar with John Greenleaf Whittier's poem "Maud Muller," which tells the story of a farm girl who had fallen in love with an attorney. (Dallin, that is a dangerous procedure at any time.) The attorney thought, "Well, perhaps I'd be more comfortable at home"; and she thought, "Well, I know I'll be more comfortable with my friends in the rural setting." Despite their love for each other, they did not marry. The years quickly came and went as they do, brothers and sisters, and the poem ends this way:

> God pity them both! and pity us all,
> Who vainly the dreams of youth recall.
> For of all sad words of tongue or pen,
> The saddest are these: "It might have been!" [1856, stanza 53]

So many "might have been's" in life are tied directly to our remaining worthy.

It has been said that when your heart tells you things of which your mind is not sure, the Spirit is guiding you. If you will live the gospel of Jesus Christ every day, your future will be exciting and peaceful, and all of your innate potentialities will be realized.

What are some of the other acts that need doing? Life is here to be lived. Jump in; never stand off at the side, watching things happen. It is far better to be an awkward, struggling performer than to be a secure observer. Just the very act of living life should make our time on earth exciting, meaningful, and full of learning.

Another act that needs doing is the seeking out and developing of meaningful friendships and relationships. Some of my most enjoyable hours are spent with friends that I met when I was your age. Dr. H. Gill Hilton, Dr. Barbara Vance, Dr. James T. Duke, and a number of others at this institution are friends from twenty and twenty-five years ago. I shudder sometimes as I wonder, "What if those relationships had not been developed? What if those delightful people had not made the effort to be friends to me, and what if I had not expended the energy to earn their friendships?" These acts that require an expenditure of energy are the acts that need doing.

The great battles of this world often are not fought on the front lines but back in the general's tent, where tears are shed as difficult decisions are made that mean the expenditure of lives and equipment. Still, those battles must be fought. Your great battles should not be fought in the back seat of automobiles when sexual temptations or moral conflicts are at their strongest; these great battles should be fought and problems overcome back in the general's tent. You must decide ahead of time how you are going to live; after the decision is made, all is easy. You will be able to travel in circles of people anywhere and feel secure, because you know that you will live the Word of Wisdom. Financially you will be secure because you know you will live an honest life and pay your tithes and offerings. You know from this moment on that you will live a secure life sexually because you have decided that there is a time and a place for everything. Make those decisions now, brothers and sisters, so that when you are on the battlefield all of the tough decisions will have already been made.

I would like to finish by sharing an experience that I had here last December. I came down at Christmastime and spoke to a small group of students, and sometime during my talk I made this comment: "The Lord forgives us in a millionth of a millisecond." I had talked of repentance, but only for a moment. Afterward a young man came up and said, "I don't believe I'm forgiven; I don't think what you said is right, Elder Pinnock."

I replied. "It is. Well, perhaps I made a mistake: the Savior forgives us instantly. It doesn't even take him a millionth of a millisecond."

The young man faded away, and I went out and got into the automobile and drove home. Several days later the telephone rang and he reintroduced himself. "I'm the young man that questioned whether I had been forgiven or not."

I said, "You were forgiven, if . . ." and we reviewed the steps.

"Oh yes," he said. "I've talked to my bishop. I have not reverted to those things I did before."

"Then you are forgiven," I told him.

But the telephone rang once again. This time I said, "Listen, dummy, you are forgiven." But oh, how he wanted that feeling, and what a struggle he was having to obtain it!

Perhaps one of the acts that we need to do even today is to clear our life from the seaweed that sometimes hangs onto it. If your transgression was serious, go to your bishop and talk with him; bishops are a marvelously equipped group of men serving the Master. You are not fair to your spirit, you are not fair to your friends or to your eternal self, and you are certainly not fair to the Savior if you carry upon your shoulders unresolved sins. May I finish by pleading with you to put your lives in order and to do all the things that we have discussed today and the other things that you know you must do, in the name of Jesus Christ, our Master. Amen.

Hugh W. Pinnock was a member of the First Quorum of the Seventy when this devotional address was given in the Marriott Center on 29 May 1979.

"Earth's Crammed with Heaven": Reminiscences

LeGRAND RICHARDS

I GREET ALL of you wonderful students and your teachers here this morning and tell you how proud I am of all of you and of this great institution and of your desire to be here for what this institution can offer to you. I appreciate the music and I appreciate that lovely prayer by Brother Ricks; I need it badly. So I pray the Lord will bless me while I stand here this morning.

In trying to think what I might say to you that would be of most interest, I decided that I would not preach doctrine to you. (I could do that—if you do not believe it, read *A Marvelous Work and a Wonder* and *Israel! Do You Know?*) I imagine that I might be the oldest person here this morning (there could be others, but I doubt that), so I figure that I have seen more things during my period of mortality than any of you have. You know that it is a habit of old people to reminisce—I thought that first I would tell you a few things out of ancient history; and then, with all these missionaries over here, I might end up with some missionary stories.

First, you have already been told by President Oaks that I am the oldest living General Authority. I want to tell you that I have known all of the General Authorities of this Church since the days of Wilford Woodruff, and I think I have heard all these Brethren preach. That is a good many General Authorities when you count all the members of the Twelve that there have been, and all the presidents of the Church. My father raised us in the country, out in Tooele, and there never passed a conference after we were old enough to sit still when he did not bring his boys—three of us—in to attend the general conferences. Of course, we did not have automobiles in those days, nor paved roads; but with the old white-top and our team we would drive in. My father wanted his boys to know all of the General Authorities of the Church, so he wanted us to attend all the conferences so we could hear them speak.

I was in the Salt Lake Tabernacle when Wilford Woodruff delivered what I think was the last talk he gave before he died, that in which he told how marvelously the Spirit of the Lord had guided and directed him through the years of his life. It has been more than eighty years ago, but I can remember to this day some of the things that he spoke in that conference. I am going to mention a couple of them; you have heard them, but I heard *him* give them.

While he was traveling with his wife in the South, once in the middle of the night the Spirit said, "Get up and move your team and wagon." He got up out of his wagon and moved his team from where it was tied to an oak—then along came a twister and picked that oak up and threw it right where his wagon had been standing. That oak had stood a hundred years, and yet while he was in his wagon that night a twister came and picked it up. And I can hear Brother Woodruff saying, "If I hadn't listened to the promptings of the Spirit of the Lord, it might have cost us our lives." Then he told, in that same conference, about bringing a group of converts from Great Britain. They landed down in New Orleans, and he was negotiating with a captain there to take them up the river to St. Louis, where they had arranged to cross the plains to these valleys of the mountains. And, he said, while he was negotiating, something said, "Don't go on that boat, neither you nor your people." So he thanked the captain and they did not embark. That boat had no more than sailed up the river when it caught fire and burned, and not a soul on it was saved. And I can hear President Woodruff as he stood there, all these eighty years ago, saying, "If I hadn't listened to the promptings of the spirit of the Lord, we wouldn't have had Brother So-and-So [naming one of the good Brethren] and Brother So-and-So"—another of the good Brethren who was with him in that group he brought from Europe.

Well, there are things one never forgets. There are impressions in my youth that have remained with me from that time to the present. My grandmother was the wife of Dr. Willard Richards, who was in Carthage Jail with the Prophet (you may have heard this story), and at that time the Prophet turned to Dr. Richards and said, "If we go into the cell, will you go in with us?" And Willard said, "Brother Joseph, you did not ask me to cross the river with you—you did not ask me to come to Carthage—you did not ask me to come to jail with you. . . . But I will tell you what I will do; if you are condemned to be hung for treason, I will be hung in your stead." But the Prophet said, "You cannot" (*HC* 6:616). I have a copy of a letter that the Prophet wrote in which he said that he had found a man who could be trusted in all things, and that man was Dr. Willard Richards.

When I came home from my first mission in 1908 my grandmother was still alive, and when I visited with her I said, "Grandma, tell me about the Prophet Joseph." And she told me what a wonderful man he was and how the people loved him and how he loved them; she told me how he used to take little children on his lap and sing to them and tell them stories; and then she told me about being in the meeting when Sidney Rigdon claimed that he ought to succeed the Prophet. She said, "When Brigham Young stood up he looked like the Prophet Joseph, he sounded like the Prophet Joseph, and we all knew who the Lord wanted to succeed the Prophet as the president of the Church." These are experiences of the past that have meant much to me in my life (even though I don't know what to say next).

Now I will skip to 1906, when my father was called to be a member of the Quorum of the Twelve. There were three men appointed in that same conference, in this order: George F. Richards (my father), Orson F. Whitney, and David O. McKay. I was at that time serving as the secretary of the Netherlands Mission, and just a few days before that conference was held, I received a letter from my father that read like this: "My son, I had a remarkable dream last night. I dreamed that the Savior came and took me in his arms, and as I found me in my Master's embrace, the love that filled my heart can't be compared with the love that a man feels for a woman. I feel the meaning of the words of the song 'I Need Thee Every Hour.'"

Then, just two or three days after I received that letter, a cablegram came to our office, the mission headquarters. It was addressed to President Grant, who was then president of the European Mission, and he was up in Berlin. We used to open the telegrams to see if they were important enough to try to relay. As for this telegram, I can quote you the exact words. It read this way: "Cowley and Taylor deposed. Richards, Whitney, and McKay appointed." When I read that, I figured that the dream my father had just had, of which I had just received word in that letter, was to let him know that he was being called by revelation.

President Grant was due in Rotterdam the next morning, so I went to the station to meet him. I handed him the telegram—I had sealed it up again—and he opened and read it, and he said, "Well, well. Cowley and Taylor deposed. Richards, Whitney, and McKay appointed." Then he said, "I wonder who this Richards could be." I could have told him but I waited for him to tell me. "There's your father, your Uncle Charlie, your Uncle Franklin"—and then he said, "I guess it's your daddy; Brother Lyman thinks he's the salt of the earth." Well, these are experiences that one does not usually forget. (Let's see what I want to tell you next.)

Out in the little country town where I was raised we used to have Sunday School conferences. I do not know whether we have them anymore. But I can remember a conference held there about eighty years ago when the visiting brethren from the Sunday School General Board were Brother Karl G. Maeser and Brother George Goddard. I thought I would mention that because of the fact that Brother Karl G. Maeser was the man who organized this institution under the direction of President Brigham Young. I cannot remember to this day what Brother Maeser preached about in that conference, but I can remember old Brother George Goddard with his great singing voice and long beard, and I can remember the songs he taught us to sing in that conference. The first one—I do not think it is in the hymnbook anymore—went like this: "Take away the whiskey, the coffee, and the tea, cold water is the drink for me," and then it repeats and goes on. That made such an impression upon me as a boy that I can hardly drink anything but cold water. I was traveling on the train headed for Los Angeles a few years back, and I went into the diner for breakfast and the waiter said, "Are you ready for your coffee?"

"No, thank you."

"Would you like a glass of milk?"

"No, thank you."

"What do you want to drink?"

I said, "A glass of cold water, please."

He said, "You're the funniest man I ever did see."

The next song that Brother Goddard taught us to sing in that Sunday School conference (that was when I did not know that I could not sing, so I tried to sing with them) is still in the hymnbook. It goes like this: "Who's on the Lord's side? Who?" (*Hymns,* no. 175; 1985, no. 260). And, brothers and sisters, right there as a boy I resolved, the Lord being my help, that I'd try to be on his side as long as I lived.

I was up in Wyoming some years ago talking in a conference of the young people, and between the morning and afternoon meetings—we used to hold an afternoon meeting then—a little fellow about six or eight years old came up and, looking up into my face, asked, "Bishop, could I shake your hand?"

I said, "I can't think of anything I'd rather do than shake yours."

And while we were shaking on it, he looked up into my face, and he said, "Bishop, my bishop will never need to worry about losing me." I could have hugged the little fellow. Isn't it wonderful to think that this little boy, in his youth, had resolved that he would be on the Lord's side all the days of his life? Well, these are great experiences. (Let's see what else I want to tell you.)

Now I think I'll skip over some of my missionary experiences. This one might interest you. While I was laboring as a district president in Amsterdam on my first mission, my companion and I were invited to the home of one of the Saints. She wanted to invite her neighbor in and wanted us to come and teach her the gospel. When we arrived, the neighbor was there, but she had brought her minister along with her to make sure that we told her the right things. Well, the minister and I had a little difference of opinion on the subject of priesthood, and right there he challenged me to a debate in his church. In those days we were not advised not to debate, and so I accepted the challenge—I was young and had plenty of fight in me.

When we arrived at his church a week from Saturday night, the church was full; all of his people were there, and all of our people. How our people had found out about it I do not know. I had not told them. I think he had spread the word around, thinking to show us up. But at any rate, he stood up and said, "Inasmuch as Mister Richards is a guest in our church we'll accord him the privilege of opening the debate, and we'll each talk for twenty minutes and continue as long as it's mutually agreeable." He asked, "Is that agreeable to you, Mister Richards?"

And I said, "Very much." I did not tell him that I would have given him the shirt off my back for the privilege of opening that debate, and he had just handed it to me on a silver platter. I did not know whether the Lord had anything to do with that or not, but I thought he did.

I stood up and said, "The last time I talked to my friend, we had a difference of opinion in regard to the principle of the priesthood. I've come tonight prepared to discuss that subject, but I do not propose to start with that subject." This is a device that has helped me in my work: I said, "If you were going to build a house, you wouldn't try to put the roof on it before you got the foundation in, would you? Because if the foundation were faulty the house would tumble anyway, so what good would the house be? I propose to open this debate tonight by laying the foundation of the gospel of Jesus Christ, and I choose for my text the sixth chapter of Hebrews, where Paul said,

> Therefore leaving the principles of the doctrine of Christ, let us go on unto perfection; not laying again the foundation of repentance from dead works, and of faith toward God,
>
> Of the doctrine of baptisms, and of laying on of hands, and of resurrection of the dead, and of eternal judgment. [Hebrews 6:1–2]

I hurried over faith and repentance; I assumed that they believed that. I preached baptism by immersion for the remission of sins until everybody in the audience was giving me accord. Then it came to the laying on of hands for the gift of the Holy Ghost, and they did not believe that. They thought the Holy Ghost just came, like the breezes that blow from the heavens.

I reminded them that when the apostles at Jerusalem heard that Samaria had accepted the word of God through the preaching of Philip, they sent Peter and John. When these apostles arrived, they prayed for the people, then laid their hands upon them, and the people received the Holy Ghost. When Simon the sorcerer saw that the Holy Ghost was conveyed by the laying on of the apostles' hands, he offered them money, saying, "Give me also this power, that on whomsoever I lay hands, he may receive the Holy Ghost." And Peter said, "Thy money perish with thee, because thou hast thought that the gifts of God may be purchased with money" (see Acts 8:14–20). Then I gave two or three other references on laying on of hands and I sat down.

The minister stood up. He never mentioned a word I had said. He started expounding on a few of the bad things that our enemies had said against us and then said, in the most courteous manner, "Now, if Mister Richards will enlighten us on these matters I'm sure this audience will be most appreciative."

I was on my feet just like that. (My companion later asked how I could think so fast; I responded, "What have you been praying for all week long?") I stood up and said, "In the days of the Savior his enemies tried to trick him with cunning and craftiness. I don't suppose there's anyone here today who'd like to see us resort to those old tactics. If I understand a debate, it's a presentation and answering of argument. Has this man answered any of my arguments?" All shook their heads negatively. "All right, my friend," I said, "you may have your twenty minutes over again."

He would not do it. I knew he could not. His wife, who was in the audience, stood up and said, "What Mister Richards is asking is fair. You ought to answer him." And even then he would not do it.

I said to my companions, "Stand up. Give me my coat and hat." (It was winter.) "One more chance," I announced. "I am willing to remain here till ten o'clock tomorrow morning, when I have to be in my own church, provided this debate can go forward on the basis that you have set up. If not, I am going to leave and ask my companion to leave and ask our people to leave, and I shall leave it with you to settle with your people for what has happened here today." And still he would not do it. So we all walked out on him. I met him on the street time and time again after that and he would duck his head so that he would not have to speak to me. Well, that is one of my little experiences there. (Let's see what else I want here.)

Now I'll tell you one of a little more recent vintage. A year ago last June, I was asked to accompany the presidency to Denver to hold a solemn assembly, and after that we went down to Farmington, New Mexico, to hold a solemn assembly there. As we were headed back to Denver to return from there, our plane landed at Alamosa with something wrong. The captain announced that we would not take off until some repair parts were shipped in from Denver, and we could either stay in the plane or go into the airport. We chose to stay. The First Presidency sat right in the front of the plane, I sat next to them, and Brother Neal Maxwell sat on the other side with one of the regional representatives of the Twelve, Brother Patterson. Then the captain came out of his cockpit, and since he knew we were all Mormons he said something about it. Brother Tanner of the First Presidency spoke up and said, "You better not let LeGrand start on him." (I'm LeGrand, you see.) That opened the door. And so I started on him.

"Captain, I can tell you two reasons why you could not be anything but a Latter-day Saint if you would just use your thinker and if you are willing to believe in the words of the holy prophets and the Savior of the world." So I told him what those two things were. They are in the forepart of *A Marvelous Work and a Wonder* that I wrote. The first was this: One of our broadcasters, Edmund C. Hill, was asked what message could be broadcast to the world that would be of greater importance than any other message, and after considering the matter he decided that to be able to say to the world that a man who had lived upon this earth had returned again with a message from God would be the greatest message that could be broadcast. I said, "The Latter-day Saints are the only ones that claim such a visit, not only of one man, but many of the holy prophets, and we built a monument back in New York to the honor of one of those men who returned again with a message from God. That was Moroni."

The other point was the statement of a Catholic prelate who visited in Salt Lake. Brother Orson F. Whitney told about his visit—he said he could speak a dozen different languages and knew all about science and religion. The prelate's comment was this:

> "You Mormons are all ignoramuses. You don't even know the strength of your own position. It is so strong that there is only one other tenable in the whole Christian world, and that is the position of the Catholic Church. . . . If we are right, you are wrong; if you are right, we are wrong; and that's all there is to it. The Protestants haven't a leg to stand on. For, if we are wrong, they are wrong with us, since they . . . went out from us; while if we are right, they are apostates whom we cut off long ago." [Quoted in LeGrand Richards, *A Marvelous Work and a Wonder* (Salt Lake City: Deseret Book Company, 1988), p. 3]

That is a good statement—anybody who stops to analyze it would find it as fine a definite statement of fact as can be spoken. That is why I quoted it to that captain.

The prelate went on to say, "If we have the apostolic succession from St. Peter, as we claim, there is no need of Joseph Smith and Mormonism; but if we have not that succession, then such a man as Joseph Smith was necessary." I always add that the Catholic church and the Bible cannot both be right because the Bible definitely declares an apostasy and a restoration in the latter days; that leaves The Church of Jesus Christ of Latter-day Saints with the only right in the world to claim to be the true church of Jesus Christ. (I still have a few minutes. Why don't you kick me on the heel if I start going too long?)

Coming back to Dr. Hart, the pilot—that talk, instead of lasting just a few minutes, lasted for two hours. He had studied for the ministry and then decided to become a pilot instead of a minister. He asked, "What if I don't join your Church in this life?"

"Oh," I said, "that's all right. We'll just let you sleep in the dirt for five hundred years, a half of a thousand, and we'll come and preach it to you in the spirit world." And when I parted with him I told him I would send him a copy of *A Marvelous Work and a Wonder,* the missionary book, if he would promise to read it, and he said he would. So he gave me his name and address, and I said, "The next time I meet you, you'll be an elder in the Mormon church."

The little stewardess was sitting right next to us, and I said, "How do you feel about spiritual things?"

"Well," she said, "I was raised a Catholic but I don't feel satisfied with my church."

I asked, "Would you like me to send you one of these books?" She said she would and wrote down her name and address.

Then one of the passengers sitting in the back of the compartment came up and asked, "Could I get one of those books?"

And I said, "You surely could." So he gave me his name and address.

Later, when we landed in Denver, another man came up, saw me hobbling with my cane, and inquired, "Where did you get that cane?"

I said, "I know where I got it, but I can't tell you the address or the name of the company. If you will give me your name and your address I'll write you from Salt Lake and tell you." Then, when he began to leave, I said, "Well, you don't get off that easy. I'm a Mormon elder, and I want to tell you what we believe. If you will just read the book I'm going to send you, you will want to join the Church."

Well, to make the story short, I sent the names to the mission president. He sent the missionaries to them, but the pilot would not let them give any of the lessons. He said, "All I need is this *Marvelous Work and a Wonder* and the Book of Mormon." So just before last June 1, he called me from over in Littleton, Colorado, where he lives, and told me he had set his baptismal date for the first day of June. Last week I received a letter from him, and in this letter—I am going to take time to read just one paragraph of it to show you what it means to call people out of darkness to the Lord's true light. Like Peter said of the Church of his day, "But ye are a chosen generation, a royal priesthood, a holy nation, a peculiar people." Why? "That ye should shew forth the praises of him who hath called you out of darkness into his marvellous light" (1 Peter 2:9). This is the one paragraph:

> The happiness I've experienced in my heart and soul since joining the Church is indescribable. I feel that meeting I had with you and President Kimball really set things into motion for me. Prior to that I had just been spinning my wheels and searching. Now I know that through the discovery of the restored truth of our Lord my life has meaning and direction. I want to work for him and do his will.

Then he went on to tell me that he had just baptized one of his daughters, that four of his family are attending our Church with him—his wife and two older daughters have not yet capitulated, but he said he would get them—and then, in the last paragraph, he asked if I would ordain him an elder next May. I suppose he had talked with the stake president, and the stake president had indicated that by May he would be ready to be an elder; and, you know, these pilots can probably fly anywhere for nothing. He said he would come to Salt Lake. So I wrote him back and told him that if he would bring a letter of recommendation from his stake president I would be glad to ordain him.

All many people need is to have someone lay things out for them so that they can understand them. I have another little story to illustrate what I mean. I toured the Colorado Mission with Brother Hinckley, a former stake president who lives here in Provo. We were holding a meeting over in Nebraska, and the leader of the Reorganized church in that particular locality honored us with his presence in the meeting, and I went up to him afterward. He seemed very interested, and I said, "You have so much to be grateful for. You have the Prophet Joseph, and you have the Book of Mormon, but you only have about half of what the Prophet Joseph taught. Wouldn't you like to know all about it? You have half a pie; we have the whole pie. I have written a book. If you will agree to read it, I'll send it to you."

A few weeks after that I received a letter back from him in which he thanked me for the book. He said, "I read it, and last Saturday my brother and I were both baptized members of your Church. Now I have sent the book to one of my friends over in Independence, one of the leaders of the Reorganized church, and asked him if he would read it." If we will just take time to tell them what we have, we do not need to worry about their joining the Church. (Let's see what else I want to tell you.)

Just a few years ago we converted a Reverend Cooke from up in the northwest—the state of Washington. He wrote a letter to my brother, who was then president of the Northwestern States Mission, in which he said, "I have always thought that I had as much authority as any man to administer the ordinances of the gospel—until I met the Mormon elders. Now I have come to feel that I must accept baptism at their hands." Then, after he was baptized, he came down to Salt Lake and to my office and said this: "When I joined the Church I did not feel I could say that I knew that Joseph Smith was a prophet, but I believed that he was. But when Brother Burroughs [and I know Brother Burroughs up there] laid his hands on my head and ordained me to the priesthood I felt something go through me like I never had felt before in all my life, and I knew that no man could do that for me. It must have come from the Lord." Then he continued, "When I think of how little I had to offer my people as a Methodist minister compared with what I now have in the fullness of the gospel as it has been restored, I want to go back and tell my friends what I have found. Now they won't listen to me; I am an apostate from their church." But he had given up his ministry (and that is an honorable calling) to run the elevator in our state capitol building so that he could join the Church. Through the window in my office he pointed to the temple and said, "I can't wait until I can go there with my wife. I want to be sure I have her forever." That is what it is when people really love truth and are called out of darkness, as Peter said, unto the Lord's true light.

While I was president of a stake in California we converted a very prominent attorney, and in one of our stake conferences I asked him if he would like to tell the people what he found in Mormonism that appealed to him. He had a deep, rich voice that just penetrated a person; he stood up and said, "If you have hunted for something all your life until you have nearly decided that it does not exist, and then you just happen to stumble onto it, you do not need anybody to tell you what you have found, do you? That is what I did when I found Mormonism." And he added, "The most beautiful thing about it to me is that the more I learn about it, the more wonderful it becomes." I have since had the privilege of setting his son apart to go on his mission. I feel such a close contact with that family that when that son wanted to marry down in the Los Angeles Temple, I consented to go down and perform the marriage for him at his request. I do not usually do that away from Salt Lake.

Brothers and sisters, the gospel is true. We now have one of our greatest leaders that I have known, and I have known them intimately from President Joseph F. Smith through Heber J. Grant, George Albert Smith, David O. McKay, and Joseph Fielding Smith to Harold B. Lee—and now we have Spencer W. Kimball. I was thrilled with Brother Grant Bangerter's talk at the conference where he indicated, "We thought we couldn't get along without Brother Lee. He was a great man and a great leader, but look what we've got today" (see "A Special Moment in Church History," *Ensign,* November 1977, pp. 26–27). God bless that noble man. It is a miracle that he is able to do what he is doing, considering the trials he has had through the years of his life.

Now, I see, it is time to close. I know this is God's eternal truth. My, how happy I am to be a member of his Church, to bear the name of Christ the Lord! I have just been reading the New Testament again; what miracles he performed, and yet all around us are miracles every day that just thrill me. As Elizabeth Barrett Browning said (and I've quoted her before):

> Earth's crammed with heaven,
> And every common bush afire with God;
> But only he who sees takes off his shoes;
> The rest sit round it and pluck blackberries.
> [*Aurora Leigh,* book 7, lines 820–23]

God help us to take off our shoes and be true to the faith, I pray, and leave you my blessing in the name of the Lord Jesus Christ. Amen. (Thank you for your attention. I went over a little.)

LeGrand Richards was a member of the Quorum of the Twelve Apostles of The Church of Jesus Christ of Latter-day Saints when this devotional address was given in the Marriott Center on 11 October 1977.

America's Fate and Ultimate Destiny

MARION G. ROMNEY

THIS YEAR BEING our nation's bicentennial anniversary, and the Fourth of July being but two months away, I have thought it might be appropriate to give some consideration to our country's fate and her ultimate destiny.

Although I was born and lived for fifteen years in a foreign land, my parents, who were United States citizens, and their fellow colonists always remembered and observed the Fourth of July. The celebration regularly included a flag and bunting parade and an oration commemorating the signing of the Declaration of Independence.

My concept of, and my feelings about, what was going on in and around Independence Hall at the time the declaration was being signed were in my youth—and still are—influenced by the words and the spirit of the poem "Independence Bell, Philadelphia." I memorized it in my youth, and I hope its lines will transmit to you something of my feelings as I read them to you now.

There was tumult in the city,
In the quaint Old Quaker town,
And the streets were rife with people
Pacing restless up and down.—
People gathering at corners,
Where they whispered each to each,
And the sweat stood on their temples
With the earnestness of speech.

As the bleak Atlantic currents
Lash the wild Newfoundland shore,
So they beat against the State House,
So they surged against the door;
And the mingling of their voices
Made a harmony profound,
Till the quiet street of Chestnut
Was all turbulent with sound.

"Will they do it?" "Dare they do it?"
"Who is speaking?" "What's the news?"
"What of Adams?" "What of Sherman?"
"Oh, God grant they won't refuse!"
"Make some way, there!" "Let me nearer!"
"I am stifling!" "Stifle, then!
When a nation's life's at hazard,
We've no time to think of men!"

So they beat against the portal,
Man and woman, maid and child;
And the July sun in heaven
On the scene looked down and smiled:
The same sun that saw the Spartan
Shed his patriot blood in vain,
Now beheld the soul of freedom,
All unconquered, rise again.

See! See! The dense crowd quivers
Through all its lengthy line,
As the boy beside the portal
Looks forth to give the sign!
With his little hands uplifted,

Breezes dallying with his hair,
Hark! with deep, clear intonation,
Breaks his young voice on the air.

Hushed the people's swelling murmur,
List the boy's exultant cry!
"Ring!" he shouts, "Ring! Grandpa,
Ring! oh, ring for Liberty!"
Quickly at the given signal
The bell-man lifts his hand,
Forth he sends the good news, making
Iron music through the land.

How they shouted! What rejoicing!
How the old bell shook the air,
Till the clang of freedom ruffled
The calmly gliding Delaware!
How the bonfires and the torches
Lighted up the night's repose,
And from the flames, like fabled Phoenix,
Our glorious Liberty arose!

That old State House bell is silent,
Hushed is now its clamorous tongue;
But the spirit it awakened
Still is living,—ever young;
And when we greet the smiling sunlight
On the Fourth of each July,
We will ne'er forget the bell-man
Who, betwixt the earth and sky,
Rung out, loudly, "INDEPENDENCE;"
Which, please God, *shall never die!*

[Anonymous, in Robert Haven Shauffler, *Independence Day* (New York: Dodd, Mead and Company, 1924), pp. 112–14]

I hope each of you, and I, have like feelings about this great land of America, about the Declaration of Independence, and about the Constitution of the United States.

In God's economy, America is now and has always been a choice and favored land. God has decreed for her a final, great, and glorious destiny. Here Zion is to be established and the New Jerusalem is to be built. From here the law of God shall go forth to all nations.

America received her first consecration as a favored land when the Lord planted here the Garden of Eden as a habitation for Adam and Eve.

A thousand years later Enoch's Zion flourished here.

And then some six hundred years thereafter this land was deluged by the Flood and left uninhabited, so far as human beings were concerned, until the Lord led to this land from the Tower of Babel a colony of people, the Jaredites, declaring as he led them that he was bringing them to a "land of promise, . . . choice above all other lands" and "that whoso should possess this land . . . from that time henceforth and forever, should serve him, the true and only God, or they should be swept off when the fulness of his wrath should come upon them" (Ether 2:7–8).

Here in this land these people, the Jaredites, built a nation of which the Lord said, "There shall be none greater . . . upon . . . the face of the earth" (Ether 1:43). They dwelt here for some two thousand years. Finally, however, they ripened in iniquity and were, pursuant to God's decree, swept off the land in a fratricidal war.

Six hundred years B.C., as time was running out for the Jaredites, the Lord brought to this land Lehi and his colony. Before they arrived here the Lord said to them, as he had said to the Jaredites, "Inasmuch as ye shall keep my commandments, ye shall prosper, and shall be led to a land of promise; yea, even a land which I have prepared for you; yea, a land which is choice above all other lands" (1 Nephi 2:20). Simultaneously he warned them that if they did not serve him, they would not prosper in the land but would be cut off from his presence.

The Book of Mormon record testifies to the fact that, when they obeyed the laws of God, they prospered, and that when they did not obey them, they were cut off from the presence of God. Finally the Nephite branch of those people, having ripened in iniquity, was destroyed by the Lamanites, who, under the curse of "their unbelief and idolatry," were scattered and became the people discovered by Columbus when he was led here in 1492 (see Mormon 5:15).

You, of course, know that the facts I have just recited are not to be found in profane history books. Nowhere in all secular history is mention made of America before Columbus. Why? Because this land has been from the beginning reserved by the Lord for those whom he himself would lead here. This we learn from the ancient prophet Lehi.

> I . . . prophesy according to the workings of the Spirit which is in me, that there shall none come into this land save they shall be brought by the hand of the Lord.
>
> Wherefore, this land is consecrated unto him whom he shall bring. And if it so be that they shall serve him according to the commandments which he hath given, it shall be a land of liberty unto them; wherefore, they shall never be brought down into captivity; if so, it shall be because of iniquity; for if iniquity shall abound cursed shall be the land for their sakes, but unto the righteous it shall be blessed forever.
>
> And behold, it is wisdom that this land should be kept as yet from the knowledge of other nations; for . . . many nations would overrun the land. . . .
>
> Wherefore, I, Lehi, have obtained a promise, that inasmuch as *those whom the Lord God shall bring out of the land of Jerusalem* shall keep his commandments, they shall prosper upon the face of this land; and they shall be kept from all other nations, that they may possess this land unto themselves. And if it so be that they shall keep his commandments they shall be blessed upon the face of this land, and there shall be none to molest them, nor to take away the land of their inheritance; and they shall dwell safely forever. [2 Nephi 1:6–9; emphasis added]

This promise Lehi received for his own descendants and for the Mulekites who also came from Jerusalem. (Mulek was the son of Zedekiah—Mosiah 25:2; Helaman 6:10; 8:21.) He followed it, however, with this solemn warning and prophecy:

> Behold, I say, if the day shall come that they [the people who came out from Jerusalem who were the Nephites and the ones

> who came at the time of the Mulekites] will reject the Holy One of Israel, the true Messiah, their Redeemer and their God, behold, the judgments of him that is just shall rest upon them.
>
> Yea, he will bring other nations unto them, and he will give unto them power, and he will take away from them [the descendants of the people who came from Jerusalem] the lands of their possessions [that is, the new nations will take away from them], and he will cause them to be scattered and smitten. [2 Nephi 1:10–11]

This remarkable prophecy not only explains why America was to be discovered only by those whom God should lead here; it also foreshadows the forfeiting by Lehi's descendants of their inheritance and the coming of other nations.

History records that these "other nations" were introduced to this land by Columbus, of whose coming ancient American seers prophesied. As early as 590 B.C., before Lehi made the foregoing prophecy, his son Nephi was given to see in vision Columbus being led by the "Spirit of God" to this promised land. Nephi thus described his vision:

> And I beheld the Spirit of God [before he had ever reached the promised land], that it came down and wrought upon the man; and he went forth upon the many waters, even unto the seed of my brethren, who were in the promised land.
>
> And it came to pass that I beheld the Spirit of God, that it wrought upon other Gentiles; and they went forth out of captivity, upon the many waters.
>
> And it came to pass that I beheld many multitudes of the Gentiles upon the land of promise [among them the Puritans in New England, the Quakers in Pennsylvania, the Catholics in Maryland, the Huguenots in Virginia and the Carolinas, and the Lutherans in Georgia]; and I beheld the wrath of God, that it was upon the seed of my brethren; and they were scattered before the Gentiles and were smitten. [1 Nephi 13:12–14]

Everyone acquainted with colonial and U.S. history knows how the American Indians were scattered and smitten by the Gentiles who came here following Columbus.

Nephi then saw and thus described our colonial history.

> And I beheld the Spirit of the Lord, that it was upon the Gentiles, and they did prosper and obtain the land for their inheritance [that is, the inheritance of the seed of his brethren who had been scattered]. . . .
>
> And it came to pass that I, Nephi, beheld that the Gentiles who had gone forth out of captivity did humble themselves before the Lord; and the power of the Lord was with them [the thirteen original colonies].
>
> And I beheld that their mother Gentiles were gathered together upon the waters, and upon the land also, to battle against them [in the American Revolutionary War].
>
> And I beheld that the power of God was with them, and also that the wrath of God was upon all those that were gathered together against them to battle.
>
> And I, Nephi, beheld that the Gentiles that had gone out of captivity were delivered by the power of God out of the hands of all other nations. [1 Nephi 13:15–19]

We know why the colonies were able to win freedom in the Revolutionary War.

Columbus, of course, knew nothing about this record of Nephi's vision. Nevertheless, he corroborates it. He put on record his convictions that he was divinely led to America. Elder Nephi L. Morris supports this conclusion with quotes from Washington Irving's *The Life and Voyages of Christopher Columbus:*

> "In the latter part of his life, Columbus, when impressed with the sublime events brought about by his agency . . . looked back upon his career with a solemn and superstitious feeling, he attributed his early and irresistible inclination for the sea, and his passion for geographical studies, to an impulse from the deity preparing him for the high decrees he was chosen to accomplish." See Irving, p. 18, vol. 1.

> "When Columbus had formed his theory, it became fixed in his mind with singular firmness, and influenced his entire character and conduct. He never spoke in doubt or hesitation, but with as much certainty as if his eyes had beheld the promised land. No trial or disappointment could divert him from the steady pursuit of his object. A deep religious sentiment mingled with his meditations, and gave him at times a tinge of superstition, but it was of a sublime and lofty kind; he looked upon himself as standing in the hand of heaven, chosen from among men for the accomplishment of his high purpose."...
>
> In the royal presence of Isabella, Irving [his biographer] says (p. 59): "He unfolded his plans with eloquence and zeal for he felt himself, as he afterwards declared, kindled as with a fire from on high, and considered himself the agent chosen of heaven to accomplish the grand design."...
>
> His own son Fernando, in the biography of his father quotes him as saying on one occasion: "God gave me the faith and afterwards the courage so that I was quite willing to undertake the journey."
>
> And the will of Columbus reads thus:
>
> "In the name of the most holy trinity, who inspired me with the idea and afterwards made it perfectly clear to me that I could navigate and go to the Indies from Spain, by traversing the ocean westward." [Nephi Lowell Morris, "Columbus and the Book of Mormon," an address delivered over KSL Radio, Sunday, 1 July 1928, and printed in the *Deseret News,* Saturday, 7 July 1928, section 3, p. VI]

We who live in America today are here because the Lord led Columbus to this land. We dwell here under the same divine decree, however, as did the ancient civilizations, who, being likewise led here, prospered when they obeyed the laws of the God of the land but who finally ripened in iniquity and, pursuant to the Lord's decree, were swept off the land. And be it known that we are as well informed of the decree as were those former inhabitants. The manner in which a knowledge of this decree came to us is as follows:

Moroni, an American prophet-historian who, about A.D. 421, closed the sacred Book of Mormon record now available to us, spent his youth and middle life in the final struggle between his people, the Nephites, and the Lamanites. As the sole surviving Nephite, he spent the rest of his life abridging the two-thousand-year record of the Jaredites. He was therefore familiar with all the lurid details of their demise. With these heartrending scenes and his own experiences upon his mind, he was given in vision a view of us who now dwell here. Knowing that his record would come to us, he wrote as he looked at us in vision:

> Behold, I speak unto you as if ye were present, and yet ye are not. But behold, Jesus Christ hath shown you unto me, and I know your doing. [Mormon 8:35]

> And this [the record that he wrote] cometh unto you . . . *that ye may know the decrees of God*—that ye may repent, and not continue in your iniquities until the fulness come, that ye may not bring down the fulness of the wrath of God upon you as the inhabitants of the land have hitherto done.
>
> Behold, this is a choice land, and whatsoever nation shall possess it shall be free from bondage, and from captivity, and from all other nations under heaven, if they will but serve the God of the land, who is Jesus Christ. [Ether 2:11–12; emphasis added]

Although the foregoing references to America's past are brief and sketchy, they clearly show that she is now and has been from the beginning a favored and choice land in which the Lord has taken a personal and peculiar interest. They make it crystal clear that if destruction or subjugation shall come to us, it will not be by a foreign foe but because we, the inhabitants of the land, shall "have reached a 'fulness of iniquity'" (see J. Reuben Clark, Jr., *Stand Fast by Our Constitution* [Salt Lake City: Deseret Book Company, 1973], p. 183).

But not only has the Almighty reserved America for a righteous people and decreed that her inhabitants shall serve him or be swept off the land; he has also, as indicated at the outset of these remarks, decreed for her a great and marvelous final destiny—namely, that out of her is to go forth to all the world his law.

Isaiah so declared centuries ago when he prophesied:

> It shall come to pass in the last days, that the mountain of the Lord's house shall be established in the top of the mountains, and shall be exalted above the hills; and all nations shall flow unto it.
>
> And many people shall go and say, . . . let us go up to the mountain of the Lord, to the house of the God of Jacob; and he will teach us of his ways, and we will walk in his paths: *for out of Zion shall go forth the law, and the word of the Lord from Jerusalem.* [Isaiah 2:2–3; emphasis added]

Zion, as used in this scripture, means America. In fact, America is Zion. At times the term is used to include both the North and South American continents. In some references the word *Zion* is used to designate the area in and about Jackson County, Missouri, where the New Jerusalem will be built, which city is itself sometimes called Zion. From Zion the law of God shall eventually go forth into all the world.

> It is this fact and this purpose, the building of Zion on this hemisphere, . . . which seem to be the dominant elements in all of God's dealings with them who possess this land. . . .
>
> Thus America's ultimate God-given destiny, planned by the Creator [and by him through Isaiah declared], is that out of her shall go forth the law. [Clark, *Stand Fast,* pp. 174–75]

This destiny no power of men or devils can thwart.

Let us now consider for a moment what the Lord has done since he led Columbus to America to move her toward her divine destiny. Reference has already been made to the early settlers, to the growth of the original colonies, to the Declaration of Independence, and to the success of the colonists in the Revolutionary War through which their declared independence was won. Later on, between 1820 and 1844, the Lord revealed a new and complete dispensation of his gospel that contains the laws of the God of this land, who is Jesus Christ. This was, of course, made imperative by the divine decree that those who dwell here must obey such laws or be swept off the land. His laws have always been given to the inhabitants of America. He gave them to the antediluvians through his prophets from Adam to Noah. He gave them to the Jaredites through the prophets from the brother of Jared to Ether. To the Nephites in a personal visitation and through his prophets from Lehi to Moroni, he revealed his laws. To this generation he has given them anew through his prophet Joseph Smith, Jr.

The giving of these laws, however, would have been abortive without a civil government that would guarantee men the untrammeled exercise of their God-given free agency. Without such a civil government men could not be bound by the laws of God even though they were revealed. As a matter of fact, free agency underlies all of God's laws. It is God's law of liberty. It is the basis of existence.

God wants men to do good, but he never forces them and does not want them to be forced. He placed in and left with them the power of election. When they do good, he honors them because they could have done evil. When they are coerced, they are entitled to no such honor. God allows men to make their own choices, and he has reserved to himself the judgment as to the correctness of their choices.

Free agency has always had rough going, however. Over it the War in Heaven was fought. In the earth it has been abridged by almost all governments, civil and ecclesiastical. Apostate churchmen, kings, and other rulers have from the beginning arrogated judgment unto themselves. They have, contrary to God's law of liberty, preempted man's right, with or without his consent, to determine what would be best for them to do and by every means within their power have undertaken to force men to do their bidding.

> We have learned by sad experience that it is the nature and disposition of almost all men, as soon as they get a little authority, as they suppose, they will immediately begin to exercise unrighteous dominion. [D&C 121:39]

On July 3, 1776, no government on earth guaranteed God's law of liberty; but on July 4, 1776, in the Declaration of Independence, that law was declared anew in the earth.

> Everywhere in America, says John Adams, the people received the Declaration of Independence "as though it was a decree promulgated from heaven." And well they might, for it was a strange and wonderful thing. "Freedom hath been hunted round the globe," wrote Tom Paine. "Asia and Africa have long expelled her. Europe regards her like a stranger, and England hath given her warning to depart. O! receive the fugitive and prepare in time an asylum for mankind." [Hugh Nibley, *The World and the Prophets* (Salt Lake City: Deseret Book Co., 1954), pp. 170–71]

The colonial patriots did receive the fugitive. They fought and won the war of the revolution to obtain freedom. They, under the inspiration of heaven and the interposition of the Almighty, established the Constitution of the United States to secure freedom, God's law of liberty, not only for all Americans but also for all men.

In this manner did God move America into position to fulfill her destiny. That it was *he* who did it, he himself affirms. In 1833 he told his people, who had been scattered by their enemies, to

> continue to importune for redress, and redemption. . . .
>
> According to the laws and constitution of the people, which I have suffered to be established, and should be maintained *for the rights and protection of all flesh* [not just for America], *according to just and holy principles;*
>
> That every man may act in doctrine and principle pertaining to futurity, according to the moral agency which I have given unto him, that every man may be accountable for his own sins in the day of judgment.
>
> Therefore, it is not right that any man should be in bondage one to another.
>
> And for this purpose have I established the Constitution of this land, by the hands of wise men whom I raised up unto this very purpose. [D&C 101:76–80; emphasis added]

In this declaration the Lord reveals three things: (1) that the Constitution of the United States was established by him; (2) that the purpose of it was to protect men in the exercise of their

God-given moral agency; and (3) that every man should eventually, under its just and holy principles, enjoy such protection.

Did time permit, we could with profit consider the Constitutional provisions that guarantee this freedom, which, pursuant to her declared destiny, is to go forth from America to maintain the "rights and protection of all flesh." I refer you who are interested in this divinely established guarantee to the late President J. Reuben Clark, Jr.'s, great speech "America—A Chosen Land of the Lord," which you can find in the book *Stand Fast by Our Constitution* (pp. 173–98).

I think I have now said enough to sustain my thesis that America has from the beginning been, and now is, in God's economy, a choice and favored land, and that he has decreed for her a great destiny. I shall therefore conclude with a statement of these basic facts.

The blessings of our constitutional freedoms were secured for us by the bounty of the Almighty through the patriotism and sacrifices of the founding fathers. They were preserved for us through the suffering and trials of the Civil War. For them we owe a deep debt of gratitude to God and our forebears.

By the grace of God we occupy this land, the blessings of which are unequaled in any other land. It is difficult for us of this generation to fully appreciate these blessings because they were not won by the shedding of our own blood, sweat, and tears, but by that of others.

There are some things, however, that we must no longer fail to appreciate. If we do so, we shall do it at our peril. Chief among these things is man's free agency, which was provided for in the Constitution as it was originally adopted and interpreted. America's destiny requires that the constitutional safeguards of this freedom be appreciated and maintained. It is imperative that they be maintained and observed here in America in order that they may go out from here undiluted to the protection of all flesh. Whether this generation of Americans will live up to its opportunity to obey and preserve them, particularly God's law of liberty—including the gospel of Jesus Christ, who is the God of this land—remains to be seen. If it does not, the wicked among us will be destroyed, as were the wicked preceding the appearance of the risen Lord to the Nephites. God will spare the righteous and raise up another generation in this land, for out of Zion the law of God will go forth.

There are those among us who feel, and perhaps with good cause, that these constitutional freedoms are being, both wittingly and unwittingly, eroded. If this be so, let it be known that with the loss of each constitutional freedom we are surrendering our inheritance in this favored land.

What can we do about it? Let me give you a suggestion in the words of the immortal Lincoln. As I read the word *laws* and I quote him, think of the laws of the gospel and those constitutional laws calculated to preserve our free agency—*God's law of liberty.* Here is the quotation:

> Let every American, every lover of liberty, every well-wisher to his posterity, swear by the blood of the Revolution never to violate in the least particular the laws of the country [and let Latter-day Saints include in that the laws of the gospel of Jesus Christ], and never to tolerate their violation by others. As the patriots of '76 did to the support of the Declaration of Independence, so to the support of the Constitution and the laws [of God], let every American pledge his life, his property and his sacred honour; let every man remember that to violate the law is to trample upon the blood of his fathers and to tear the charter of his own and his children's liberty. Let reverence for the laws be breathed by every American mother to the lisping babe that prattles on her lap. Let it be taught in schools, in seminaries, and in colleges. Let it be written in primers, spelling books, and almanacs. Let it be preached from the pulpits, proclaimed in legislative halls, and enforced in courts of justice. In short, let it become the political religion of the nation. [John Wesley Hill, *Abraham Lincoln—Man of God,* 4th ed. (New York: Putnam, 1930), p. 73]

Now, my beloved brothers and sisters, young and old, let us—who know and believe so much more than others about the fate and ultimate destiny of America—lead the way by precept and example to the realization of that great destiny, I humbly pray. And I leave with you my blessing, in the name of Jesus Christ. Amen.

Marion G. Romney was second counselor in the First Presidency of The Church of Jesus Christ of Latter-day Saints when this fireside address was given in the Marriott Center on 2 May 1976.

Truth

RICHARD G. SCOTT

I HAVE PRAYERFULLY selected my topic for today with the desire that it benefit both student and missionary on this campus. I know what I would communicate but find it difficult to choose appropriate words to underline the principles I would share with you. Therefore, I appreciate most sincerely the prayer that was offered in my behalf at the beginning of this session. I would speak on the topic "How to find and confirm truth, and how to gain the courage to apply that truth in our lives."

Each one of us wants to be a self-sufficient self-starter in life. We realize that to avoid undue dependence on others we must have a platform of absolute truth, something unshakable that provides a foundation when all things whirl and conspire about us. In our university careers, and later on in our professions, we find so many people who would counsel us to take this path or another path; and often that counsel is at variance with teachings we have learned in the Church. Theories of science are proposed that seem at variance with gospel principles. How, then, can we find for sure that which is true? I have found in my life two ways to find truth—both useful, provided we follow the path and the laws upon which they are predicated.

The first let us call the scientific method. That involves a group of facts and statistics, combined and analyzed, from which is distilled a theory or a postulate or what might be called a principle. Often the reverse is true: We advance a principle, then perform experiments to establish its validity. The scientific method is a sound and most valuable way of arriving at truth. There are two limitations, however, with that method. First: We never can be sure we have absolute truth, though we often draw nearer and nearer to it. Second: Sometimes, no matter how earnestly and sincerely we apply that principle, we come up with the wrong answer.

I recall years ago as a university student reading about Niels Bohr, who first postulated an atomic explanation of matter—a nucleus of neutrons and protons surrounded by spinning particles called electrons. As scientists and experimenters tested that theory, they developed great contributions in the field of chemistry, and the periodic table was organized using that theory as a key; but further investigations proved that it was not a satisfactory explanation of the truth. More scientific endeavor has brought us nearer and nearer until now there is a tremendously expanded understanding of matter. Yet anyone would admit that we are far from the essence of truth.

Sometimes mistakes are made. Let me give you an example of a professor from a well-known Eastern university who spent two years of his time researching basic documents in the Church to discover information about the documentation of Mormon history. He was sincere and honest and invested much of his time; yet what do you think of these two conclusions, among others, that he reached? "It is not possible for a loyal member of the Mormon Church to write an objective history of Mormonism because of inherent restrictions that require the views of ecclesiastical leaders to be accepted totally," and "It is not possible to develop a true scholar or gifted intellectual from the ranks of loyal Mormons because each is required to follow the views and counsels of the Church leaders." You and I know that this is false. Yet he was sincere. He applied the scientific method and got the wrong conclusion because he lacked the insight that you and I share: that inspiration is what provides the commonality of feeling in the Church and not the dictum of its leaders.

Some deny the fact that there is any method of finding truth other than the scientific method. I remember, early in the days of nuclear engineering, when we were experimenting to confirm some of the hypotheses. One day I was in an area where a swimming pool had been built, and down deep in it were aluminum plates with uranium-aluminum contents arrayed. Three of us were taking turns at the controls, and I remember the thrill of excitement that came to me as we moved the control rods. I happened to be at the control panel when the count-rate meter indicated that the reactor had gone critical; and as I looked down into the pool I could see that Cerenkov radiation, the iridescent blue indicating that in fact there was a controlled chain reaction. That may not appear much to you now with today's familiarity with physics, but it was a scientific thrill for me.

Later, we experimentally measured cross sections of materials to determine their nuclear constants. We used a beam of high-energy neutrons from one of the graphite pile reactors, deflecting it with a crystal into an experimental apparatus. A young janitor approached the experiment evidencing total disdain for what we were doing. He did not understand it, nor did he want to understand it. In kind of an accusatory way he indicated that we were just wasting time, kidding people, doing that which had no real meaning. To show his disdain he reached up to touch the crystal that deflected the beam and to whirl it. Had he not been stopped, that powerful, dangerous beam of high-energy neutrons would have sprayed the room. His if-you-can't-see-it-taste-it-smell-it-feel-it-hear-it-then-it-doesn't-exist attitude is all too prevalent in the world today when we talk about things of God, things that really matter.

That brings me to the second way of finding truth, and that is simply to go to the origin of all truth and ask. This differs from the scientific method in that certain principles must be applied. You have observed that scientists who in their private lives may do anything but follow gospel standards can be successful in the scientific method of evaluation. This is not so when we talk about finding truth—pure truth—directly from the source. Two ingredients are essential: first, faith—unwavering faith; second, obedience—a willingness to apply true principles and to keep God's commandments, that we may open the avenues of clear communication with God. Through such communication we can receive a positive, certain knowledge about a decision with which we have labored, about which we have asked, and for which we have sought confirmation from the Spirit. Such communication can be so powerful as to be undeniable. We can be certain that it is true as private inspiration comes directly from the Lord.

Sometimes the Lord reveals truth to us when we are not actively seeking it, when we are in danger and know it not. I remember that on one occasion I had been driving for long hours alone on high Bolivian mountain roads a single lane wide. As I approached a sharp turn an impression came into my mind: "If my wife were here she would tell me to honk the horn." I did, and as I turned the corner I saw a jeep skidding to a halt; it had heard the warning sound. Had I not done it I would have been in trouble. Not two hours later the same thing happened, this time with an ambulance.

The Lord gives us truth when we live righteously. Sometimes it comes in response to an urgent, sincere prayer for help when we need guidance. I remember one night in the mission field, after kneeling in prayer with my lovely wife, having thanked the Lord for the blessings of the day, I had a strong impression that one of the missionaries was in trouble. I tried to think who it could be but could not. I excused myself from my sweet companion and went up onto the flat part of our mission home roof. All night long I labored, reviewing in my mind each companionship, everything I knew about every missionary, and pled with the Lord that he might let me know where that missionary was that needed help. Finally, as the dawn began to break, I was impressed to know in which part of the mission he lived. That, of course, was all I needed. I went there and through appropriate interviews found and helped the individual the Lord wanted to help. Yes, God answers prayer and gives us truth when we live obediently and exercise the requisite faith.

Let me summarize: The scientific method is useful, but it does not guarantee obtaining pure knowledge and could possibly lead us down blind alleys. I find a combination of the scientific method and that of seeking pure truth by prayer to be a tremendously effective way of solidifying a foundation of knowledge in our lives.

May I share with you some of the comments made by other Brethren on this topic? Elder Hugh B. Brown said on one occasion:

> There is dawning upon this age what might be termed a scientific spirituality—a new type of mind that studies the truths of faith with the care and caution and candor of science, yet keeping the warmth and glow and power of faith.
>
> Spiritual insight is as real as scientific insight. Indeed, it is but a higher manifestation of the same thing. [*CR,* April 1967, p. 49]

Remember that we do not attempt to understand the laws of physics by rejecting all previous efforts to explain and record them and then set about to develop our own theories about everything. We search out that which is already established, learn the existing laws, and conscientiously apply them as instructed. The same applies to spiritual laws.

There are sources of pure truth other than direct prayer. Examples are pure testimony from righteous friends, parents, or relatives; insight and inspiration given to a stake president, bishop, or mission president when we are in need; and the scriptures—oh, what a powerful source are the scriptures!

With regard to the scriptures, President Romney has given us this excellent counsel.

> So I would suggest that you do study the gospel and study it every day. You should never let a day go by that you don't read it.
>
> . . . I do not know much about the gospel other than that which I have learned from the standard works. When I drink from a spring, I like to get the water where it comes out of the ground, not down the stream after the cattle have waded in it.
>
> . . . I appreciate other people's interpretation, but when it comes to the gospel we ought to become acquainted with what the Lord says and we ought to read it. You ought to read the gospel;

> you ought to read the Book of Mormon and the Doctrine and Covenants; . . . and all the scriptures with the idea of finding out what's in them and what the meaning is and not to prove some idea of our own. Just read them and plead with the Lord to let us understand what he had in mind when he wrote them.
>
> After we have done that, you have to live it. You can't learn the gospel without living it. Jesus did not learn it all at one time. He went from grace to grace (see D&C 93:12–14). [Coordinators Convention, April 13, 1973]

A knowledge of truth is not sufficient—we must find the courage and strength to apply that knowledge. Consider for a moment a man, heavily overweight, approaching a bakery display. In his mind are these thoughts: *The doctor told you not to eat any more of that. It's not good for you. It just gives momentary gratification of appetite. You'll feel uncomfortable the rest of the day after it. You've decided not to have any more.* "I'll have two of those almond twists and a couple of those doughnuts and two of those chocolate ones." *One more time won't hurt. I'll do it just once more and this will be the last time.* Truth is of little value in our lives if we do not apply it.

We gain the courage and strength to apply truth as we live close to our Father in heaven and as we form a personal relationship with him. President David O. McKay once said, "The greatest comfort in this life is the assurance of having a close relationship with God" (*CR,* April 1967, p. 84). Truth and its application bring peace and satisfaction and stimulate self-reliance.

May I share with you some other observations from the Brethren on this subject of how we gain truth and how prayers are answered? The Lord has said, "I will tell you in your mind and in your heart, by the Holy Ghost, which shall come upon you and which shall dwell in your heart" (D&C 8:2). That is the vehicle through which pure truth is transmitted. Every soul in the world can benefit temporarily from the guidance and inspiration of the Holy Ghost, but only those who are obedient to the gospel, who are baptized, and who receive the gift of the Holy Ghost by confirmation have that companion as a right eternally. One of the best sources of counsel from the Lord regarding prayer is found in section 9 of the Doctrine and Covenants, verses 7 through 9.

For prayer to be answered we must first formulate a decision and then present it to the Lord for ratification. Specifically the Lord has told us that

> If it is right I will cause that your bosom shall burn within you; therefore, you shall feel that it is right.
>
> But if it be not right you shall have no such feelings, but you shall have a stupor of thought that shall cause you to forget the thing which is wrong. [D&C 9:8–9]

As you study that scripture and others that apply to the principles of prayer, you will find that nowhere does it say when the Lord will answer. Some of us misunderstand. We urgently plead for an answer. We pray with sincerity, following the steps outlined—and nothing happens. Permit me to share something with you that I feel is sacred. I have found by personal experience and have had confirmed so repeatedly that I know it is true that when we follow the laws of prayer given us of God, one of three things happens. First, we will feel that peace, that comfort, that assurance, that certainty that our decision is right; or second, we will feel that uncomfortableness, that stupor of thought, and we know that what we have chosen is wrong; or third—and this is the difficult one—we feel nothing.

What do you do when you do not feel an answer? I have come to thank the Lord with all my heart when that occurs, for it is an evidence of his trust. I positively know that as we apply our decision as though it were confirmed powerfully from on high, one of two things will certainly occur at the appropriate time: either the stupor of thought, or the peace—the confirmation.

May I share two experiences to demonstrate what I mean? One day a very close friend came to my home. He was a bishop, very much enjoying his calling. He had an opportunity for employment in another part of the country and was undecided about whether or not to go. We discussed the principles just reviewed. He went home and made a decision to move. He felt no confirmation of the correctness of that decision, but moved to the new job anyway. His employment was good and his family comfortable, yet he continued to feel somewhat ill at ease, not knowing for sure whether he had made the right decision. A week passed, then a month, then additional months. One day one of the Brethren was assigned to reorganize the stake in the area where he now lived. He received his confirmation from the Lord when he was selected to be the new stake president.

The other experience came as I followed, as carefully as I knew how, the principles we have discussed. One of the most sacred responsibilities of a mission president is the assignment of companionships, for it must be done through inspiration. On one occasion, having carefully followed the same procedure as always, I invited a missionary into my office and said, "Elder, you're going to be thrilled with your new assignment."

His eyes lit up with enthusiasm. Then, just as I was about to give him his assignment, a powerful impression came to my mind: "No, not there; you can't send him there."

The more he stared wide-eyed at me, the more uneasy I became. I said, "Just a minute, Elder; I'll be right back," and, of course, I went to another room and prayed to find out where he should go.

I know that when we live righteously, exercise faith, and supplicate the Lord, using the proper principles, if we feel no confirmation immediately we should act on our decision. If that decision is consistent with gospel principles and our other teachings, one of the two feelings will surely come. First a scriptural statement from President McKay:

> It is true that the answers to our prayers may not always come as direct and at the time, nor in the manner, we anticipate; but they do come, and at a time and in a manner best for the interests of him who offers the supplication. [*CR,* April 1969, p. 153]

I find great comfort in that statement of the prophet.

During a general conference session, President McKay told of a personal experience from his life that illustrates this point. He said that he was out hunting cattle and while climbing a steep hill he stopped his horse to let it rest. In his own words,

> An intense desire came over me to receive a manifestation of the truth of the restored gospel. I dismounted, threw my reins over my horse's head, and there, under a serviceberry bush, I prayed that God would declare to me the truth of his revelation to Joseph Smith. I am sure that I prayed fervently and sincerely and with as much faith as a young boy could muster.
>
> At the conclusion of the prayer, I arose from my knees, threw the reins over my faithful pony's head, and got into the saddle. As I started along the trail again, I remember saying to myself: "No spiritual manifestation has come to me. If I am true to myself, I must say I am just the same 'old boy' that I was before I prayed." I prayed again when I crossed Spring Creek, near Huntsville [with the same result]. [*CR,* October 1968, pp. 85–86]

Then he added that much later on, when he was in the mission field, a singularly spiritual experience came during the equivalent of a zone conference today. A powerful, unmistakable witness came in answer to his supplication. It came when he needed it, when it was more important to confirm other promptings of the Spirit.

Knowledge is power, and the glory of God is intelligence. Permit me now to share from our current prophet some comments about this matter of gaining pure knowledge. President Kimball calls it spiritual knowledge.

> Knowledge is that power which raises one into new and higher worlds and elevates him into new spiritual realms.
>
> The treasures of both secular and spiritual knowledge are hidden ones—but hidden from those who do not properly search and strive to find them. The knowledge of the spiritual will not come to an individual without effort any more than will the secular knowledge or college degrees. Spiritual knowledge gives the power to live eternally and to rise and overcome and develop and finally to create.
>
> . . . Spiritual knowledge is not available merely for the asking; even prayers are not enough. It takes persistence and dedication of one's life. The knowledge of things in secular life are of time

> and are limited; the knowledge of the infinite truths are of time and eternity.
>
> Of all treasures of knowledge, the most vital is the knowledge of God: his existence, powers, love, and promises. . . .
>
> . . . God and his program will be found only in deep pondering, appropriate reading, much kneeling in devout, humble prayer, and in a sincerity born of need and dependence. . . .
>
> Desirable as is secular knowledge, one is not truly educated unless he has the spiritual with the secular. The secular knowledge is to be desired; the spiritual knowledge is an absolute necessity.

Now listen as President Kimball explains how we gain this knowledge:

> It is my prayer that we learn to master ourselves by obedience to the Lord's commandments by the control of our physical appetites, and by placing first in our lives service to God and our fellowmen, so that the hidden things of the spirit may come to us and that we may attain perfection with the Father and the Son. Many have seen God in the course of history. All of us may do so eventually through our righteousness. [*CR,* October 1968, pp. 129–31]

In discussing these principles with you today I have had one desire: that somehow in the mind and heart of each of us there might be generated, as though we were talking to ourselves, this sort of conviction: "I am truly and deeply loved of the Lord. He will do all in his power for my happiness. The key to unlock that power is in myself. While others will counsel, suggest, exhort, and urge, the Lord has given me the responsibility and the agency to make the basic decisions for my happiness and eternal progress. As I read and ponder the scriptures daily and with sincere faith earnestly seek my Father in prayer, peace will envelop my being. This, coupled with full obedience to the commandments of God and selfless service to and genuine concern for others, will purge fear from my heart and condition me to receive and to interpret the divine aid given to mark my path with clarity. No friend, bishop, stake president, or General Authority can do this for me.

It is my divine right to do it for myself. I will be at peace; I will be happy; I will have a rewarding, productive, meaningful life."

As you prepare for your future in the academic and professional worlds, or as you embark now to serve the Lord, remember that God will grant truth as we live to merit the inspiration of the Holy Ghost in our lives. I know this. I know that pure truth flows from God.

Last Friday President Kimball, his counselors, and the Quorum of the Twelve announced to the world a new revelation. I know positively that that revelation came from God. I know that because of the application of the principles that I have discussed. I know positively that the Lord gave that revelation to the president. Now countless spirits who otherwise would not have had the blessing of the priesthood—those who are beyond, those who are here, those who are yet to come—will enjoy the blessings that only can be obtained in the temple because a prophet so lived his life as to be an instrument in the hands of God to bring new truth to his children on earth.

I am grateful for this privilege to be with you today. It is a sacred responsibility to come to this choice institution where truth is taught through the medium of the Holy Ghost and where one can expand the testimony and instruction in the laboratory and classroom by quiet pondering and meditation. I know that God lives. I know positively that he lives. I know that God answers prayer. He answers prayer so clearly and concisely that we can write his counsel down as though it were dictated to our mind and heart, for I have done that. I know that God answers urgent prayer when there is a need. One example will illustrate.

One day I was interviewing a young lady for an assignment in the mission—a choice young lady, a recent convert to the Church. As I reviewed her personal history and asked her the questions about her personal life, she answered as though she were reviewing her personal history page by page. Then, it seemed, she skipped several important chapters. Nothing she said told me that, but I had that strong impression in my heart that she was leaving something important out.

I went back to ask questions about that area, but no matter how I phrased the question I got the same result—no comment on that area. As I anxiously tried to communicate with her, a very powerful impression came to me—to my mind and to my heart. I knew specifically what had happened to her. She had been betrayed by a trusted doctor who had taken away the most precious gift: her chastity. Being a new member of the Church, she had not known what to do as you and I do. She had sought the Lord, asked for help, anguished over her efforts for repentance without fruition.

I began to feel impressions to counsel her, and she became nervous and turned her head to the wall so that all I could see was the back of her hair. Yet specific counsel flowed forth, and I gave it to her. Finally an impression came that I communicated to her. "I don't need to talk to you any more, do I? You have made a decision."

She whirled around and asked, "How could you possibly know that? I want to bear to you my testimony." And as she poured out her love for her Father in heaven and her conviction of the Church's truthfulness, there flowed between us a power, a real power and a strength. Neither she nor I wanted that moment to end. I discovered again how the Lord could use a servant as an instrument to answer the urgent desires of someone who wanted to do right but had no idea of how to proceed. He answered her prayers unequivocally.

Yes, the scientific method is worthwhile when combined with spiritual insight based on faith and obedience. We do have a source of pure truth to edify, to clarify, and to ease our way. Of this I bear solemn witness, in the name of Jesus Christ. Amen.

Elder Richard G. Scott was a member of the First Quorum of the Seventy when this devotional address was given in the Marriott Center on 13 June 1978.

The Powers Within You

BARBARA B. SMITH

THIS IS AN overwhelming sight. And I would like you to know, my dear brothers and sisters, President Holland, President Vernon, President Gardner, and all of you, how much I have enjoyed the music and how pleased and honored I am to participate in this fourteen-stake fireside tonight, because I want to tell you what an exciting and challenging time it is in the history of Relief Society. It is a time of great growth, great expectations, and great needs. The sisterhood of Relief Society must be strengthened and unified now just as much as during the administration of any of the wise Relief Society presidents of the past.

Relief Society has reached its present position of status and influence under the inspiration and guidance of the prophets and apostles, and it is a great blessing to the women of the Church worldwide. Relief Society must stand as a bulwark and a fortress against the penetration of the extreme viewpoints regarding women that have become political and social issues. It must develop in each woman an understanding of not only her magnificent potential, her irreplaceable contributions, and her eternal destiny, but those of each man as well.

Problems are not unique to our times. Look at the life of President Zina D. H. Young, the third general president of the Relief Society. She was bright, observant, and deeply religious. Even so she suffered sickness, trials, tribulations, and sorrows. She witnessed the burning of the homes of the Saints in Nauvoo before the exodus. Her father and mother both died as the result of persecutions against the Mormons. She had two children by her first marriage. Then, later, she married Brigham Young and raised four of his children along with her two and one daughter born to them.

President Brigham Young gave Zina the mission of establishing the silk culture in the territory of Deseret. The silkworms were extremely repugnant to her, but in spite of that she successfully completed that assignment. Her love of the Lord and her determination to follow the direction given by the prophet made it possible for her to do what she was asked to do, and I am sure that she had to develop some special strengths in order to be able to do it. I can't tell you how grateful I am that I don't have to handle silkworms—just Phil Donahue.

Last week a beautiful young woman sent me a book entitled *Hope for the Flowers* (Trina Paulus [Paramus, New Jersey: Paulist Press, 1972]). As I read it, I thought, "It's too bad that Sister Zina didn't have this book. It might have given her some new insights about worms." Let me share its message with you.

It tells of a tiny striped caterpillar and how he joined a pile of other squirming, pushing caterpillars who were trying to get to the top of the pile. It was only when he talked to a certain yellow caterpillar that the two of them decided that getting to the top wasn't really what they wanted most. So, they climbed down and away from the others. They enjoyed being together, and they ate and grew fat until one day they became bored, and they wanted to find out if there was more to life. The striped caterpillar decided to find out by climbing again to the top of the caterpillar pile. The yellow caterpillar felt ashamed that she didn't agree but decided it was better to wait until she could take action she could believe in. So he climbed, and she wandered aimlessly until she saw a caterpillar hanging upside down on a branch caught in some hairy substance. She said, "You seem to be in trouble. Can I help you?" "No," said the hanging caterpillar, "I have to do this to become a butterfly."

"Butterfly? What is a butterfly?"

"It's what you are meant to be. It flies with beautiful wings and joins the earth to heaven. It drinks only nectar from the flowers and carries seeds of love from one flower to another. Without butterflies the world would soon have few flowers."

The yellow caterpillar exclaimed, "It can't be true! How can I believe there's a butterfly inside you or me when all I see is a fuzzy worm? How does one become a butterfly?"

The hanging caterpillar said, "You must want to fly so much that you are willing to give up being a caterpillar."

The yellow caterpillar began fearfully but continued the process until at length she became a butterfly. Then she helped the striped caterpillar learn who he was and leave the pile to become what he was really meant to be.

Like the caterpillars who will one day become butterflies, you have the magnificent potential to develop the powers within you and become greater than most of you dare dream. "God has . . . made us the custodians of some great powers," said Sterling W. Sill (*The Power of Believing* [Salt Lake City: Bookcraft, 1968], p. 6). You have the power and the capacity to perform so well that you can inherit all that our Father has if you begin the process and continue until you become what you are really meant to be.

Each individual is entitled to choose which path to walk and thereby determine the ultimate destiny of his or her life. Some of you might question so bold a statement: "That can't be true. I want to be a great quarterback like Jim McMahon or a miraculous receiver like Clay Brown, and I can't do it, no matter how determined or diligent I am."

It is not of such choices I speak. I speak of the destiny of your life and of the eternal truth that you *can* choose to use the powers within you to have a happy life of continual growth and development that leads to eternal progression or choose to follow the crowd of other people struggling to get to a top that is nowhere.

Tonight let's consider just three of the great powers of which you are custodians. Perhaps then you can begin to understand the process necessary to become what you are really meant to be.

First, you have great physical powers. Look at you; notice your hands, your arms, your legs, your feet, your face, your eyes, your ears, your mouth, and your nose. You must admit that you are a magnificent creation when you realize how intricate these components are and what you can do because of them. If by any chance there is more of you than you would like to see, you can do something about it. And, if you do, it will make a great difference in how you feel about yourself.

Recently I was in Washington, D.C., where I met a woman in her thirties who has not yet married. She is stunning, tall, and full of enthusiasm. She is running an oil recycling business. This young woman told me about her recent campaign to lose weight. I think that she had taken off more than forty pounds. "I can't begin to tell you what it has done for me," she said. "Having decided to reduce my weight and then having successfully done it have made it easier for me to relate to other people because I feel so good about myself. It is exciting."

Her example serves to illustrate that physically you have the power to choose the options available to you. You who have five or ten or more pounds that you would like to lose can do so in different ways. You can take in fewer calories, or you may desire to put yourself on a consistent program of exercise, or both. The point is that you have the power to lose weight and thereby increase your capacity to do what you want to do.

I like the statement made by Bryant S. Hinckley, father of Elder Gordon B. Hinckley. He said:

> When a man makes war on his own weaknesses he engages in the holiest war that mortals ever wage. The reward that comes from victory in this struggle is the most enduring, most satisfying, and the most exquisite that man ever experiences. . . . The power

> to do what we ought to do is the greatest freedom. [*That Ye Might Have Joy* (Salt Lake City: Bookcraft, 1958), p. 83]

I hope at some time you all will feel the reward of such a victory and that you will recognize the miracle of your mortal bodies in helping you to gain this newfound freedom.

"Think for a moment," said B. H. Roberts,

> what progress a man makes within the narrow limits of this life. Regard him as he lies in the lap of his mother . . . a new-born babe! There are eyes, indeed, that may see, but cannot distinguish objects; ears that may hear, but cannot distinguish sounds; hands as perfectly fashioned as yours and mine, but helpless withal; feet and limbs, but they are unable to bear the weight of his body, much less walk . . . and yet, within the short span of three score years and ten, by the marvelous working of the wondrous power within . . . what a change may be wrought! From that helpless babe may arise one like unto Demosthenes or Cicero, or Pitt, or Burke, or Fox, or Webster, . . . or from such a babe may come a Nebuchadnezzar, or an Alexander, or a Napoleon, who shall found empires or give direction to the course of history. [*Mormon Doctrine of Deity* (Salt Lake City: Deseret News, 1903), pp. 33–34]

The miracle of the mortal body became apparent to me one afternoon when I was holding my first baby. It was a girl, and suddenly she seemed to stop breathing. I tried to force air into her lungs. I cried to the Lord in desperation, and after only a few seconds that seemed like an endless hour, she began to breathe normally again. The problem was diagnosed as an enlarged thymus gland that needed treatment. I shall never forget how grateful I was for the miracle of life and for the power of the body that I knew that day. I determined to do my very best to help her use her life as the Lord intended when he gave her to me to care for and love.

I know now the powers within these bodies, and I know they are powers not only to create life but to live it in such a way that mortality will be a happy and meaningful experience. When these miraculous systems malfunction—and maybe only then—we fully appreciate the complexity of the systems that give the body life. Only as we struggle to understand the body in order to treat the ailments it falls heir to in this life do we fully appreciate its remarkable nature and the intricate interrelationships that exist. The human body is most remarkable. It can walk, run, jump, climb, swim, ski, play, jog, and on and on, but not the least of these remarkable capabilities are its compensatory powers. We find these powers as we observe some of our friends and acquaintances—or even ourselves—who have birth defects, accidents, or illnesses that cause the functions we counted on to be lost so that other parts of the body have to substitute.

You'll hear from Curt Brinkman during this week. You honored Curt at Homecoming last year because he had broken some records in the famous Boston Marathon. Curt was a good basketball player before his accident, but afterward he did not dwell on what his body could not do. When he had no legs, he trained his arms and built strength in them to compensate for his missing legs. He found another way to use the powers within him, and he became a champion.

I want you to know the full joy of your mortal body. The power is within you to do an infinite variety of things. It is like a never-ending kaleidoscope of experiences that are available to you regardless of your challenges or your problems. When one avenue of activity is denied by a physical impairment, there is still a rich variety of alternate choices available to you.

It is the masterful creation of our bodies that gives us these wonderful abilities because we are the literal offspring of our Heavenly Father. He, whose spirit children we are, organized these mortal bodies and provided us with a powerful instrument capable of vitalized mortal living. However, Elder LeGrand Richards cautions:

> There are those who think their bodies are their own and that they can do with them what they will, but Paul makes it plain that they are not their own, for they are bought with a price, and that "if any man defile the temple of God, him shall God destroy; for the temple of God is holy, which temple ye are." [*A Marvelous Work and a Wonder* (Salt Lake City: Deseret Book, 1950), p. 380]

You do have great physical powers within you to create life, to control your abilities and capacities, and to compensate for disabilities; and these physical powers require you to take good care of your bodies. At the very least you should obey the Word of Wisdom, eat properly, sleep and exercise regularly, and abstain from taking anything into your bodies that will destroy your powers, for you will be held accountable for them as you strive to become what you are really meant to be.

Now consider your mental powers. Think of your infinite capacity to learn, your ability to control your attitude toward learning, and your ability to adapt to and draw from the happenings of each day. No mother can watch the progress of her child without being filled with wonder at his endless desire to learn. It is one of the joys of being a parent.

There are a hunger and a frustration that accompany the young child's eagerness to grow and learn. You have all watched a child struggle to walk. Again and again he tries: up on his feet, down on the floor, bumps and hurts, cries of pain and frustration until at last he walks. At first he holds on to the offered hand for support, and then he pushes it away. A child must go through the process if he would grow and gain a sense of achievement.

This fundamental principle applies to you if real learning is to occur. Each of you must reach out for strength from others, then struggle and stretch to the limits of your own capacities to feel the ultimate sense of achievement.

With that realization, look back over the centuries of our experience in mortality and see the great learning that has come to us from others. I mentioned my recent trip to Washington, D.C. While there I had the opportunity to visit the National Air and Space Museum. It is a huge structure, housing all the tangible machines of flight that are part of our national legacy. Within those walls are housed many dreams. The history of our conquest of the moon is documented there in countless projects and written records. It is just one of the tiny fragments of human inquiry that have yielded enormous amounts of knowledge.

In the earliest records of human desire to go to the moon are stories of drinking a magic potion and being wafted to the moon, or harnessing giant birds that could pull a raft carrying a man to the moon. Some even thought about covering men with suction cups so that, as the dew would evaporate from the cups, the traveler could be lifted to the moon. Then came a reflection of our technological progress, the thought of gliding, and finally the realization that a person might be shot from a rocket to the moon.

More than 300 years ago the necessary principles of physics were beginning to be known, and Kepler declared that when we had developed the technology to build machines to go to the moon, men would come forward to ride those machines. They did, and the moon once whimsically described as being made of green cheese suddenly became a real place—barren, foreboding, made of rocks and boulders with no living thing on it.

In the process of conquering the distance to the moon, many things were discovered. As the hardware was developed to lift the rocket from the earth and hurl it through space, the first major discoveries with computers were made. From the roomful of equipment it took to do the first computer calculations developed our present pocket calculators.

Walk the corridors of this great university and look into the libraries and the laboratories, and you will find more projects designed to overcome the ignorance and the unknown than could have even been dreamed about a few short years ago. Remember that knowledge builds upon knowledge. There is no end to the capacity of men and women to learn. The great vision of the gospel is that we grow in wisdom and in knowledge and in favor with God and man. You must put yourself to that task because you have the power.

When the Lord sent Adam and Eve out into the world from the Garden of Eden, he said to them, "Multiply, and replenish the earth, and subdue it" (Genesis 1:28). So here we are in the midst of the work of subduing the earth. There is only one way to subdue the earth. It is to learn enough to dispel ignorance and to gain enough wisdom that we might apply what we know for the benefit of all people.

There is most often an urgent desire for knowledge in us when we are young. I smiled at my young grandson who, long before he went to school, used to take science books to his mother and say, "Read these to me."

She would ask, "Don't you want a storybook?"

He would reply, "No, mother, I don't know anything about science, and I want to learn."

At this great university you have unnumbered opportunities to learn. You can select courses, you can study in the library, you can attend concerts and plays and lectures. You can engage your friends and your professors and teachers in conversation. If you fill your time well, you will learn many great and important things at a pace you may never be able to sustain again in your lifetime.

There are no handicaps that cannot be overcome.

I was told that when J. Willard Marriott, the man for whom this great structure was named, returned home from his mission, he found that the cold of a very severe winter had killed most of his father's flock of sheep. He asked his father to buy more sheep, but his father was very hesitant to make such a large investment again. He reminded Willard that he and his brothers would be in school and that there would be no one to stay home full time with the sheep. And so young Willard volunteered to stay home instead of going away to college. For two years he watched the sheep, but his desire for an education was so compelling that he registered for home study classes and while out in the field studied hard enough to complete his first two years of college.

Joseph Larsen, a fine stake president in Illinois, was injured while serving his country. The accident left him without the use of his legs, confined to a wheelchair. But he, with the help of his lovely wife, went on to finish his education, and he is now a dean at the University of Illinois. He is a spiritual giant among the brothers and sisters of his stake. His capacity to learn did not end when his ability to walk ended. He kept going.

A delightful sister, Ruth Knudson, took me on a tour through the National Gallery of Art. When her husband passed away, she decided that she would make good use of her time alone. She studied art history. It was so fascinating to her that she wanted to tell others about it, so she began conducting tours through the various galleries. Then she took a group abroad to study art. People began coming to her home and requesting private lessons or group instruction, whichever she would give. Now her life is rich and full as she continues to seek more learning about art in order to be filled enough to constantly teach others.

Continuing education is one of the gospel concepts for an enriched life. We can learn in so many ways. For example, one of my daughters was visiting with Sarah Boyer recently and observed that Sarah's little girl had a new and attractive braid in her hair. My daughter remarked how lovely the little girl's hair looked, and Sarah said that she would teach her how to do it. Sarah commented: "When I realized how many years of combing and setting hair I would have with five little girls, I thought I might as well learn all I could about caring for their hair, including a lot of different and charming hairstyles." Isn't that delightful? I wonder why I didn't think of that. I had four daughters.

Another family from this area keeps their learning alive by acquiring things like telescopes, looms, greenhouses, and potter's wheels, and they accompany each new piece of equipment with an intensive study so that they can master a new skill. Imagine how many happy, productive hours they spend together.

Classes are available; books are available; constant, never-ending media stimulation is available. All these things can work to our good if we desire to continue learning. Once I made the statement to President Kimball, after I returned home from Mexico, that I wished I could speak Spanish. His quick reply was, "Well, you can learn, can't you?"

At first I thought, "Oh, no, not at my age, I can't," and then I realized that of course I could learn.

I haven't learned Spanish yet, but I know that I can. We all can come from the unknown to the known. We can develop skills, but we must remember that one of the significant tools for learning is our ability to control our own attitudes. Fortunately, we have the power within us to control and establish our own attitudes. All the knowledge in the world will not help us if we resist learning. But there is no end to our capacity to learn if we apply ourselves diligently and eagerly to the task.

A slight change of attitude to a new point of view can open up a whole new world to you. I can remember descending into the Los Angeles airport one day. I was seated next to a landscape architect. I was thinking about the myriad of houses and buildings below us, and he looked across at me and said, "Can you imagine how many sprinkler heads there are down there?" The landscape problems of a big city had never entered my mind before that, but occasionally I think about them now.

Perhaps the most important point I would like to discuss with you regarding your intellectual powers is the fact that you have the power to grow from your day-to-day experiences. At one time or another, you will all have the occasion to choose between a life of bitterness or a life of beauty. You have the power within you to make such a choice, and the Lord has promised that you can count on him for sufficient help to have an abundant life if you choose to live by the principles that lead to your personal growth and development.

Brother Marriott turned the circumstances that kept him from school into great personal discipline and a learning experience. President Larsen changed his life in a wheelchair to a life with sufficient optimism that he could stand tall in spirit and intellect even though his legs would no longer hold him. Sister Knudson accepted her situation and receives abundant satisfaction as she is sought out for her deep insights that bring happiness to herself and to others.

This great adaptive quality is part of the power within us that can shape our lives into contributions and excellence if we so choose. When we use our mental powers wisely, we can more easily become what we are really meant to be.

There is a third great power within you, the power for enormous spiritual growth—the infinite possibility for perfecting yourself. One way you can develop your spiritual power is by sharing the gospel because the gospel has the principles upon which all growth is predicated. Once we understand those concepts, we need opportunities both to teach them and to live them.

Another way to develop your spiritual power is to render acts of loving kindness and compassionate service. They are only of real value to you when they are given out of personal choice, not pressure. Albert Schweitzer wisely said, "The only ones who will ever be truly happy are those who have *sought* to serve."

For example, my former bishop and his wife entered the Missionary Training Center this week to prepare for their mission to Nigeria. Their daughter also entered the MTC this week to prepare for her mission to Peru. This family is well aware of the conveniences and luxuries they will give up, but they are eager to serve the Lord by loving and serving his children. The Lord wants us to be mindful of each other and to be dependent upon each other, and so to one he has given a particular spiritual gift and to another a different gift so that we might bless each other.

Recently a visiting teacher helped prepare a blind sister to go for the first time to the Seattle Temple soon after its dedication. She did not assume the responsibility of the bishop but tried to explain each part of entering the temple for one's endowment in such detail that the sightless woman could feel calm, peaceful, and spiritually in tune. Again, I mention Relief Society because it serves two fundamental purposes. It gives us a chance to be schooled in the art of sharing our talents and in giving loving service.

In the Doctrine and Covenants, we read:

> I say unto you, that as many as receive me, to them will I give power to become the sons of God, even to them that believe on my name. [D&C 11:30]

You may think, "That can't be true! How can there be that great potential in you or me when all I see is a struggling, imperfect human being?" And I can only say, as did Lorenzo Snow, "Godliness cannot be conferred but must be acquired" (Truman Madsen, *The Highest in Us* [Bookcraft: 1978], p. 9).

You must want that blessing so much that you have faith in his word, resist worldly enticements, seek him in prayer, listen to the promptings of the Holy Spirit, and proclaim his gospel within the reach of your influence, and in the process you will help develop the spiritual powers within you.

The power *is* in you. From the Doctrine and Covenants again, we read:

> Unto as many as received me gave I power to do many miracles, . . . power to obtain eternal life. [D&C 45:8]

Nurture your spiritual powers. It is the only way you can become what you are really meant to be.

Where do you begin to develop your physical, mental, and spiritual powers? Begin in your home. Whether you are single or married, whether your home is an apartment, a house, or a dormitory, begin in your home. Your home is the place where you go each night, but it is more than that. Your home is the place where you grow in physical stature, in mental abilities, and in spiritual strengths. The scriptures clearly teach the importance of the home and the training that takes place there. Let's consider for a moment Doctrine and Covenants, section 88, verse 119:

> Organize yourselves; prepare every needful thing; and establish a house, even a house of prayer, a house of fasting, a house of faith, a house of learning, a house of glory, a house of order, a house of Cod.

I like to apply those words to establishing a house where gods-to-be can be taught and trained, where they can develop the habits and attitudes that will prepare them to live in a celestial home in the hereafter because they have learned how to pray and develop a sweet dependence upon the Lord, to fast and draw near unto him, to learn of him and his ways so that his purposes can be the direction of their lives. I feel that the phrase "prepare every needful thing" is very important. What is a needful thing? How would you describe every needful thing? Is it a needful thing to have a regular place designated to study in your home—a specific desk, a table, a favorite chair? Is a budget a needful thing? Is it a needful thing for you to learn how to pay your tuition and your rent and still have enough money for books, transportation, and entertainment? Is it a needful thing to have good food if you would increase your physical abilities and strengths? Is it a needful thing to have food prepared that is pleasing to look at—or just satisfying to the appetite?

Sometimes in our hurry to get everything done, fast foods have become the order of the day. We think of dinner at McDonald's—at least I'm told that they feed more people in America than any other food service except the army. I think dinner at McDonald's should be the exception rather than the rule unless, of course, your name happens to be McDonald. I hope that you will use the many resources available to you to help you supply your kitchen with good things to eat—nutritious snacks, super soups, and money-saving meals. Use the ideas that have proven successful to enrich your living.

Come with me vicariously into three homes. Let's look in unobserved to see how these homes are organized to foster the powers within those who reside there. We'll go first into the home of a young mother who is a concert pianist. She is preparing right now to play with the philharmonic orchestra of her state. She has a baby-sitter caring for her three little sons while she spends these last few days in uninterrupted practice. Ordinarily she would limit her practice time at the piano to the hours when the children are in bed, but she is well aware that a flawless performance demands hours and hours of highly concentrated preparation.

She loves music. She wants her children to love it too. Each mealtime is accompanied by classical recordings, opera, symphony, world-renowned vocalists, or choirs. She is following the pattern set by her own mother. As soon as the children are old enough, they will accompany their parents to special musical events in order to firmly establish great music as an important part of their lives. Perhaps we should take our leave now, but it is to be hoped that her example will give you a thought about how you might cultivate learning by planning a time, a place, and a way to make the learning you desire possible.

We'll enter quietly into the next house because the fourth-grader who lives there is sobbing out the aching of the hurt he experienced today in school: "My teacher told me that I am the worst penman in the whole class!" If there is dismay at the teacher and her lack of consideration for that young son, the mother doesn't show it—only compassion and understanding. She carefully weighs her words, and then she says, "I'm sorry. I know it hurts to have someone point out your errors and your weaknesses, but I have a thought. Why don't you practice your penmanship each day until you are the very best in the class?"

Her son's tear-filled eyes begin to shine with a ray of hope. He asks, "But, how can I do it, Mother? When would I write? What will I write?"

"Every night after school you can work at the kitchen table until dinner time. Why don't you begin by copying your favorite scriptures? Or you might write words from the dictionary or even newsworthy events from the newspaper. You will learn a lot, and if you write very carefully and try to form each letter perfectly, you will soon be a beautiful penman. It can only happen with practice. You'll have to try really hard."

That determined little boy begins. He works hard every night. By the end of the year he comes home elated. "You were right, Mother! My teacher said today, 'Theron, you are the very best penman in the class!'"

He invested the time. The place was established. He was given the encouragement. All of them are important elements of organization—needful things—if learning is to take place.

It's Christmas Eve as we join this next family. They are at home in a strange city. It's new to them. The father has to complete his professional training, and so the whole family had to be uprooted. At Christmastime, it is very difficult for them to be away from their extended families. They have just finished dinner as we enter the house, and so we'll follow them into the family room.

The father says: "Children, Christmas is a time of great love. Our Heavenly Father loved us, his children, enough to send his Only Begotten Son into the world on that Christmas Day so long ago. He was to be the example of righteous living. He was to teach us how to grow close to our Heavenly Father. We must live worthy of that precious gift. This Christmas Eve I would like to give you a gift that is available to you only because Jesus was born. Because of him I hold the priesthood of God. With that power I would like to give each of you children a father's blessing tonight. We will start with the oldest."

One by one the children go to their father. They receive blessings suited to their special needs. Then we see each child, even the three-year-old, stand and tell how he or she has been blessed by the life of Jesus. The parents then testify to their children of the abundant blessings they have received from Jesus Christ.

I believe that those children will always remember this Christmas Eve. I believe that the example set by the parents of faith and prayer will be a directional force in the lives of their children. It is a needful thing to organize and to plan such experiences to be a part of one's life. They don't just happen.

Someone once said, "All human power is a compound of time and patience," and Benjamin Disraeli said, "All power is a trust" (*Vivian Grey,* book VI, chapter 7).

You should realize that time and patience are necessary for organizing your life and calling forth your powers. It may begin with something as simple as bringing order to your desk, to your drawers, or to the room where you are. You can leave each room better than it was when you entered it simply by picking up and by straightening it. Some people leave a trail of books, papers, clothes, boots, purses, and so forth, from the front door to the bedroom if that is their destination. They expect someone else to pick up after them, or they decide that they will retrace their steps at another time and begin picking up their belongings. Neither of these actions is worthy of the kind of living of which I speak. It's good to believe in a future time, but it's better to surround yourself with beauties and memories born of order.

President J. Reuben Clark, Jr., suggested that our homes are holy places and that we should approach them as if coming to an altar. Ask yourself what you have done to make your home an altar—a place that sanctifies or prepares those who are there for celestial living. Do your actions focus on developing loving relationships? Are there kindly acts of concern each day? Does your routine bring about maintenance of that home and practices of provident living? Do your pursuits bring about learning and refinement? Are the relationships within that home those that can be forever?

What is a home? To one of my friends it is a place where children are cherished and memories are born. Home is where she and her husband put priceless antiques they seek out. Home is where friends and family gather to share love. Home is a framed newspaper account of her grandmother's funeral service or an oil painting of a scene she knows and loves. Home is an attic turned into an upstairs playroom that is just filled with things meant to bring happiness to children. Home is a collection of books that have lofty thoughts they make theirs. Home is a kitchen where good food is prepared and gratefully enjoyed. Her home is a place where you feel love and faith and dreams that have become a reality.

When President Ronald Reagan delivered his Inaugural Address, it was essentially based on faith in the American people. He said, "Act worthy of yourselves," and he told us that we are "too great a nation to limit ourselves to small dreams."

So it is for us as Latter-day Saints. We too must act worthy of ourselves and the glorious vision of truth and eternity that has been restored to us. That vision of eternal growth and gentle, loving persuasion is too great a dream to let go of when we hunger in our hearts to be one with our Savior.

The power is in you to reach out and claim those blessings.

Tonight, remember that beyond anything you have ever accomplished is the challenge of living the principles of heaven in such a way that you connect the powers in you with the powers of heaven. Melvin J. Ballard said: "Men came to the Saviour to see what God was like; we stand to show men what Christ was like"

(Melvin J. Ballard, *Crusader for Righteousness* [Salt Lake City: Bookcraft, 1966], p. 112).

You have the powers within you to be Christlike. It is what you are meant to be, I humbly testify, in the name of Jesus Christ. Amen.

Barbara B. Smith was president of the Relief Society of The Church of Jesus Christ of Latter-day Saints when this fireside address was given in the Marriott Center on 1 February 1981.

"Deep Roots Are Not Reached by the Frost"

DWAN J. YOUNG

It is an honor for me to be with you today. Although I didn't attend the Y, I have great pride in this university. I am proud of what you accomplish. I am impressed by your spirit and your enthusiasm and your unity. I hope that you take advantage of every moment that you are here. Take advantage of every opportunity, because this is a great university.

I feel it is a great responsibility to offer some thoughts to keynote the women's conference that will be held this week.

The interesting theme taken from the *Fellowship of the Ring* by J. R. R. Tolkien—"Deep Roots Are Not Reached by the Frost"—suggests many things. Because I am the general president of the Primary, it is not surprising that I would first think of children. And then as I contemplated the words of the theme, I also thought about trees. As I explored the thoughts that came to my mind, I found myself wanting to say something to you of growth and potential; something about hanging on in adversity; something of the life-giving, healing balm of loving service; and something of the challenges of life and the great promises of the eternities to come.

Our family spends most of our vacation time in the Bear Lake valley, where we have a cabin. When our children were young, one of our favorite activities was to go exploring the mountains in our open Jeep. Many a day we would pile into the red Jeep, all seven of us and the dog, and off we would go. There were no restrictions in those days, and so we were able to go almost anywhere. One day, when we were about twenty-five miles up St. Charles Canyon, we came upon a Forest Service sign pointing the way to the Englemann Spruce. We decided to see what the Englemann Spruce was. So we stopped the Jeep and walked up the narrow path. Truly, we were not expecting what we found at the end of the trail.

The Englemann Spruce is magnificent. It is a beautiful, thriving tree with deep blue green needles more than an inch in length. Its trunk is straight and more than one hundred feet tall. The tree is nearly twenty feet around. We all took hands and encircled the tree. We had to stretch to reach around that mighty trunk. The Forest Service estimates this tree has been growing there for more than two thousand years. Each of us standing there holding hands and feeling a little awestruck by this magnificent tree thought different things, I'm sure. I wondered about how it grew to be so large.

It is fascinating to learn how trees grow. Trees are the biggest plants in the world. They never stop growing as long as they live. Every new tree begins its life in a flower. There are many kinds of trees, and within each kind there are many different sizes and shapes. Only a few ever grow to be the size of the mighty specimen we had encircled. The *World Book Encyclopedia* says:

> A seed starts to grow when a grain of the pollen dust of a tree flower is caught on the sticky pistil of a flower of the same kind of tree. When a tree seed begins to grow, a new tree is 'born.' This tree inside a seed is extremely small, but it has all the essential parts needed for a tree. It has a tiny white thread which will some day turn into the trunk. This thread has a root tip at one end and a bud at the other end, plus two tiny leaves. This baby tree

> is packed into a tiny parcel with a good supply of food. It is covered with a weatherproof coat. When the seed is ripe, it leaves the parent tree and goes traveling. . . . Tree seeds often open and grow on top of the ground or lying on leaves, if the spot is wet enough to soften their hard seed coats. Then, by a wonderful law of nature, the thread-like stem expands and grows longer and stronger. The end with the root tip turns down pointing into the ground. Even if you turn over an opening seed so that its root end points up it will turn down in a few hours, as though pulled by gravity. At the same time, the tip with the bud and the leaves turns up, as though pulled by the light of the sun.

It was hard to believe that this mighty spruce could have started as one tiny seed, but of course it did.

Those of you who have studied botany know what happens in the process of growth. A tree develops a crown. The uplifted trunk and outreaching branches and network of twigs make a broad, tall frame for the leaves. The leaves soak in the sunlight. The leaves use air, water, and sunlight to make food for the plant. A tree also develops a root system. The roots are the fastest growing part of a tree. Roots are longer and usually have more branches than the crown above them. They collect water in the damp ground and send it up the trunk to the leaves. The roots also serve as a mighty anchor that holds the tree upright.

The roots can only grow as fast as they get energy from the leaves in the form of sugar, vitamins, and hormones. The food-making operation of the leaves is controlled by the amount of water sent from the roots. There is in the tree a marvelous example of the constant interdependency and a graphic example of how the continuance of small acts leads to remarkable growth and strength. Our giant tree seemed almost indestructible, but of course it wasn't and it isn't. Just let the day come when the giant reaching, searching taproot cannot find a steady source of water, and the tree will begin to wither and fade. Death would not likely come by one mighty blow, but more likely by a gradual withering away.

Well, we cannot go on all morning talking about how trees grow, but there's one other fascinating fact that I learned as I prepared for this moment today. The root system provides a long, strong taproot that pushes ever downward in a search for more and more water, and to give stability to the tree. But the chief water-collecting part of the root system is made up of tiny, pearly white hairs called root hairs. The root hair is as fine as a spider's thread. It grows so fast, the encyclopedia says, that you can see it lengthen if you watch the plant under a microscope. Root hairs grow just back of the tip of the root. They appear suddenly, wherever there is moisture. Root hairs push between soil particles. When it finds a particle that is covered with a film of moisture, the root hair flattens and wraps around the particle to suck up the water. New hairs are constantly coming out and old ones are withering. The root hairs are constantly radiating outward to increase the absorbing surface so that the tree might enjoy enough of the life-giving water.

Knowing that the Englemann Spruce reached more than one hundred feet in the air, just think what an amazing root system it has developed in the two thousand years—a system that we could not see, but that stretched down below us and reached out on every side.

I don't know what each of my children thought about this great tree as we stood encircling it with our stretching arms, but I do know that they remember the tree.

There are many things to think about when one looks at trees. I couldn't help reflecting on all that happened during the life of this tree, stretching back to just a few years before the birth of Christ—before cars, before television, before E.T. and Mork, and before Pac-Man. Interesting, isn't it, that this tree was here on the earth when the Savior came into the world to fulfill all that had been prepared before the foundation of the world?

There are some fascinating parallels in the life of the tree and in the life of a child. It occurs to me that children too come into the world very much like a flower—fragile and beautiful. There is in the newborn baby a special quality of innocence, potential, and vulnerability that evokes a very special tenderness. I never hold a baby without an overwhelming sense of wonder. The miracle of life overpowers me, and I find the infant beautiful no matter how different and unique it may be.

Just as the fertile seed of the tree possesses all of the essential parts needed to be a full-grown tree, so the unborn child from its inception has all the essential parts needed to become a full-grown human being. Inside each baby, as inside each fertile seed of the tree, there is the potential for mighty growth. Just as the seeds of the tree bring forth after their kind, so we too come forth after our kind.

We should never forget that we are children of God, and that means that there is within us the necessary power to become like our Father. It is an eternal principle—God has brought forth his own kind in us, and we have the potential to become as he is. This means that there is no end to our growth and development. I think it is a concept that gives comfort and hope to our lives.

We must never forget that we have this eternal potential. Achieving potential is one of the fundamental purposes of life itself.

Knowing then that we have this potential, we should not question our fundamental worth. One of the most significant contributions that the Primary makes in the lives of our children, and I believe in the lives of our officers and teachers, is to give us all these first straightforward statements of belief.

It is not a coincidence that the Primary song "I Am a Child of God" is so greatly loved around the world. "I am a child of God" is a simple statement of a magnificent concept. You can understand it, I can understand it, and all the children of the world, no matter what their language, can understand it:

> I am a child of God,
> And he has sent me here,
> Has given me an earthly home, With parents kind and dear.
> Lead me, guide me, walk beside me, Help me find the way.
> [Naomi Randall, "I Am a Child of God," *Sing with Me,* no. B-76]

Almost all the work of Primary is designed to help our children find the way.

First, all of us must understand what we have come on earth to do. We're here to gain wisdom and knowledge. We're here to learn to love and to give service one to another. Being able to repeat the simple statements that summarize these great concepts is not all there is to learning. Learning also requires an application in daily life.

Life is a wonderful adventure, and working with the Primary children has brought back into my life a renewed enthusiasm for living. Children have a simple way of dealing with life. It is an approach that should not be lost. A child learns most when he or she is taught how to apply a moral teaching. Let me share with you an experience of my childhood. It made one of the ten commandments forever a part of my life. I speak of the commandment, "Thou shalt not steal." As a little girl, I worked in a small grocery store that my father owned and operated. One day while I was stocking the shelves, I noticed some little candies called "Guess-What's" on the counter. There was penny candy on the counter every day, but on this day that I shall never forget, I found myself wanting to have one of those little "Guess-What's," but I had no penny to pay for it. Somehow the wanting got the best of me, and although I knew it was not right, I picked up one of those little tempting candies and walked away. I cannot tell you how dreadful I felt. I knew I had done something wrong. I knew that—because I was nine years old—my baptism would not cancel out this wrong deed. I felt terrible. I made up my mind I would never, ever take anything again that did not belong to me. I had been taught about honesty, and in that moment the Spirit confirmed the truth of that teaching by the terrible, disquieting spirit that raged within me as I violated that law. Children learn very rapidly, and what they experience stays with them a very long time.

Let me tell you about an incident that happened last October in Washington, D.C. I was there for the Women's Legacy Concert. During the day, a group of us went to the National Museum of Art. We stopped for lunch at the Gallery, and as the waiter brought the bill to me he said, "Do you want me to fill in the amount, or do you want to do that?" For just a moment, I did not catch the importance of his question. Then it came to me. He was giving me a chance to pad my expense account. I was distressed by the suggestion, and the teachings of my childhood came back to me—Be Honest. My own standard of honesty was what counted. It was a matter of integrity with me.

Integrity is built by little actions. When my son, who is a counselor in the priests quorum presidency, declines to leave a meeting on Sunday in order to go to the corner ice-cream store, he is building his own character. When we get up and leave a movie that is offensive to our own standards of decency, we're developing strength of character. Like the tree, we're sending small root hairs out, and one day that massive system will be strong enough for us to stand firm against raging torrents.

I think of a little girl in England who dared to do right. The little girl's name is Lisa. She is an eleven-year-old girl in Primary and has been a member of the Church for three years. Lisa came home from school feeling very excited. She had been asked if she would read in the school assembly the following morning. She said, "Mum, I've been asked to read this tomorrow, but some of the words are wrong." The mother read the paper, and one paragraph referred to God and the Holy Ghost being one and the same person. The rest of it was correct, but just this paragraph was incorrect. They talked it over and decided that they would send a letter to Lisa's teacher, explaining that this paragraph was contrary to Lisa's beliefs and that she would feel much happier leaving this part out.

They waited rather anxiously for Lisa to return home from school to see what had happened. She came home with a big smile. Yes, the teacher had let her read the part, and, yes, she had let her leave that statement out. Also the teacher had thanked them for the letter, saying that she could understand her feelings, and then she said, "Could you please send some material to me and tell me more about what Mormons believe?"

The next day Lisa took a Book of Mormon, *Meet The Mormons,* and *A Marvelous Work and a Wonder* and gave them to the teacher. She found the books so interesting that she asked Lisa and three other Mormon girls in the school to present an assembly on the Mormons.

All of this came about because Lisa dared to be different and do right. Would you have the courage Lisa had?

When Jesus said we could not enter the kingdom of God except we become as a little child, I'm sure he was urging us to keep our sense of wonder. I'm sure he was reminding us to remain teachable. I feel sure he was encouraging us to keep our sense of accepting faith and our curious search for what makes the world go around. We can learn much from children.

If you do not have the opportunity to associate with children in your family, or if you do not serve in Primary, then you must take some action yourself. One young woman I know (her name is Gerry Avant, and you have probably read her byline in the *Church News)* found herself in a situation where there were no children close to her. She did not want to be deprived of that experience, and she decided to do something about it. She arranged a clown party for the children of her neighborhood. The party was so successful that one little girl came to Gerry and said her family was moving, but she did not want to go because she would miss the next clown party.

More importantly, two of the little girls from two different families became Gerry's friends. They would come over to her house to play. Gerry has a large unfinished basement, and she provided them with puppets and some help in writing a script. Then the girls made a puppet stage from some large, empty cardboard cartons. After awhile they decided to invite the girls' families over for a family home evening. Gerry offered to buy cookies, but the girls wanted to use her kitchen and make brownies. She agreed. I tell you about this party because I think Gerry did an innovative and fun thing that enriched not only her own life, but the lives of some children.

There need be no barriers between adults and children, and oh, how the world's children need us to be mindful of them!

The deepest taproot of any human life is the one we might call faith. Do you remember Alma likening the word to a seed? This passage tells us how important it is to prepare a place for the seed to grow. Let me tell you about a stake Primary president in Hawaii who had prepared herself. Last fall her six-year-old son was run over by a car. Though the emergency medical team arrived before he died, she told me that when she picked up his little body and held it close, she knew he would not live. Others who knew her marveled at her great strength in the face of this terrible tragedy. "How did you get prepared to meet the loss?" I asked her. This is what she told me:

> In the summer before the accident, I began to slip into a feeling of deep depression. I tried to talk myself out of it, but I could not. I prayed and I thought, and I had the strong impression that I was not doing my scripture reading. Another strong impression came to me: I was not attending the temple regularly. I resolved to do something in response to these feelings. I began to read my scriptures regularly, and I began to go to the temple twice a month. As I began to do them consistently, a strength and a peace came to me. When the accident happened, I was fortified. I could go on because I knew that he had died a celestial being, and I could become more nearly like him if I kept closely tuned.

That's one person's experience, but it illustrates how she sent out her little root hairs to find more of the life-giving water that sustains.

We have talked about growth and potential, about gaining strength from adversity. When we are converted, we can stand alone against the storms around us, secure in the knowledge of the revealed truth. Then we can reach out and serve others. Acts of service can be very small or very large, but all should be done in the spirit of increasing our awareness of another's burdens.

This building of one's ability to give loving service does not need to wait upon a master plan. It can begin today. We always start where we are and then develop a plan to direct our efforts.

One of the most rewarding experiences I have had this year came when I decorated some rooms in a rest home with gas-filled balloons. These simple, colorful ornaments brought cheerful smiles and happy eyes.

At Christmastime I accepted an invitation to participate as a sub for Santa. I went to a grateful but humble little home. They had done all they could, but needed some help. Our family provided the finishing touches. But what I want to tell you about is the gift this little family gave back to the world. They had a little home in the middle of an industrial area. I did not go inside the home, but the outside was brightly lighted with Christmas lights adding a cheery holiday glow to that dreary, dismal neighborhood.

So let me urge you to realize that your first task to prevent the frost from killing your roots is to fill up with faith and testimony, to develop deep and complex root systems that make you sensitive and thoughtful of others. These two principles will give you the kind of strength and magnificence we saw in the giant Englemann Spruce on that day so long ago.

Now may I share with you my deep concern for the children of the world. Who is caring for them? How will they get the loving nourishment they need to grow up into strong moral citizens? We all know what the Lord's plan is. He wants all his spirit children to come into the world where they can be cared for by a loving father and mother. He wants them to have stimulation for growth and refinement. He wants them to be taught the eternal truths of the gospel so they can stand firm against the winds of circumstance. He wants them to know the principles of salvation so that they can be about the business of working out their own salvation. I firmly believe that each of us has a responsibility to take the Lord's pattern and make it operative in our lives. We all belong to family units, either as a parent or as a child, and we should soberly address our attention to making those family units the place of hope and renewal that our Heavenly Father has taught us they can become.

But there are people and children whose circumstances in life are not favorable. The growth of the number of women in the workplace has shifted the care of children to alternate arrangements. More children now have mothers working out of the home full-time than has been the case in America before. Arrangements for children are made in day-care centers, with other relatives, or some other caretaking situation. Unfortunately, millions of school-age children have become latchkey children. That means they come home to empty houses and unsupervised hours of waiting. Many others of preschool years are left locked in their apartments while mothers go out to help provide the financial support for the family.

These are not ideal conditions for children. Study after study is carefully, painstakingly documenting for us the great need for infants and children to have loving, one-to-one care during their formative years.

Dr. Benjamin S. Bluhm of the University of Chicago declares that a child has gone 50 percent of the way in organizing the thinking patterns that we call his intelligence by the time he has reached the age of four, and the next 20 percent occurs by the age of eight.

Bruner observed that the child learns from careful, constant modeling, preferably of the mother. A skill is learned, reinforced—then the child reaches further. For this to be successful the child needs time—a lot of time—with some one person who cares enough and has time enough. Children without this one-to-one care do not develop so well.

Dr. Lamb, at the University of Utah, has recently compiled some of his studies into a book concerning infant social development. He found that the kind of response given an infant sets up lifetime patterns of expectancy. When a young child grows up in a home where the adult interaction is sensitive and caring, then the child comes to expect this relationship with other adults.

I read an article last year in *Time* magazine written by Roger Rosenblatt entitled "Children of War." He interviewed children in Ireland, Lebanon, Israel, Cambodia, and Vietnam. In spite of the terrible conditions in which they live, the children have something in common—a fierce desire to survive. In all their suffering and sorrow, these children still believe in goodness and in the need for good to overcome bad. Two things we might remember from these children: (1) They want to live, and (2) they reach out instinctively for the good. That does not surprise me for I know, as you do, that children are really celestial beings who dwell among us, saved in the celestial kingdom if they die before eight years of age. These children should be an example to us as they look forward with hope to a brighter day.

Another who experienced sorrow and suffering was the Prophet Joseph Smith. He once said that he felt like a lone tree standing on the plain. He learned early in his life to send his roots deep so that his faith would steady him. He learned to develop a widely spread system of roots that could constantly nourish him. Think of the sensitive awareness he had of people. Think of the constant development of awareness of other people that made him sensitive to their needs. The people who knew him said he was a man of love and unceasing compassion. He was a man of prayer who sought the Lord, and the results were that people reached back to him and sustained him, and the Lord heard his prayers and came unto him.

These things we too must do here and now. We must seek the Lord, and we must become sensitive to the needs of others. Then we must give service to one another. Service is the life-giving water that renews our souls and lets us continue in our growth. There are plenty who need our loving concerns: the young, whom I've mentioned specifically, and many others who are around you every day. There is the power within us to do much good, for we are the children of God.

I would like to observe that the ways you will use the ideas I've expressed and the ideas that you will hear from your conference speakers during the week are many and varied. But I hope that some of the things that are said will find their way like seeds into the soil of your heart and they will grow and grow until they give sustenance to your soul.

> All that is gold does not glitter, Not all those who wander are lost, The old that is strong does not wither, Deep roots are not reached by the frost.

May we grow strong and tall in our convictions. The day may come when we will have to stand as a lone tree against the sky.

Let us become as that Englemann Spruce, each a mighty witness for the truth, I humbly pray in the name of Jesus Christ. Amen.

Dwan J. Young was general president of the Primary when this devotional talk was given in the Marriott Center on 15 February 1983 as a prelude to the Eighth Annual Women's Conference.

Living Flames, Not Dead Ashes

S. DILWORTH YOUNG

I WAS INVITED during the week by the *Universe* to name a subject about which I might speak, and I was hard put to do it; so, finally, I recalled reading somewhere a statement by a French philosopher, a one-sentence statement. I have never read the works of this philosopher—I do not even know his name—but I liked what he said as the subject about which I wish to speak this morning: "From the living flames of our campfires of the past rather than the dead ashes." That is the subject.

Ashes have no life. Flames are constantly moving, changing, and challenging. Anybody who sits at a campfire can watch but never tire of the variety of the flames that arise from the burning wood. And after the fire has died down and he has gone through the action of killing it with water or whatever, running his hands through the dead ashes, he finds that the ashes are not very much once they are dead. I debated for some time as to whether or not I should come to you with a doctrinal subject, but you get a lot of that—nearly all of the Brethren who come here to speak to you talk about the doctrines or variations of the doctrines—and I thought perhaps I could tell you young folks what is really in my own heart, as if I were speaking to my own. And I can take advantage because I am old enough now to be able to do it and not have people think that I am eccentric. One debates whether to hide his earphone and his contact lenses and his teeth, which are extractable (he cannot do anything about his hair so he does nothing about that), and stands before you in the latter part of life trying to tell what he has learned. So here is what I have learned from the living flame.

In righteousness, one may be guided by the spirit of the Holy Ghost in his personal affairs if he seeks such guidance and if these affairs are honorable and honest. I want to call your attention to the fact that there is a place in section 89 of the Doctrine and Covenants that says something like this: "All [those] who . . . keep and do these sayings" (the Lord has been speaking of tobacco and liquor and other noxious substances, as well as wheat and corn and rye and barley—and there might be one added that is not a part of this particular section: "Retire to thy bed early" [D&C 88:124]), "walking in obedience to the commandments, shall . . . run and not be weary" (D&C 89:18–20). I have talked to several athletes of my acquaintance who wonder why they are running weary; but they do not seem to realize that they are not walking in obedience to the commandments. We are told in section 93 of the Doctrine and Covenants that if we will do all the things we ought to do, we may see the face of our Savior (see verse 1). On the same basis you may be guided by the Spirit of the Lord, the Holy Ghost, in your personal affairs if you are honorable and honest and keep the commandments.

I have discovered that one is guided sometimes even if he does not ask for it. Nearly all of the occasions in my life when I have had great events foretold me by the Spirit, I have never invited them myself or asked about them. They have just come. I can see why that is: Because every person who joins the Church and is a member of it in good standing has a right to receive the constant companionship of the Holy Ghost. He is given the right at baptism and he keeps that right as long as he is righteous. I have come to the conclusion that this Spirit and whatever influence he uses to reach us is more anxious to help us than we are anxious to be helped. I found that out quite early. So you may be sure that if you are doing your normal things in righteousness, there will come to you intuitions, feelings, revelations that will guide you if you can understand that Spirit and how you're having it. It takes a little work to understand when it is there, but you can learn it.

I found that it is true in that very important thing called marriage. In one case (I have been married twice, as you might know) it came without asking. I did not ask for it, but the guidance came anyhow. In the other case it came after asking, but just as clearly as in the previous case. So I know that if you need guidance, whether or not you seek it, if you are righteous and have not made previous decisions, you will receive guidance. Of course, if you have already made up your mind, you will not; but if you have not made up your mind and are wondering, you will.

I have found that it is true in Church assignments. I knew in 1945, two months before I was called, that I would be a member of the First Council of the Seventy. I can remember my feeling at the time. I was standing near the grave of my mission president, who was a member of that council, paying my respects to his family, and it came to me that I would succeed him. I gave my head a shake and said to myself, "Don't be a fool. No such thing can happen." I fought it, but it didn't do me any good to fight it because the more I fought it the more strongly the impression came. On the day it occurred I could have told you the exact language that would be used in the call, and it proved to be so.

I received a call to preside over the New England Mission, and the method by which I found out had nothing to do with that mission—it was so far removed from it that I could hardly believe it—but a month before I received the call, right out of the clear sky, when I was thinking of something else entirely, I had a very distinct revelation that that would happen.

I name these two incidents not because I am exceptional; I think it is also true of men who become bishops. A woman told me a few days ago that she had a premonition—not a premonition but a warning—that she was going to be made teacher of a certain

Sunday School class, and she was. It does not matter what the calling is; you can receive knowledge ahead of time that you are to receive it if you have the Spirit of the Lord in your heart.

I found that it is true in civic affairs, the most noteworthy of which was an occasion when I was to serve on a grand jury. I had every excuse in the world not to serve. If I served, my Boy Scout camp would not open. It could not, because in the days of the Second World War we could not hire a man to help get it ready, for there were no men to hire. So I had to get it ready personally. There were seven or eight hundred boys expecting to come to that camp. When I saw my name in the newspaper among forty others who might serve on the jury, I said to myself, "Well, I won't serve." But as I said it to myself, I knew perfectly well that I would and that no matter what I said to that judge I would not be able to escape it, and that proved true.

I found many times in my life when these things have come to me, with and without asking. But I found out also that if I was not righteous or was not doing righteous things at the moment, it never happened. Whether one asks or not, one must live so the Spirit can dwell in him. That is the key to the whole thing—living so the Spirit can dwell within you. And, of course, you know what that means—that means, in plain, common English: Behave yourselves.

As I look back upon my life I see that I have been protected or helped in danger and crisis. I look back, and although at the time I did not see it, now I see that I could not have made it without that assistance. For example, as a boy eight or nine years old, I was standing with some other boys—my brother and two others—in a semicircle, and the boy at the other end of the crescent had a Sears and Roebuck twenty-two caliber single-shot pistol (two dollars and fifty cents with tax), and he was showing us how Buffalo Bill used to shoot. Buffalo Bill was supposed to pull his pistol and fire in this manner [illustrates]; but the spring on this pistol was broken, and my friend had an elastic band around the hammer and around the trigger guard. The way he did it was to pull it back and let it go with his thumb. He was firing this pistol down into City Creek Canyon when all of a sudden I felt my arm go numb. I looked down and saw a red spot forming on my arm right there [pointing to left biceps]. Then my hand went numb, and I realized that I had been shot. That is what I said as I ran for home; but afterward I thought, had that pistol turned one-sixteenth of an inch farther I would have had it. Now I do not say that the Lord kept that pistol from turning, but something did.

I climbed Longs Peak one time with a group of men. Longs Peak is 14,255 feet high, and as one gets above the thirteen-thousand-foot level, he finds, unless he is used to it, that his legs go numb about every fifth step. One can go four or five steps and then his legs go numb, and he has to wait for them to come alive before he can go farther. It took us about an hour and a half or two hours to go the last thousand feet.

Up on top I noticed that there was a ridge apparently running down in a direction that, if I could get on it, would save me the hours of going around the way we had come. Against the advice of my companions, I decided that I would take that shortcut. So I dropped down off the peak onto a series of ledges that were waist high, just like a giant staircase, and before very long I was a thousand feet down. Then I ran into ice. During the evening before there had been an ice storm up there. It was clear ice; one could not see it on the rocks, and the first thing I knew I slipped. I caught myself and then began to worry; for I could see when I got there that I could not make that ridge. There were glacial cirques on both sides thousands of feet deep, and I was caught. I cannot tell you how panicked I was. I was terribly frightened. I realized that the only way I could escape was to work my way, somehow, back to the top. Every so often I could hear a whistle blow up on top; that meant that one of the men was still up there. I will not describe the things I went through to start back upward to get out of the particular danger I was in, but finally I got to where I could move. I went up that thousand feet in twenty minutes without even losing my breath. You will say, perhaps, that it was adrenaline, but it was not; and when I got to the top there was Golden Kilburn, a man who was with us, waiting. He said, "I couldn't leave. I knew you were in trouble, so I decided I would not go down this mountain till I found out where you were." And I found out there the value of friendship, too, and of the loyalty and devotion of those who care for you.

One time, on the way to Mexico to attend the funeral of my brother-in-law, we were driving along from Cortez, Colorado, south toward Gallup, New Mexico. It was January, and the thermometer was by the actual count ten below zero. We had a Chevrolet with no heater in it. We were so bundled up in blankets that we could hardly move. There was a ground blizzard, and the snow was drifting across the road so that one could hardly see it. I was going along about fifty miles an hour, the lights penetrating not more than seventy-five or eighty feet in front, when all of a sudden there loomed up in front of me on my side of the highway a horse, with another horse directly behind him, starting across the road.

There was no time to stop. To this day I do not know what happened. All I know is that the horse jerked his head back as I went by on the left side of the road, then I was back into the right-hand side again. My life was spared, and so was that of my wife. I did not do it. There was no time to do it. There was no time to think; but some guiding hand had forced me to turn that car into the left-hand lane and back again, and some guiding hand had kept it from skidding as it went around. By all the laws it should have skidded off into the borrow pit or I should have struck the horse. At ten below zero, we would never have survived.

Sister Young had a stroke two days after we got home from a trip we took to Mexico. It incapacitated her for the rest of her life, and I had the honor and the great pleasure of nursing her for the five or six more years she lived. Had she had the stroke two or three days before in Coatzacoalcos, Mexico, in the southwest corner of the Gulf of Mexico, we never should have gotten her out alive, but mercifully it waited till she got home.

When I was young, I came home from a mission and needed a job. I got married and was working for a hundred and twenty-five dollars a month when I heard there was a job in Scouting in Ogden.

An old friend, Howard McDonald, past president of your university here, met me on the street and wanted to know if I wanted that job.

"What is it?" I asked.

He said, "You get paid for being a Boy Scout leader. Lots of fun. You direct the Scout work in a community."

The only thing I had ever done in Scouting was to help my little brother in a fire-by-friction situation. I showed him how to make fire by friction in our kitchen, and all I succeeded in doing was boring a hole through our kitchen linoleum. So I said that I was not interested; but all the way home that night I thought, "Well, why not? Maybe I could do it. I don't know what it's about." So I applied to the president of the local council in such a manner that he was not impressed—anything but impressed. I was frightened, I was stuttering, I was hesitating, I did not know what to say, I could not give him any reason for wanting the job, I did not know what the job was, but I said, "I want it."

He looked at me casually, and finally he said, "Well, we are going to receive written applications, so if you want to write an application we'll read it."

So I wrote the application, and to my surprise I was invited to come to a meeting where I could be interviewed. There were eight candidates, all of whom had had years of experience in volunteer Scouting. I had had none. At the time, however, I suddenly became very calm, very sure of myself. I did not have the least fear. When my turn came to speak—each of the others had taken at least thirty minutes each, so it took nearly all day to hear them, and I was the last one—the president reminded me that they were all tired. So I said, "I don't know a thing about this job, but I know that I can learn to do it rapidly," and then I sat down. To my surprise, I was one of two picked out of that crowd to appear before the board; and with that much of a statement before the executive board, against a man who had had fifteen years of experience, they chose me.

Looking back upon it, I can see the steps by which I was inspired to say the things I said and not say the things I should not have said to get that job. It proved to be good. I had it for twenty-three years before I became a member of the First Council of the Seventy. I am certain as I stand here that the Lord directed me to that job through Howard McDonald and others, and that I was given it, not because of any qualification—not at all—but because somehow I was supposed to have it. I can bear you my witness that you yourselves (only in your case get prepared; this is not 1923) will find the opportunity that will take you to your life's work so that you can have the joy.

Well, the campfire flames mount. I have learned some guideposts in that period of time, and I would like to pass them on to you. The first one is: "One must always tell the truth." Dr. Jeremiah Jenks, a great psychologist of his day, let me have that one time. I was at a big meeting and he was speaking about honor and dignity and truth-telling. Incidentally, you might be interested in knowing that he was the man who was instrumental in seeing to it that the Boy Scout Law contained "A scout is reverent" and also that the oath had "I will do my duty to God." Otherwise we would have been kind of pagan in our Boy Scout business. He was a great Christian. But he was speaking, and a man in the audience raised his hand and interrupted him and said, "Dr. Jenks, should one always tell the truth?" thinking about the little white lies one tells about how good the dinner was when it wasn't, or "I've got to go somewhere; I've got to quit talking on the phone," or all those other things we do.

Dr. Jenks, aged then about seventy-five, looked out at that man and smiled and said, "Young man, if the truth is told in a courteous manner, the truth may always be told."

I give you a quick illustration that I have told before many times. Many years ago I was driving home late one night from Provo to take care of my sick wife. I was very nervous because I had prepared things for her to last until six o'clock at night, and I was starting home from Provo at eleven o'clock at night, so she had already been without help for five hours. I was fit to be tied. I passed through Salt Lake City (I had not been arrested so far between there and Provo), and started up the highway toward Ogden, got as far as Farmington junction, and turned off on the hill road, newly paved at that time though not straightened out. With that I stepped on that accelerator and got the car going seventy miles an hour. I passed the road where Hill Field takes off going seventy-two or -three; it was downhill a bit, and going down the hill I think I increased to seventy-eight or eighty. And then I noticed in my rearview mirror the flashing lights of a patrol car. I pulled to a stop and got out and walked back fifteen or twenty feet, extending my hands so he could see I was not armed, and he came up and stopped a few feet away and got out.

"I guess you're arresting me for speeding," I said.

"Yes, you were doing better than sixty miles an hour when you passed the Hill Field road."

"I was doing better than seventy miles an hour when I passed the Hill Field road," I corrected him. "But give me a ticket; I've got to go. My wife's sick, I'm in a hurry, and I'll pay the fine gladly, but let me get out of here. I've got to go home quickly, so just give me the ticket."

He said, "Don't get your shirt off. Stand still a minute. I'm not going to give you a ticket." He had not asked for my name. He just stood there.

I said, "Well, thanks for that."

He continued, "I'm going to give you a warning ticket. That means you don't have to go to court unless you do it again. On one condition."

"What's the condition?" I asked.

"That you drive within the speed limit the rest of the way home, so you will get to your wife."

I said, "I'll do it."

So he gave me the ticket, and when he handed it to me it had my name on it. He smiled, stuck out his hand, and said, "My name's Bybee. I used to be one of your Scouts at Camp Kiesel."

All the way home I said to myself, with each turn of the wheels on my car, "What if I'd lied to him? He knew I was doing seventy. Policemen do. He knew I was going too fast, and he knew I was his Scout executive years before, too." I did not know that he knew any of this, but if I had not told him the exact truth or tried to hedge at all he would have lost respect. He would have given me a ticket, and I would have had no influence on that man ever again.

And so it is with you. You are always doing seventy, no matter where you go or what you are doing, and you had better admit it. Then you will get a reputation for honesty and honor, and it is so great that it will save your life many times. If you get in crises—your word against someone else's word—and if you have a reputation for being truthful, it will save you. That has been my experience.

You must be absolutely honest, of course; that goes along with truth-telling. You cannot afford to do one thing that is not absolutely honest. I commend to you the one thing that many people are not honest in and that is truth-telling in examinations. I do not think that any teacher is ever fooled by a boy who cheats. The boy fools himself. But if he tells the truth, his fifty-percent grade is more honored by the teacher than the ninety percent he might have gotten if he had lied; and what he doesn't know he doesn't know anyhow. That is part of truth-telling.

There are many other phases, of course. You must set your ideals so high . . . well, you have to set your ideals as high as the Lord said to set them: "Be ye . . . perfect, even as your Father . . . in heaven is perfect" (Matthew 5:48). And then, if you do that and live up to some of them, you will be able to live up to many of them. Some of them you will compromise in spite of yourselves, but you will not compromise enough of them to jeopardize yourselves if you have them high enough. But if you only have them half-high and start compromising, you do not have much, and you are left desolate and barren. So set your ideals as high as you possibly can set them in conduct and handling yourselves and doing what you ought to be doing. If you do that you will find things happening to you that will surprise you.

I can say, now that I am getting to the stage where I am old enough to testify to it, that the greatest thing next to heaven itself is a clear conscience, as far as your personal life is concerned. When one is my age, he looks back upon the things he has done wrong and says to himself over and over again—or I say to myself over again—"Why did I do that? Why did I do that?" and there never is an answer. And I suppose that is what hell is like. You never get the answer—and that is futility. But if your conscience is clear, how happy your old age is! It is a time of such rejoicing that you cannot possibly imagine how wonderful it is. You know what things you have to do and what you get if you do them without my naming them over one by one—these become the pearls you count. A man never needs to apologize to any woman for the way in which he treats her or has treated her in the past. He knows his mind is clean, and therefore his speech is clean.

Vulgar talk is a great temptation. Little half swear words, the *damns* and the *hells,* come easy, I guess. They have done so to me. I punched cattle once and discovered the cattle did not know any of my language, so I tried the language they knew. I wish I had tried my cleaner language on the cattle a little longer. They might have learned something, and I would certainly have saved myself trouble. It is a temptation. Once one of my present associates got irritated and, in saying something over the phone about getting us to move faster, he used a little word with it that made us want to move faster; but to my surprise one of my colleagues, listening on a collective phone, said, "I don't like that. I don't think he ought to use that word. We don't need that here. We'll move without it." And that was just a very simple word. I learned the lesson that there are men in this world and women in this world who want to have clean minds, and want to have clean thoughts, and are insulted if you violate their ideal. You can find them; you don't have to look very far for them. Just be that way and they will gravitate to you.

Live in such a way that you can pray. Most people pray, but I am talking about being able to pray with the assurance that you can be heard. We say our prayers, but are you praying and am I praying with the assurance way down deep that what we are saying is heard where it ought to be heard? That only comes with clean living, with what we call repentance. We must truly repent of our sins, start to make ourselves better, and try to live cleanly; then we are heard. The Lord can hear us and he will hear us and he does hear us, and then what I said in the beginning takes place: the Holy Ghost works on you, whether you want him to or not.

When you do these things, you will have another great compensation come to you. Your life will be such that when you listen to leaders speak—leaders such as the president of the Church or the apostles or the bishop of your ward or your class teachers—you can discern whether that person speaks by the Spirit or not, and that is vital in your life and in mine. We Latter-day Saints can have no other standard than this, that we live in such a way that we will be able to discern when people are speaking by the Spirit. If you have that you have a pearl of great price, and you will understand and know the way by which you may become perfect. Brigham Young is reported to have said once, "The important thing is not whether I am speaking by the Spirit of the Holy Ghost in conference, but whether or not the congregation can detect the spirit by which I'm speaking." He was more worried that the audience would not have enough spirituality to hear what he was saying by the Spirit than he was that he speak by the Spirit, and I am worried about the same thing right this minute. I hope that I am speaking by the Spirit; and if I am not I hope that you in this congregation will all have enough discernment to know whether I am or am not, or what I am and am not. Anybody who speaks from the pulpit in this university ought to stand that test, and you ought to be the testers and be able to do it.

Brigham Young had a dream once, and I think it is the epitome of what I have been trying to tell you:

> Joseph stepped toward me, and looking very earnestly, yet pleasantly, said, "Tell the people to be humble and faithful, and be sure to keep the Spirit of the Lord and it will lead them right. Be careful and not turn away the small still voice; it will teach them what to do and where to go; it will yield the fruits of the kingdom. Tell the brethren to keep their hearts open to conviction, so that when the Holy Ghost comes to them, their hearts will be ready to receive it. They can tell the Spirit of the Lord from all other spirits [Now, here's how you can do it, too.]; it will whisper

> peace and joy to their souls; it will take malice, hatred, strife and all evil from their hearts; and their whole desire will be to do good, bring forth righteousness and build up the kingdom of God. [That's how you can know whether or not you have the Spirit.] Tell the brethren if they will follow the Spirit of the Lord, they will go right. Be sure to tell the people to keep the Spirit of the Lord; and if they will, they will find themselves just as they were organized by our Father in Heaven before they came into the world. Our Father in Heaven organized the human family, but they are all disorganized and in great confusion. [And then, finally,] Tell the people to be sure to keep the Spirit of the Lord and follow it, and it will lead them just right." [*Manuscript History of the Church,* 23 February 1847]

Just imagine; the president of the Church has a dream or a vision in which the Prophet Joseph comes to him, and he spends all that time telling him one thing over and over again. That is what it is, brethren and sisters, young folks.

One last thing: I shall tell you how you can measure your spiritual discernment. Nephi became ecstatic one time, and he prayed to the Lord and praised the Lord and sang paeans, psalms, and kept becoming more spiritual and more spiritual, and finally he made a great statement, a great prayer: he said something about "wilt thou do this for me?" "wilt thou keep my soul?" "wilt thou feed me?" and went on like that, "wilt thou do this?" Then, finally, he said, "Wilt thou make me that I may shake at the appearance of sin?" (2 Nephi 4:31). He was so spiritual that the least deviation from having the Spirit, which is sin, he could discern, and that is what he wanted most of all.

And so with you and me. Let us learn to shake at the very appearance of sin, and we can measure our spirituality by how much we do that. If we do not shake, we are not very spiritual, and if we shake, we are. And the more we shake at the appearance of sin, the more we are spiritual.

After all, the final thing is that the Father and the Son do live and guide us, and the Church established by Joseph Smith is the Church of Christ, the only Church of Christ. That is the great testimony, to know that President Kimball is the real prophet of

God our Heavenly Father and his Son, and to follow after and keep the commandments of the Lord that our prophet teaches us and to know when he speaks by the Spirit. I know that he does, and I know these things are true, and so do most of you, I suspect. May we all unite together and go forward and earn our place in the kingdom of our God by keeping the Spirit and understanding, I pray in the name of Christ. Amen.

S. Dilworth Young was a member of the First Quorum of the Seventy when this devotional address was given in the Marriott Center on 17 May 1977.